ADVANCE PRAISE FOR
SEARCHING FOR SOLIDARITY

Perhaps the most powerful affective force of our current times, solidarity pulls us radically together but may also pull us radically apart. In this beautiful homage to the generative capacities of solidaristic relations, Noor Ghazal Aswad takes us well beyond strategic or formulaic paradigms of solidarity to show us the heart of our alignments, our passions, and our commitments to others. *Searching for Solidarity* is a spiritual balm for our now and a rousing, inspiring disquisition for our futures.
—Jasbir Puar, author of *The Right to Maim: Debility, Capacity, Disability*

Radical subjects are involved in intense struggles for freedom and justice, at risk of being arrested, tortured, and killed. Starting in Syria, this lucid book weaves personal struggles with the political to tell the story of the radical subject, and represents the author's own fluctuation between the insider's commitment and outsider's melancholy.
—Yassin al-Haj Saleh, Syrian writer and dissident, author of *The Impossible Revolution: Making Sense of the Syrian Tragedy*

This is a book that affect inquiry (and beyond) sorely needs. Situated in case studies drawn from Syrians' resistance, Ghazal Aswad's writing arrives as a fully realized grappling with affect in its myriad imbrications—both tragic and joyous—with social movements, liberatory struggles, "thick" solidarities, "post"-memories, and political potentialities. Ghazal Aswad continually upends many of our too readily assumed ways of moving with and against the transnational grain of critical/political discourses. Tough-minded and deeply moving, *Searching for Solidarity* is revelatory in every sense.
—Gregory J. Seigworth, coeditor of *The Affect Theory Reader*

In stunning prose and with a compelling argument, this book offers a trailblazing account of solidarity as an affective force of openness to the testimonies, memories, and hope of distant bodies that fight in revolution. Remarkable in its clarity and courage, it brilliantly demonstrates how and why turning our emotion and attention to radical subjects and their struggles of resistance holds the best promise for a new emancipatory politics.
—Lilie Chouliaraki, author of *Wronged: The Weaponization of Victimhood*

Solidarity is collective defiance, collective resistance, and collective hope. As such, if it is the case that "where there's hope there's life," then it is also the case that "where there's solidarity there's collective life." This book explores crucial radical affects and, in the process, weaves them into our existence.

—Ghassan Hage, author of *The Diasporic Condition: Ethnographic Explorations of the Lebanese in the World*

Searching for Solidarity contributes to important conversations concerning whiteness and nationalism, testimony and witnessing, public and private memory, territoriality, and hope and community. Ghazal Aswad illuminates the radical subject as both theorist and object of study, who works at moments of political rupture and envisions new political possibilities.

—Mary E. Stuckey, author of *For the Enjoyment of the People: The Creation of National Identity in American Public Lands*

With *Searching for Solidarity*, Noor Ghazal Aswad seeks to shape how we see those who undertake revolutionary work. Her combination of the personal and the political exemplifies current critical work in rhetoric studies—and BIPOC rhetorics and rhetorics of the Global South in particular.

—Ana Milena Ribero, author of *Dreamer Nation: Immigration, Activism, and Neoliberalism*

SEARCHING FOR SOLIDARITY

INTERSECTIONAL RHETORICS
Karma R. Chávez, Series Editor

SEARCHING FOR SOLIDARITY

REVOLUTIONARY DREAMS AND
RADICAL SOCIAL MOVEMENTS

Noor Ghazal Aswad

THE OHIO STATE UNIVERSITY PRESS
COLUMBUS

Library of Congress Cataloging-in-Publication Data

Names: Ghazal Aswad, Noor, author.

Title: Searching for solidarity : revolutionary dreams and radical social movements / Noor Ghazal Aswad.

Other titles: Intersectional rhetorics.

Description: Columbus : The Ohio State University Press, [2025] | Series: Intersectional rhetorics | Includes bibliographical references and index. | Summary: "Analyzes the rhetorics of Syrian revolutionary materials—protest banners, films, and more—to put forth a theory of solidarity that prioritizes the lived experiences of transnational radical subjects over abstract ideals, offering a new way of viewing liberation struggles worldwide"—Provided by publisher.

Identifiers: LCCN 2025024915 | ISBN 9780814215982 (hardback) | ISBN 081421598X (hardback) | ISBN 9780814284445 (ebook) | ISBN 0814284442 (ebook)

Subjects: LCSH: Solidarity—Social aspects. | Solidarity—Political aspects. | Revolutionaries—Syria—Case studies. | Social movements—Syria—21st century—Case studies. | Protest movements—Syria—21st century—Case studies. | Rhetoric—Social aspects. | Syria—History—Civil War, 2011—Case studies.

Classification: LCC HM717 .G43 2025 | DDC 303.48/4095691—dc23/eng/20250615

LC record available at https://lccn.loc.gov/2025024915

Other identifiers: ISBN 9780814259603 (paperback) | ISBN 081425960X (paperback)

Cover design by Ashley Muehlbauer
Text composition by Stuart Rodriguez
Type set in Minion Pro

To my parents, and to all those who
dared to dream of a life of dignity

CONTENTS

ILLUSTRATIONS

INTRODUCTION

Statement Number One
The Syrian people will not be humiliated
Statement Number One
We sure won't stay like this
Statement Number One
From the Houran comes good news
Statement Number One
The Syrian people are revolting.
—Underground anthem of the Syrian Revolution

Recently, I came across video footage of Youssef al-Jader, nicknamed Abu Furat (Father of the Euphrates), a colonel who defected from the Syrian military and joined the Free Syrian Army after his battalion was ordered by the Assad regime to attack civilians in the revolutionary village of Al Hiffa in June of 2012. In the video, Abu Furat sits on some roadside pavement in military camouflage, holding a walkie-talkie while flanked by armed rebels. Havoc wreaks in the background. The whirling sound of bombing is incessant. As a window right behind him is smashed by an unknown assailant, my beating heart clasps itself. I am taken back to the heady rush of emotions I had when I first witnessed the footage ten years ago. This time, however, I observe it with a foreboding awareness of what is to come.

After leading a successful assault on Aleppo's infantry school in one of the major battles against the Assad regime, instead of taking a triumphant tone, Abu Furat sat down and counted sentimentally on his fingers the reasons for his sorrow:

> Honestly, I am bothered. Those tanks are our tanks. And the ammunition is our ammunition. Those fighters are our brothers. I swear to God, every time I see a person killed, from our side or theirs, I feel sad. Because if that bastard had resigned, Syria would have been the best country in the world.

But you clung to your throne, you bastard. Why? You killed people when we were telling you we were peaceful, and you were saying we were armed gangs. And we officers sat on our beds watching, while you called people terrorists. We are not terrorists. You are the one who wants us to become terrorists.[1]

The victory would prove bittersweet. A few minutes after his speech, Abu Furat was killed by a tank shell, along with at least twenty-four rebel fighters.

Writing about the video in the present, I navigate a profound rift. I am thousands of miles away, in a faraway continent and in another temporality, but I can still feel the atmosphere of the moment. Notwithstanding the nightmare the revolution would become, I carry remnants of the immense faith we had in the revolution and the gratefulness toward people like Abu Furat who were willing to sacrifice their lives to topple the Assad dictatorship of over fifty years.

The revolution *was* personal. It either brought Syrians together or tore them apart. Even family members could become strangers, and blood would become water. It came seemingly out of nowhere. In the early days of 2011, the "Arab Spring" cascaded like dominos across the region—starting in Tunisia, to Egypt, to Yemen, to Bahrain, and then to Libya,[2] all against deeply entrenched authoritarian regimes. We watched with bated breath to see if the wind of freedom protests would spread to Syria. Many were skeptical, taking the absence of political resistance over the years as assent toward the persecution of the Assad regime. Syria was the country least expected to fall susceptible to revolutionary fervor, generally known to be the most authoritarian state of all. Under the Assad dictatorship, Syria had become a single-party police state where civil society was severely curtailed and the military was intricately infused with the regime.

Though discontent had slowly burned for decades, it wasn't until the torture of fifteen schoolchildren in the sleepy town of Daraa for antigovernment graffiti on the walls of a school that the proverbial camel's back was broken. Even Syrians, long hardened by the repression of a totalitarian regime, were stunned to see the violence of the state turned on the most innocent among them. We watched, incredulous, as the exceptional unfolded out of the

---

1. Alarabiya, "Killing of Abu Farat."
2. Although the "Arab Spring" is how the wave of prodemocracy movements that took place in the region are popularly referred to, it is conceivably problematic given how the term "Arab" ignores the region's cultural and ethnic diversity, and the fact that it was not a unitary process but one that unfolded in dramatically different ways in each country.

monotonous rhythm of everyday life and aggrieved and disenchanted Syrians took to the streets in protest. As put by the musical icon Samih Choukair, "the youth, oh mother, heard that freedom was at the gate, so they went out to chant for it." And so, the 18th of March 2011 marked the unofficial start of a beautiful revolution,[3] one which would enact a theory of its own agency and possibilities, an expression of a liberatory moment in history where people rose from under an authoritarian regime's historic eclipse. Protests spread exponentially to the cities and towns in Syria. Ultimately, millions gathered on the street in protest motivated by a yearning for dignity, collectively forming the most significant challenge to the Assad regime in decades. A peaceful revolution was birthed from the night of authoritarian terror.

The regime's response to the revolution was swift and unforgiving, unleashing hell upon civilians. The military were given shoot-to-kill orders against protestors, sniping from rooftops and shelling residential neighborhoods. Though initially only appealing for political reforms, as Syrians were goaded further into revolt, they began to cry out for an overthrow of the regime. From the first bullet, Syrians furiously documented the Assad regime's violent response, uploading millions of images, videos, blogs, and tweets online as events unfolded. In light of the overwhelming amount of documentation of events on the ground, in a *60 Minutes* interview, United States Ambassador for War Crimes Stephen Rapp provocatively reported that evidence about the regime's human rights abuses was so extraordinary that it was stronger than that used to convict the Nazis in Nuremberg.[4] Tallying the ceaseless surge of casualties soon became an exercise in futility. By 2016, stating it was impossible to keep count of the ever-growing casualties, the United Nations abandoned the count. Their official records, dating back to 2014, paint a haunting picture of over four hundred thousand lives lost—a number that, in its starkness, barely scratches the surface of the tragedy. After this, the dead were "not merely nameless, reduced to figures. They are not even numbers."[5] Today, local

---

3. There are heated debates among activists about where and when the revolution really started. Some insist the 15th of March 2011 was the start of the revolution because of a protest which took place in al-Hariqa in the capital city of Damascus. Others insist this was not a revolutionary protest but a gathering to object to someone's killing by the regime, and that the small town of Daraa was where the revolutionary fervor catalyzed after two civilians were killed by the Assad regime. This debate also speaks to questions about the socioeconomic and regional character of those in the struggle.

4. CBS News, "Former Prosecutor."

5. Abouzeid, *No Turning Back*, xi.

human rights organizations estimate 1.2 million souls perished in one of the century's most harrowing genocides.[6]

But our shared humanity did not guarantee a recognition of our suffering, nor did it make solidarity inevitable. The sheer amount of documentation of the monstrosities wrought on the Syrian people did not ensure anyone noticed or grieved the loss of Syrian lives. Nor was it able to recuperate their loss. We were living in a world oblivious to our struggle. The mounting number of dead did not matter. In fact, it appeared deliberately numbing, facilitating exhaustion in face of the magnitude and relentless intensity of state violence.

In the summer of 2012, President Obama announced Bashar al-Assad's use of chemical weapons would be a "red line" that would "have enormous consequences" and "change his calculus" on intervention.[7] But when footage of twisted bodies wrangling on the floor, twitching and foaming at the mouth after exposure to sarin gas came out, Obama stepped back on his words. The regime became emboldened by the international community's determination to turn a blind eye. Waleed al-Muallem, a Syrian diplomat who would later serve as deputy prime minister from 2012 to 2020, brazenly told international observers investigating crimes in the country that the regime would "drown them in the details. Let them learn how to swim!"[8] The orgiastic footage of atrocities in the accelerated news cycle caused "too much information," which counterintuitively generated uncertainty about the regime's crimes,[9] while others blamed Syrians for not doing a better job telling their story. No safe havens, no-fly zones, or humanitarian corridors were enacted to protect civilians, and a deadlock at the United Nations Security Council prevented Syria's referral to the International Criminal Court in The Hague.[10] Later, Syrians

---

6. The regime's response to the revolution was so incredibly violent that the UN Secretary General Ban Ki-moon exclaimed, "We no longer count days in hours, but in bodies." Hashemi and Postel, *Syria Dilemma*, 4. Just a few months after the revolution commenced, United Nations Human Rights Chief Navi Pillay referred Syria to the International Criminal Court, citing the five thousand people killed and fourteen thousand detained. See BBC, "Syria Should Be Referred to ICC." She called on the international community to take protective action before the country would be driven into a "full-blown civil war." United Nations Human Rights, "Pillay Urges United International Action." No action was ever taken. For more on the various tolls counting the numbers of the dead, see Salahi, "Will We Ever Really Know."
7. PBS, "President Blinked."
8. Syria Stream, "In Less than Three Minutes."
9. Wedeen, *Ideology*, 79.
10. On December 18, 2015, the United Nations proposed a road map for peace under Security Council Resolution No. 2254, calling for a Syrian-led political transition and free and fair elections to be held in Syria within eighteen months. To date, the resolution has never been implemented.

would call on the international community for weapons and military aid for the Free Syrian Army—all to no avail.[11]

To date, there have been no truth commissions, reconciliations, or harms addressed as has been the case in some other countries that have suffered mass collective trauma from unimaginable institutional and societal abuse.[12] For many years, it appeared the regime had won the war on the Syrian people. Even after the countless number of dead, Bashar al-Assad remained as president of the country he had burned to the ground. Once a political pariah, countries around the world reinstated diplomatic ties with the regime, giving Assad the red-carpet treatment and welcoming him back like a long-lost friend into the fold.[13] Syrians were left starving and, as an old Arab expression puts it, "aysheen men elet al mawt," alive only because death has not claimed them. It was as if nothing happened. In the words of disappeared dissident Samira Khalil, "the world has closed its heart and gone away."[14]

It was not until late November 2024, in an unexpected turn of events and an abrupt closing chapter, that the regime fell when the world least expected it. The city of Idlib, the last stronghold of the revolution, which was garrisoned and left to plunder by the regime (bombing of civilians in Idlib occurred almost daily), was in the end the very spring from which Syrian rebels trained in secret and emerged to fight for their land. In an opportune moment, rebels advanced to Aleppo, then Hama, then Homs, and then finally, the capital,

---

11. By late 2012, around half of the armed groups were operating under the Free Syrian Army, an umbrella term for a leaderless resistance of competing brigades. Some of their first tasks were to protect peaceful protestors and people in the neighborhoods where protests took place and make continued demonstration possible, as well as allow for burial of the dead. Other times, they closed off territories so that those whose names were revealed to the regime could escape. With time, the Free Syrian Army grew to over seventy thousand armed rebels defending against Assadist assault. See Alford and Wilson, *Khiyana*.

12. More than forty countries have used truth and reconciliation commissions (TRCs) after situations of civil war or genocide. Some of the most well-known are the TRCs established in South Africa in 1995 for the victims and perpetrators of apartheid; the one established in Greensboro, North Carolina, which investigated the November 1979 massacre of anti–Ku Klux Klan protesters by Klan members and Nazis; and the Gacaca courts Rwanda established after the 1994 genocide for both judicial accountability and community-driven reconciliation. Moreover, the International Criminal Court (ICC) has not been able to prosecute those involved in crimes in Syria because Syria has not ratified the Rome Statute and so the ICC does not have jurisdiction over crimes committed there. While the United Nations Security Council can override this requirement and refer Syria to the ICC, China and Russia have continually vetoed resolutions to refer Syria to ICC.

13. In 2021, despite its record of deliberate and systematic attacks on Syrian healthcare facilities and personnel, the regime was appointed to the World Health Organization's executive board. In 2023, Syria's membership in the Arab League was reinstated after a twelve-year suspension, completing the symbolic triumph of the former political pariah.

14. Al-Haj Saleh, *Impossible Revolution*.

Damascus. After thirteen long years of asking the international community for help, Syrians took matters into their own hands in an advance that was largely bloodless. The regime, weakened by years of war, was a skeleton of what it once was. When their long-time loyal allies Russia and Iran failed to prop it up and keep Assad in power, the regime collapsed, like a spiderweb, in one fell swoop. The army, mostly made up of conscripts coerced into service, did not give up much of a fight and deserted their posts en masse. Assad neither resigned nor apologized but fled in secret to Moscow without informing even his closest officers or extended family members.

Syrians wept tears of joy, incredulous that a regime that had appeared impenetrable had finally crumbled. Refugees abroad could at long last return home to loved ones from whom they had been separated for years. Political dissidents, prisoners of conscience, and those who had been forcibly disappeared were released in the thousands from the labyrinth of Assad's notorious prisons. Syrians dared to dream again of a beautiful, prosperous, and dignified Syria.

In the end, Syrians took their own freedom. As former child prisoner Omar AlShogre sums it up, "We fought alone, we dreamed alone."[15] No country ever supported our struggle or encouraged it. The United Nations failed to release a single detainee, return a single refugee, or compel the regime to implement even minor reforms. Our advocacy was ignored, and the world watched us die. There was no consideration of the existence, aspirations, and well-being of Syrians. Not even after our liberation did the world emerge from its moral stupor, choosing instead to debate and question the ideologies of fighters and reasons for their success or offering lukewarm platitudes of congratulations laced with concerns about the geopolitical implications of the tyrant's fall. For Syrians, they muttered, the worst was surely yet to come.

The Dilemma of Solidarity

Even as we are overjoyed, the unhealed wounds of trauma remain. Beyond the insurmountable sacrifice of human lives for freedom, those who suffer feel immense pain when sites of repair are neglected by those who might stand in solidarity, often experiencing as much anger, indignation, and humiliation toward the people and institutions that fail to come to their aid, acknowledge their hurt, place blame appropriately, and offer solace as they experience

---

15. Hasan, "We Fought Alone."

toward the original wrongdoer.[16] For those whose lives have been destroyed, this forms a "second harm" or bystander complicity compounding the original violation—an instance when "failure to hear abounds."[17] A three-year-old boy's haunting last words before succumbing to his bomb wounds in a hospital convey the sentiments of those who saw the world watch them be killed and do nothing: "I will tell God everything."[18] But his words fell like coals in the black night.

Just because an emotional response is appropriate when hearing of the Syrian struggle, this does not mean we will be moved to feel it, or that we are able to hear their stories. The international community's response to the revolution casts the relationship between a preponderance of evidence and the impetus for solidarity in a troubled light. *Searching for Solidarity* pauses on this impasse to think through how we might heed the calls of those in liberatory struggle. It is preoccupied with the conditions and realities that impose themselves in a way that renders reparative justice and affective reconciliation difficult, unlikely, and quite possibly impossible for those who gave up their lives for the cause of liberation. I consider generative ways for our affective dispositions to exist within the liberation paradigm, crossing geopolitical locations and colonial differences, with the understanding that certain feelings emerge under some conditions more than others.[19] *How might we*, this book asks, *create possibilities for solidarity within the fragile political economy of emotion, attention, and the proliferation of fake news and damaging discourses about those in resistance?*

As an intervention, this book explores how we might affectively arrive at solidarity, together. Who is the "we" this book addresses? At first glance, one might say it is anyone who cares about the woes of others, regardless of their political stripes, affiliations, or creed. But this book's reach is far more ambitious. It seeks to awaken those who are distant, who have forgotten, who are indifferent but if given the chance, have the potential to be unsettled and awakened to the lives of others. With this in mind, this book argues solidarity is an emotional, ethical, and political capacity cultivated through attention to certain bodies. In a word, solidarity is made possible through an interventionist consideration of those who underpin the revolutionary phenomenon—this book's "radical subject." Though this claim might appear simplistic, it invites us to reconsider much of our critical practice and ways of knowing.

---

16. Walker, *Moral Repair.*
17. Stauffer, *Ethical Loneliness.*
18. Katouh, *As Long as the Lemon Trees Grow.*
19. Million, *Therapeutic Nations.*

Above all, the book's main contention is that by collectively awakening to and feeling the weight of these radical subjects, we enable alternate groundings for solidarity. The radical subject, the chief protagonist of the revolutionary moment, is a subject whose affectivity in situ induces solidarity. As revolutionary subjects, they imagine liberatory futures and take decisive actions to dismantle oppressive systems, frequently facing the risk of injury, imprisonment, and death. Their affective force forms a communicative affect that transitions one from neutral separation toward contemplation of the truths and realities of distant others. Oftentimes, their stories elicit a rush of affect, a felt change in intensity channeled through the body, which moves one to expression or action. Through consciously centering the radical subject, an attachment to those once ghosted through hegemonic frames is created. In listening to them, the dichotomy between rationality and emotion is bridged, bringing to the fore latent feelings, thoughts, and desires that solicit the emotional response necessary for solidarity. We sense their precarity, and their traumas impact us profoundly.

This book operates on the premise that solidarity is not discovered by happenstance but is processual and created by hearing certain subjects as authoritative. To phrase it differently, solidarity is an empty shell if not accompanied by a heeding to the radical subject. Solidarity here is not a process that has already happened or a linear point of arrival—the active participle in this book's title names an ongoing search for solidarity. In the context of this book, solidarity does not gesture to elite humanitarianism, politics of pity, or an admirable feeling of goodwill toward those who have suffered. Those conceptions of solidarity, akin to today's "thoughts and prayers," hearken back to an eighteenth-century culture of sympathy, where benevolent action relies on a theory of human goodness legitimated by colonial modernity.[20] Instead, I seek

---

20. The eighteenth century witnessed significant social and intellectual transformations that impacted the way people understood and maintained human connections. As societies shifted from more traditional, close-knit communities to larger, more impersonal social structures due to urbanization, industrialization, and the rise of market economies, the question of how to sustain social bonds in this new context became pressing. Within Enlightenment moral philosophy, thinkers such as David Hume and Adam Smith articulated solidarity through the language of sympathy, describing it as a natural human inclination that underpins moral judgments and social interactions. Importantly, they based sympathy on "resemblance," stressing face-to-face interactions and human sociability based on similarity (in race, class, gender, moral capacity, etc.) and proximity (socially, geographically, or culturally). This created a hierarchy where solidarity was extended more readily to those who could be seen as reflections of the self and offered a problem for those who were too different, or whose suffering didn't register as legible, relatable, or "worthy." As such, this made sympathy a powerful but limited—and often colonial—form of solidarity, one that assumed a giver and receiver, a subject and object, and thus was often structured by imperial and racial hierarchies. The "culture of sympathy" functioned to affirm European moral authority, while masking domination as care. See Hume, *Treatise of Human Nature.*

a justice- and action-oriented solidarity, be it a no-fly zone, a strike, a demonstration or rally of support, policy initiatives, or otherwise, that incites change from a place not immediately connected to happenings on the ground. Some term this a "differentiated solidarity" between metropolitan and (anti)colonial locations that breaks from conceptions of the world as a homogenously imagined collective.[21] Others describe it as a "thick solidarity" that does not gloss over differences—be they racial, socioeconomic, or geographic—or take liberatory struggles as universal.[22] In this sense, solidarity is inherently transnational in nature, as it acknowledges and addresses global inequalities. Black and woman of color theorists, such as Chandra Mohanty, Lila Abu-Lughod, and Rose Brewer, among others, theorize a feminist solidarity that crosses borders and builds political alliances across First World–North and Third World–South. This kind of solidarity must also be interventional, what Hannah Arendt refers to as "a principle that can inspire and guide action," and more trenchantly, which alleviates ethical loneliness and a sense of abandonment.[23] Therefore, when I refer to solidarity, what I am signaling is (1) political solidarity, a politicized form of solidarity partial to revolutionary movements and built on internationalism, global consciousness, or both; (2) material solidarity, aid for victims of natural disasters or human-caused conflict; and (3) rights solidarity, which revolves around human rights abuses and the actions of states or extralegal forces to lobby and influence the states in which violations take place.

On Affect

Most debates about solidarity building concentrate on shared beliefs and identities, rather than on the meaning-making mechanisms and affective impacts through which solidarity occurs. The coarticulation of the affect of those in liberatory struggle with the impetus for solidarity has remained relatively untouched. Approaching the radical subjects' affective register is particularly important during periods of revolution when those oppressed become negligible in the "mass sensorium" of discourses.[24] Due to the subdued and

---

21. Rothberg, *Implicated Subject*, 151.
22. Liu and Shange, "Toward Thick Solidarity."
23. Arendt, *On Revolution*, 89. For more on ethical loneliness, the experience of being abandoned by humanity and being denied redress, read Stauffer, *Ethical Loneliness*.
24. Lauren Berlant describes the "mass sensorium" as that which induces a "variety of collective affective responses to the shapelessness of the present that constant threat wreaks." Berlant, *Cruel Optimism*, 8.

subduing features of "war rhetoric,"[25] acquiescent publics suffer from compassion fatigue and become content with inaction, passivity, and numbness. Extensive footage of atrocities induces the "non-sustainability of grand emotions" toward humanitarian causes, especially the longue-durée kind.[26] As such, solidarity in this book is an affect-laden process in which one transitions between states, narrowing (and minimizing the deleterious effects of) the distance between those in metropolitan and (anti)colonial localities. As I will show, this transition is an inherently hopeful one, bridging the abyss between ourselves and those in liberatory struggle, who have the potential to impact us profoundly.

Searching for Solidarity inhabits the intersections between social movement theory, rhetorical studies, and affect studies. Affect theory, within the realm of cultural studies and critical theory, is a valuable lens from which to understand how sensations and intensities shape our experiences and interactions with the world. Affect theory goes back to Baruch Spinoza's *Ethics*, published in 1677, which talks about affect as the body's capacity to affect and be affected. Spinoza suggests affect is the force that influences our bodies and minds, operating below conscious awareness, subliminally, in our bodies. Affect emphasizes the interconnectedness of mind and body and can overcome the duality between the two.

But the "affective turn" would not take place until the mid-'90s, when various philosophers more thoroughly engaged with the term, signaling a move away from the "linguistic turn" of the mid-twentieth century, which focused on language, signification, and representation. Although affect theory is hardly unified in its scope or methodology, it shares a common departure from traditional approaches that prioritize cognition and rationality and that center the mind-body dualism dominant in Western thought.

Brian Massumi, one of the most influential affect theorists, suggests that affects are not emotions but rather the potential for emotions, the raw intensities that exist before they are labeled or articulated within an ideology.[27] For him, affect is contrasted with personal, conscious, emotional experiences, or "feelings," which have narrativized form. Another influential scholar in affect theory is Lauren Berlant, who explores how affect shapes our attachments and desires within a cultural context. Their work focuses on the everyday experiences of affective life and how we form bonds with people, objects, and ideas, emphasizing the complexities of affective attachments, which can be

---

25. Ohl, "In Pursuit," 197.

26. Chouliaraki, *Ironic Spectator*, 70.

27. Massumi, *Parables for the Virtual*; Massumi, *Semblance and Event*; and Massumi, *Politics and Affect*.

both sustaining and oppressive. Berlant's work invites us to reconsider the mundane and ordinary aspects of life, and the affective currents that underpin our experiences. In line with these conceptions, Melissa Gregg and Gregory J. Seigworth write about affect as "in-betweenness," suggesting affect as contagious and sticky, spreading between bodies and worlds.[28] Sara Ahmed similarly argues affect is best understood not by what it is but by what it does.[29] For Ahmed, affect is not solely located within individual minds but orients us toward others in anticipation. It is an inside-outside relation that spatially circulates in and between bodies. For her, affect is less about the subject's interiority or autonomy and more about the affective processes—both between and within bodies, as well as how and why some bodies generate affective responses of varying potentialities in a particular context over others.

Feminist scholars such as Sara Ahmed and Judith Butler have critiqued the bifurcation of affect from discursive meaning, writing in contrast to the work of Brian Massumi, who suggests that affect is preconscious and distinct from emotions and critical judgment. Both of them indicate the intimate connection between affect, meaning, and agency, thus shedding light on possible connections of affect to ethical responsibility and critical inquiry. This is the strain of affect centered in this book, by which I mean how the affect of radical subjects bridges the cognitive with the embodied to mobilize actions of solidarity that challenge oppressive systems of tyranny, domination, and abuse.

Becoming Acquainted with the Radical Subject

Who exactly is the radical subject, you might ask, this mysterious subject who holds the potential to foster solidarity? What are the parameters and features of their existence? Have we seen them before, in passing perhaps on the street, on the news as "terrorists," or are they complete strangers? Why should we care about them and how might they change our habitual ways of knowing? While I provide answers to these questions in the chapters to follow, I would like to offer a brief overview here. To put it simply, radical subjects are the master figures of the revolutionary phenomenon, who envision alternative liberatory futures and act with agency to disrupt oppressive systems, often at the risk of injury, imprisonment, and death. Agency is paramount, an agency which does not exist as an essence or natural category but arises in the willingness to make history amid opportunities created from extraordinary events

---

28. Gregg and Seigworth, *Affect Theory Reader*, 1.
29. Ahmed, *Cultural Politics of Emotion*.

in history. As radical subjects discern the exigencies of oppressive situations, they act to alleviate oppressions.

Radical subjects are not theoretical figures. They are real people, with real names, who engage in high-risk dissent across a spectrum of revolutionary activity as they revolt to create beautiful lives. They are protestors, poets, intellectuals, dissidents, journalists, human rights activists, first responders, or militants who take up arms against authoritarian, colonial, and imperial forces. They are archivists, architects, archaeologists, lawyers, and forensic photographers, engaged in memory and reconciliation work toward transitional justice. They do not exist as a priori but come into being as revolutionary actors when it is a question of struggle. They rally one another, "Raise your voice! Raise your voice! We'll live in dignity or die!" Even when prospects are grim, they see no other choice but to manifest irrational faith in revolution. As put by human rights lawyer and disappeared dissident Razan Zeitouneh, "even with fear that you can clearly see in their eyes, [they] speak about the moment of freedom with great certitude that no one could feel unless they are a true . . . revolutionist."[30] Their visionary determinism, at times bordering on nihilism, extends corporeally to how they behave, feel, and think—all of this to render more likely another world that becomes possible in the now.

These subjects, who form the backbone of this book, are identified through conceptual effort. They are Indigenous to their lands, their speaking resists normative scripts of resistance, and their actions form a risk to their own life and their family's life. Their simultaneous precarity and agency permits for a more complex recognition of liberatory subjects—they are not just "impotent victims . . . but insurgents."[31] In movements of the unknown and insignificant, they have no political weight or rights before revolution, but their morality and devotion lends credence to their proofs. Among their communities, they gain cultural esteem and are celebrated with folkloric tales of their bravery and courage. They are the effects of their sociopolitical, historical, and cultural contexts, but they are able to push the limits of these frameworks. However, their liberation struggle and participatory politics are undermined in a multitude of ways. They are ignored, viewed as mysterious, seen as controversial, misunderstood, and worse, beset with false assumptions, conspiracy

---

30. Zeitouneh, "True Justice."
31. The Afro-Colombian decolonial feminist Beth Ruth Lozano uses these words to describe "black women" in the territory-region of Colombia's Pacific coast and in Buenaventura of the collective Red Mariposas de Alas Nuevas Construyendo Futuro. See Walsh, *Pedagogías Decoloniales*, 273–90.

theories, and demonizing accusations. Therefore, radical subjects are very often occluded subjects struggling for recognition in the international arena.

Though this book is inspired by the Syrian liberatory struggle, radical subjects are not only Syrian. They exist around the world, perhaps with different-sounding names and different skin colors and with different moods, sensations, and experiences. They are akin to Malcolm X, Sojourner Truth, Wangarī Maathai, Frantz Fanon, Steve Biko, Rosa Parks, and Muna el-Kurd but also countless others who remain unknown but who have the visceral affect necessary to induce the solidarity process. With this in mind, this book draws on the phenomenal and the discursive, or what might be termed the embodied rhetoric of the radical subject, that is, the *lived lives* and their *lives as talked about,* to offer a new theory of solidarity.

I take a distinctly rhetorical approach to a revolution that has tended to be the domain of political scientists, anthropologists, and journalists. While for some, the word *rhetoric* insinuates the fluffy words of politicians and their deceptive practices, specifically words that are not followed by action, in this book, *rhetoric* is used differently. *Rhetoric* here allows us to address phenomenological questions—how those in struggle define for themselves their corporeal resistance to omnipresent historical oppressors but also how they actualize their struggle metaphysically. To achieve this, the book relies on a loose archive of texts created by radical subjects, including oral histories, documentaries, grassroots prorevolutionary news, social media activities, activist artwork, interviews, poems, posters, music, protest slogans, and autoethnographic texts.[32] Through listening closely to radical subjects in this fashion, we take seriously their epistemic perspectives, cosmologies, and insights. In the process, radical subjects transition from objects of study to theorists with much to teach us about theories of solidarity. We are drawn into their ethical realm, acknowledging their ethos as well as recognizing them as political theorists on solidarity.

As will be argued throughout this book, their rhetoric is not just an instrument of persuasion or equipment for revolutionary activity but has an affective intensity expansive of cultural, social, and intellectual thought. The force of their affecting bodies, what Spinoza calls "affectus," leaves a lasting impression, "affectio," that produces the capacity for solidarity. In this sense, solidarity is a relational phenomenon built on recognition of the radical subject, their affect, and their ability to affect.

---

32. Translations from the original Arabic are my own, unless indicated otherwise or if they appear in English in the original citation.

Moving Forward: The Tenets of Solidarity

This road to solidarity is not a methodology in the precise sense of the word but a critical practice necessitated by the presence of the radical subject. *Searching for Solidarity* suggests a move away from the noise Lauren Berlant calls a "mass sensorium" of discourses or what Foucault calls "discursive formations" to a more deliberate orientation that limits and fixes our vision on radical subjects. To put it more bluntly, this book interrogates the idea that everybody everywhere, at any time, who feels entitled to voice an opinion (and educate others) on what is happening on the land of others, matters in the same way. When confronted with endless possibilities of texts and subjects, a pressing awareness of what really matters may never materialize. Only in acknowledging the recessed possibilities of certain voices, voices that are often racially ordered and segregated, might we disrupt the silences perpetuated by the logics of the mainstream and induce an unexpected affective shift within us toward those who are, more likely than not, distant strangers we would never meet. The indispensable "bloom-space" needed for the convergence of awareness, knowledge, and affect necessary to generate solidarity is produced.[33]

Radical subjects are potent to this process—it is through their acknowledgment that alternate groundings for solidarity are made possible. As a mode of critical practice, this kind of intervention is instrumental to resolving controversies surrounding transnational social movements, which fall into the confrontation between two worldviews.[34] As Jasbir Puar writes in the context of disability, "efforts to 'diversify' and multiply the subjects of study" often lead to a reinscription of the prevailing discourses, be it on race, nation, gender, or region.[35]

In this vein, this book introduces an explicit hierarchy that values the radical subject in their own emancipatory movement. I put forth radical subjects, the very subjects who are deemed impediments to solidarity, at the center of the pressing task of conditioning and sustaining the affective conditions that make solidarity likely. My guiding claim is that the same subjects who carry the conditions of impossibility for solidarity carry the conditions for its possibility. In what follows, each chapter maps a dimension of the affect

---

33. Gregg and Seigworth describe affective "bloom-space" as an in-between space of burgeoning plenitude which has the quality of the "not yet." Gregg and Seigworth, *Affect Theory Reader*.

34. "Transnational" here is a relational concept that implies thinking across, over, and against borders that (dis)connect nations. Shohat, *Talking Visions*, 46–47.

35. Puar, *Right to Maim*, 14.

of the radical subject when liberatory struggle is at play. These tenets, to be unpacked in the chapters to come, are pivotal to setting solidarity in motion:

1. Turning toward the radical subject (orientations of affect)
2. The radical subject's testimony (cognitive affect)
3. The radical subject's postmemory (genealogies of affect)
4. The radical subject's peripherality (spatialities of affect)
5. The radical subject's hope (communities of affect)

Each of these tenets discloses an aspect of the affective life and affectivity of the radical subject. They also index the radical subject's affect as infinitely more complex and uncontainable than can be explored in a single discourse of affect. Though these tenets appear absolute, acknowledging them is in no way meant to obliterate the incredibly rich consciousness of revolutionary experiences, and even the conflicting subjectivities of what revolution means among the multitude, but it does speak to the sanctity of those who live liberatory struggle. Together, acknowledging these tenets advances us to a positive vision of politically and ethically driven intellectual work toward emancipatory ends. Interrelated and invoking one another, they propose an innovative heuristic for critical inquiry that opens possibilities for circling out of dominant narratives that obscure those in liberatory struggle.

Guide to the Book

Allow me to present a brief overview of the chapters to follow.

Chapter 1, "On Orientation: Disrupting Erasure and Ideologies of Exceptionalism," sets the stage for the book by demonstrating the critical affect manifested in an orientation toward the radical subject. It calls into question prevailing relational systems and frames of reference, in particular how radical subjects are positioned and solidarity averted among seemingly benevolent groups. The chapter delves into the multifaceted reactions that unfolded in response to the targeted killing of Qasem Soleimani, the commander of Iran's Quds Force, by a United States drone strike in Baghdad, Iraq. The event sparked a flurry of debates, reactions, and protests within US American and Syrian contexts. These responses reveal how those invested in solidarity and social justice remain locked within their own impulses and notions of exceptionalism. "Reverse moral exceptionalism" is explicated as a nationalistic tendency of self-critique and anti-imperialism that leads to an unintended dismissal of the experiences and agency of radical subjects. Though reverse moral exceptionalism may be thought of as virtuous, it saturates the space available for others and brings about indifference to radical politics. Drawing from Sara Ahmed's concept of affective orientation and Merleau-Ponty's notion of "towardness," this chapter ends by arguing for an intentional turning toward radical subjects and the multitudes of their affect. I propose that such an orientation takes us out of the ethnocentric social realities, worlds, and milieus in which we exist and into unforeseen forms of engagement and responsibility.

The intervening chapters then tackle a different affective quality of radical subjects and dimension of their existence that is affectively generative in leading us past layers of misinformation, horror, corruption, and deceptive layers of smoke to mobilize and conscientize solidarity transnationally. Each chapter offers various theoretical precepts (or tenets) about radical subjects and their ability to summon us on the route toward solidarity.

Chapter 2, "On Testimony: Reclaiming Affective Politics," attends to the affective quality of the radical subject's epistemologies, or "lived knowledge." Beginning with an exploration of the characteristics that define the radical subject within critical theory, this chapter elucidates their testimonial form of affect. The chapter confronts the limits imposed by critical sensibilities at the current conjecture and which hinder a full comprehension of the radical subject's significance. It reveals how progressive "inclusionary" efforts impede a shift in master narratives and perpetuate patterns of doubt that render radical subjects vulnerable to the distortions of a globalized economy and its epistemic insecurity. Fundamentally, dominant orientations in contemporary critical work cannot recognize the powerful stature of radical subjects, relegating them to the unserious, unruly, and untrustworthy. I argue for an epistemological corrective: the necessity of foregrounding the radical subject in a world of intricate news media, disinformation campaigns, and the surplus of information and expert opinion.

Beyond the lived knowledge attained in the active processual present discussed in chapter 2, chapter 3—"On Postmemory: Our Hearts Haven't Been Quenched Yet"—explicates the role of knowledge legacies inherited from those with ancestral power in shaping the affectivities of radical subjects. Here, I navigate the genealogies of radical subjectivities—the spatialities where they take root and flourish within the suffocating confines of authoritarian context. The chapter centers around my own family encounters with the "Events," a period of Syrian history marked by the Hama Massacre of 1982. Drawing from Marianne Hirsch's concept of postmemory, the chapter unravels the notion of "latent credibility," a potent etho-affective force born from the inheritance of historical traumas and ancestral acts of resistance, which enriches the affective salience of the radical subject. In ending, I underscore the imperative for a heightened sensibility to the affective density and historic moorings of the radical subject.

Chapter 4, "On Peripherality: Mobilizing Affective Geographies," introduces the "elastic periphery" as an affective territory where radical subjects around the world are relational and, together, central to a global revolutionary project. The chapter draws on the Palestinian liberation movement and the Black Lives Matter movement to consider the potency of translocal discourses of solidarity and the new modes of deliberation they provoke. Radical subjects deftly navigate the complexities of solidarity across different liberatory struggles to combat a lack of receptiveness to their cause, whilst imbibing an affective sociality that challenges dominant geographic and hemispheric logics.

In chapter 5, "On Hope: Bloom-Spaces and the Circulation of Solidarity," the radical subject's "hope talk" is conceptualized as a multidirectional site of affectivity with salience in the lifetime of struggle and for the intersubjective demands of solidarity creation. I explore the taking-place of hope, and its mode of operation, within the atmosphere of radical politics and within larger-scale collective flows of hope. In this chapter, belief is the necessary response to the radical subject's motifs of hope and resistance in confronting injustice.

In the conclusion, I offer some final thoughts on the unpredictability and imperfection inherent in acts of solidarity, especially in radical revolutionary contexts. Reorienting our sensory and cognitive apparatus toward the struggles of radical subjects requires an approach that embraces a commitment to ongoing negotiation and adaptation.

In sum, the driving quest of this book is to think anew how one might arrive at solidarity and its implications for the exercise of political judgment. The time has come for something different to be done, something different than before: new ways of attunement to those who might set into motion the affect needed for solidarity with geographically separated subjects. At its heart, this book argues for solidarity as an active, affective, and political force cultivated through attention to the lives of those on the front lines of liberation struggles. Imbuing each page is the guiding question: What are the emancipatory possibilities of embracing the very subjects who elicit unease and distrust? Each chapter offers a unique perspective on different dimensions of the affect of those within the crucible of revolution. By acknowledging their testimonies, memories, peripherality, and unyielding hope, we begin to unravel the tapestry of solidarity as lived and breathed by those entrenched in the struggle. Thus unfolds a journey through the landscape of liberatory struggle, forming not just an invitation but an imperative—to listen, to feel, and to think with those whose voices echo the hopes of a world reborn.

CHAPTER 1

On Orientation

Disrupting Erasure and Ideologies of Exceptionalism

> In the end, we will remember not the words of our
> enemies, but the silence of our friends.
>
> —Martin Luther King Jr., "The Trumpet of Conscience"

In the early hours of the 3rd of January 2020, Qasem Soleimani, the commander of Iran's Quds Force, the external operations branch of Iran's Islamic Revolutionary Guards Corps (IRGC), was killed by a targeted United States drone strike in Baghdad, Iraq. His death was confirmed when pictures of his severed arm with its signature amulet ring on his *digitus medicinalis* were made public. In the aftermath of the strike, Twitter exploded with the hashtag #WorldWarIII, concerned that Donald Trump's actions would cause such a world war. Debates raged about the legality of the strike, how it might play into the 2020 presidential campaign, its relationship to enduring patterns of US American imperialism, and potential consequences for the Iran-US relationship. By the next day, antiwar protests broke out in over seventy cities across the US, with protesters holding Iranian flags in solidarity. When Iran retaliated by attacking two US American military bases, there was a sigh of relief that no US Americans were killed, after which attention to the incident subsequently died down.

While the "American left" was in a frenzy of skepticism regarding the killing of Soleimani, Syrians, Iraqis, and Iranians celebrated his death.[1] Iranians

---

1. The term "American left" is an essentializing term. However, it is difficult to circumvent since it is prevalent in most of the discourse. I am aware of its analytical limitations, but for lack of a suitable alternative, I retain it with the caveat that it is not a historically specific discursive formation.

in the impoverished Sistān o Balūchestān province celebrated with pizza, congratulating mothers who lost their children at his hands, with the hashtag #FreeIran2020. Iraqis rejoiced, taking to the streets in jubilation to celebrate the death of a figure who had just two months prior been responsible for a deadly crackdown on protesters incensed about corruption and foreign Iranian influence.[2] In Idlib, Syrians passed out sweets to celebrate his death. Syrians were less influenced by the "Trump effect" (i.e., subconscious bias due to popular notions of Trump's tendency toward impulsiveness and rash decision-making) than was the US American left, and less likely to place the US as the center of analysis.[3] These grassroots expressions were not naive to the fact that President Trump had not acted in their defense but recognized how, for a cataclysmic moment, US American interests had coincided with theirs and justice was served.

The inability to contemplate the consequences of Soleimani's life or to engage in a nuanced critique of the assassination was an erasure of suffering at Soleimani's hands. After Soleimani's assassination, Syrians watched the US American left's sudden apprehension over the region, as if they were not already engulfed in a raging conflict in which an excess of 1.2 million Syrian lives had been lost. Their hesitancy to jump on the World War III bandwagon was guided by their intimate awareness of the scale of Soleimani's atrocities in the region and his sectarian cleansing of their villages and cities. Soleimani was involved in starvation sieges on the rebel-held cities of Madaya and Zabadani, enhanced the Assad regime's chemical weapons capabilities, and waged brutal assault on Syrians for over eight years. For Syrians, Soleimani was not just an Iranian general but a figure who haunted their existence. As a strong supporter of the Assad regime, he had an influential presence in the country. Riad Farid Hijab, the former prime minister of Syria, stated after his defection that "Syria is occupied by the Iranian regime. The person who runs the country is not Bashar al-Assad, but Qasem Soleimani."[4]

Regardless of the reasons behind Trump's actions and the legality of his behavior, Syrians were incensed at the lack of solidarity, even if only rhetorical, with the actual victims of Soleimani's repression by a left seen as their likeliest and potentially strongest allies. To some, this marked a blind spot, a collective myopia unable to see the tragedy and ironies of conditional solidarity with brown bodies in the region.

2. Al-Aqeedi, "World Paid Attention," 2020.
3. Hamid, "American Self-Criticism," 2020.
4. Sadjadpour, "Iran."

Reverse Moral Exceptionalism

In this chapter, I develop the key term "reverse moral exceptionalism" to describe a contemporary tendency to vigilantly insist on one's nation as behind every malevolent event of significance on the world stage. Reverse moral exceptionalism is dedicated to a critique of the imperiality of one's nation-state, akin to what the German Swiss psychiatrist Karl Jaspers terms "political guilt," a citizen's sense of collective responsibility for the deeds of their government.[5] As a nationalistic ideology, it is a political proclivity to err too much on a critique of the self (or one's nation) and the supericonicity of one's country as a rogue imperial actor on the world stage. I use the descriptor "nationalistic" deliberately here: Although reverse moral exceptionalism does not rely on an ideology of loyalty or vigorous support for one's nation-state, arguably, it still reflects an identification with one's nation-state above others and a general sense of national consciousness. Although exhibiting an admirable attempt to take on the burden of responsibility for the imperiality of one's nation-state, it exhibits a Western proclivity to establish dominance and saturate the space available for the testimony of those outside the nation-state. As a normative interpretive framework, reverse moral exceptionalism induces an inability to listen to the testimony of what others have suffered on their own terms, revealing the narcissistic and liberal discourses of solidarity offered to radical subjects when one stands too comfortably on the certainty of a moral high ground.

Traditionally, moral exceptionalism is rooted in the conviction that the US is an outstanding nation and guiding light for the rest of the world. In other words, the US or "America" is not only unlike any other nation but is an exemplary nation with a superior role to play in history. This ideology is so ingrained in US American national identity that it is "a natural part of the language."[6] Though US American moral exceptionalism is ubiquitous in political and cultural discourse, it predominantly revolves around the morality of US military actions and foreign interventions. However, it is hardly monolithic in character. There are a multitude of US American exceptionalisms, each "sufficiently distinct to justify further study."[7] As such, this chapter attends to moral exceptionalism in progressive discourse as an important dimension yet to be addressed.

---

5. Jaspers, "Question."
6. McCrisken, *American Exceptionalism*, 190.
7. Edwards and Weiss, *Rhetoric of American Exceptionalism*, 6.

Given that moral exceptionalism is commonly associated with conservative and centrist (i.e., liberal) groups, it tends to operate invisibly and without recognition in progressive spaces. I select the US American left as a case study of the peculiar manner in which this disorientation occurs, so that "just-minded people" are oblivious to the devastation of those in liberatory struggle. Though formulated from the particulars of this case, the analysis demonstrates a broader phenomenon of the "gentle back-door cruelties of 'nice people'" who are unable to act as containers for the pain of others.[8] In fact, Syrian radical subjects have long been critical of "the Left, writ large."[9] Despite attentiveness to local oppressions related to prison reform, women's rights, racial justice, and healthcare, the US American left has not attained an equivalently progressive stance with transnational radical subjects. This "progressive dystopia" has been attended to in various settings,[10] but in the context of radical subjects is due to a myriad of factors, to be discussed in the next chapter, which stymie a recognition of the emancipatory qualities of revolutionary struggle.

Underscoring this chapter is the exigency for privileging the radical subject as the principal locus of meaning-making within the complex global networks and systems in which we are enmeshed. In sum, this chapter demonstrates the importance of an intentional turning toward the radical subject, by showing what happens when this orientation is averted. Here, I draw from Sara Ahmed's phenomenological model of affect as an intentional "making room" for others.[11] In theorizing affect and space, she borrows from the French philosopher Merleau-Ponty, who uses the ambiguity of the French word *sens*—which combines the meanings of "direction" and "sentience"—to show how establishing a field of spatial significance not only determines what bodies are reachable but also creates responsivity to other bodies. Social relations can be disturbed and altered by not following expected paths, disorientating us and putting certain subjects within reach that might seem far away. For Ahmed, "towardness" is a mode of directionality which extends oneself.[12] As an angle of arrival, it allows us to access the affect of another, similar to when walks into a room and "feels the atmosphere." What we feel depends on the angle of our arrival.[13] This chapter enters into the intentionality of how we position ourselves within structural processes and networks of social relations and direct our attention toward others in anticipation of their affect. It

8. Levina, "Whiteness"; Smith, *Killers of the Dream*.
9. Wedeen, *Ideology*, 160.
10. Shange, *Progressive Dystopia*.
11. Ahmed, *Queer Phenomenology*, 2.
12. Ahmed, *Queer Phenomenology*, 115.
13. Gregg and Seigworth, *Affect Theory Reader*, 14.

is not intended to make judgment on the appropriateness of US actions or to prioritize a Western perspective on the "East" but rather to explore the schism that exists between outsiders and those in liberatory struggle when we fail to direct our attention with intentionality.[14]

Simply put, reverse moral exceptionalism is a failed orientation toward radical subjects that occurs when the exceptional evil of the nation-state is conjured to assuage guilt and redeem oneself. This normative interpretive framework errs too much on the side of reinforcing supericonicity of one's nation-state as a rogue imperial actor on the world stage, ensuring a jadedness, if not a paralysis, toward radical subjects. "Supericonicity" here refers to an extremely high level of iconicity, where a symbol or image strongly resembles or directly represents all of the thing it stands for. This orientation shapes the political contours of our social imaginaries: In its "awayness" from the radical subject and "towardness" to oneself, it interferes with the ability to be permeated by the affectivity of radical subjects.

In what follows, I theorize reverse moral exceptionalism as a tendency that unintentionally culminates in a hermetic sealing of indifference to the radical subject. Next, I overview some of the literature on how race operates within US American nationalist subjectivities. I then detail the discourses of radical subjects on the occasion of Soleimani's assassination. This provides a frame of reference through which reverse moral exceptionalism may be deciphered in the reaction of the US American left. It is intended to be situated against, read alongside, and juxtaposed with a cross-section of the US American left's discourses on the assassination. This section probes the unexpected forms in which mythic narratives of exceptionalism persist in (non)encounters with radical subjects. Drawing these together, I reflect on the limits and absences that arise when we do not turn direct our energy toward radical subjects.

Exceptionalism, Whiteness, and Erasure

Reverse moral exceptionalism reveals the unexpected material and discursive ways in which radical subjects become nongrievable. Reverse moral exceptionalism is often conditioned by race, specifically as an underlying logic of whiteness loyal to visions of US American greatness. Here, reverse moral

---

14. Admittedly, this is a challenging topic, considering Trump's exclusionary discourses in which he directly appealed to voters' racial and ethnic prejudices against Arabs, Muslims, Latina/o/x people, and a host of "others" during his presidential election and subsequent time in office, and of course, the reality of the US as an imperial actor (in terms of its economic, military, and cultural presence) in various countries across the globe.

exceptionalism is attached to structures of whiteness and geospatial articulations of power rather than being an intrinsic characteristic of white bodies. In this sense, whiteness is national, and at times international, in scope, rather than at the level of white embodiment. Even those who disavow racism are inculcated within ideological systems that set the groundwork for an anticolonial discourse paradoxically justifying oppressive regimes and oppressive actors. Whiteness and its concomitant forms of exceptionalism shape how Western subjects respond to perceived crisis abroad, producing US subjects who center their own identities, pre-existing political legacies, and histories of colonial conquest, even when motivated by ideals of justice and antiracism. Whiteness takes form through its orientation toward itself: It is oriented "around" or toward itself.[15] US American nationalist subjectivities "internalize the colonial relation" even when attempting to "repress this interiorized colonialism."[16]

Intervening against whiteness in the discourse of the US American left also means addressing the limits of a racially provincial whiteness discourse of "white is bad, brown/black is good." Through not attributing agency to brown and black bodies, reverse moral exceptionalism posits colonizers as victims and distorts understandings of inter-racial collusion in transnational contexts. As a point of departure, it challenges notions of a singular "moral exceptionalism" that unilaterally maps the US as an unrivaled humanitarian actor. Though the term may appear nonsensical, in the marrying of the terms "reverse" and "moral exceptionalism" is a tension productive to deciphering how the radical subject is constituted under such ideologies. Moral exceptionalism and reverse moral exceptionalism are two sides of the same coin in that they both are based on an ethnocentrism that approaches the world from a position of dominance and prevents a more nuanced understanding of events on the ground. However, while moral exceptionalism is predicated on self-admiration, reverse moral exceptionalism is predicated on self-flagellation. In its dedication to a critique of the imperiality of one's nation-state, it unintentionally saturates the space available for the testimony of others. Therefore, reverse moral exceptionalism is centered on a similar logic of exceptionalism, but one which operates opposite to its intention, leading to a blindness to the multisided truth of the malicious aspirations (and actions) of others.

---

15. Dyer, *White*.

16. Renée Bergland talks about a US "obsession" with internalizing the national space. She argues this is one of the central characteristics of nationalism. This nationalized subjectivity vanishes Native Americans and marginalized others. Importantly, this tendency is not confined to "bourgeois white men" but extends as a broader inclination to "internalize the same hierarchies" among women, people of color, workers, and others. Bergland, *National Uncanny*, 13.

In its overdetermination of the banality of national evil,[17] reverse moral exceptionalism places one's nation-state as the only actor capable of making history in a zero-sum equation of evil in the world. As the egoistic nation is inserted universally as the object of analysis, an orientation toward other subjects is averted. Without this orientation, we fail to capture the dynamics of the interlocking colonial systems that must be dismantled to achieve universal emancipation. Reverse moral exceptionalism therefore anchors the unwillingness to entertain risk, uncertainty, or something other than what we expect or want to hear. The radical subject is deprived of their significance, discounted as unworthy of intellectual engagement or curiosity, and affective connections are severed. In the inability to suspend one's nation from the equation, radical subjects are disembodied, the capacity for attentive listening obstructed, and openings for solidarity constrained. In this vein, Soleimani's assassination provides insight into how exceptionalism inculcates deafness to revolutionary discourse, such that even those with "progressive" positions domestically are not able to exit a generalized callousness toward the extinguishing of the lives of others.

The Perspective of Radical Subjects

In this section, I examine reactions of radical subjects to the assassination of Qasem Soleimani. This includes footage of the reaction to the assassination, social media posts, and coverage of the assassination in prorevolution Syrian media outlets such as *Enab Baladi, Al-Jumhuriya,* and *Orient TV.* The analysis affectively articulates the social imaginary of their political discourse: first, grassroots euphoria and communal dance; second, agency reclamation in the face of oppression; and third, an argument for heterarchical colonization, that is, how colonial power hierarchies are entangled with one another rather than in one monolithic colonial world-system. The latter highlights how colonial power operates through multiple interconnected and overlapping hierarchies, where various colonial actors and systems interact—sometimes competing, cooperating, or reinforcing one another—across diverse spaces and times.

---

17. Hannah Arendt famously coined the concept "banality of evil" in reference to the war crimes trial of Adolph Eichmann, the Nazi operative who organized the transportation of millions of Jews to concentration camps. For Arendt, Eichmann was "neither perverted nor sadistic" but "terrifyingly normal." She suggested he was part of an amoral system that encouraged him to commit evil acts without much thought or reflection. The term is considered paradoxical but points to the commonplace and everyday nature of evil in the world. Arendt, *Eichmann in Jerusalem.*

Together, the alluring chants, spontaneous gaiety, dark satire, harrowing sorrows, and agentic vernaculars underscore the colossal incongruence between radical subjectivities and that of the US American left.

Affective Joy and Celebration

Upon the news of Soleimani's assassination, expressions of joy and conviviality ignited in public spaces. A carnivalesque mix of bodies filled the alleyways and streets, replete with clapping, dancing, and drumming. In the hustle and bustle of the streets of Idlib, Atareb, and Suwaida, tray after tray of sweets were distributed with hearty congratulations on the news, with placards stating: "On the occasion of the death of Soleimani, from Syrian revolutionaries." Arms clamored over each other for a piece of baklava in a communal act of "breaking bread."[18] The Syrian Revolution's flag was held high as revolutionary anthems roared from the speakers. A banner emblazoned with the words "the revolution goes on" metaleptically claimed the assassination as rooted in the revolutionary struggle against despots and tyrants.[19] The collective effervescence of the crowd intimated revolutionary discourse against Soleimani's world-destroying violence and the affective conditions that marked the news of Soleimani's death.

A news report captured the charged affect of this moment. A man looks brazenly at the camera: "I mean, a man who kills children, what do you expect our reaction will be? Aside from happiness and pleasure?"[20] Another individual prays that "God would attach the rope to the bucket," a local proverb sketching a rope tied to a bucket that has reached the bottom of the proverbial well, conveying the hope that the next criminal in line would find a similar end. One man wishes that "Hassan Zemmera" (Hassan the Horn, in reference to Hassan Nasrallah and his long speeches) and Bashar al-Assad would follow.[21] The activist and former detainee Hanadi Zahlout poetically mirrored these sentiments in rhythmical Arabic: "If our eyes could see the spirits of cities, we would have seen this morning Aleppo in her glorious long dresses of silk dancing."[22] Across these voices, the assassination is presented as divine karma for an individual who had long acted with impunity.

18. Syria Plus, "Syrians Distribute Sweets."
19. *Euronews,* "Victory"; and *Euronews,* "Watch."
20. Orient TV, "Opinions of the Syrian Streets."
21. Syria Plus, "Syrians Distribute Sweets."
22. Zahlout, "If Our Eyes Could See."

Satiric subjectivities also inscribe the response to Soleimani's death. Yakeen Yaser Bido, a prominent female journalist in Idlib and former Orient reporter, refers to President Trump as "Abu Ivanka al helweh," father of pretty Ivanka, as she appeals to him in an ingratiating tone to bring their cheer to its climax: "*Sayra we sayra* [it is happening and it is happening, i.e., you are already in the heat of the action]. Continue your good deed with aircraft over Damascus . . . complete our joy, as we have become strangers to something called joy!"[23] In response, her friend, the Idlibi journalist Salwa Abdel Rahman, who goes by the pen name Sali Flowes, congratulates her, envious that they both missed out on the baklava:

> They all ate sweets on the killing of Soleimani, but Yakeen and I did not . . . !
> And so, we decided to drink maté instead and to pour on the sugar. And, we are postponing our celebration. We said perhaps we wake up in the morning and sweeten ourselves with the news of the killing of the animal Bashar.[24]

Ali Ferzat, the founder of *al-Dumari* (*The Lamplighter*), known for his antiregime caricatures, which deploy humor to laugh at the absurdity of life under authoritarianism, also published several cartoons of the assassination. In one, a man kicks Soleimani to the skies, only to find Soleimani being kicked back down to earth by a foot, presumably God's, looming from a cloud (see figure 1). Aside from the obvious politics of insult and black humor, the message is unapologetic: Even the heavens do not want Soleimani. A few days after Soleimani was buried in his hometown of Kerman, Ferzat published another cartoon, of President Trump urinating on the headstone of Soleimani's grave.[25] In the comments, Ferzat blends disrespect and satire to challenge the power dynamics at play, writing, "I wish I could do the same, but sitting."

The communal singing, dancing, drinking, eating, and sarcastic overtones reveling in Soleimani's burial all indicate the mobilization of Syrian revolutionary heritage and celebratory rituals on Soleimani's death. These carnivalesque practices, once harshly curtailed by the state, had become quintessential revolutionary practice over the longue durée of the revolution. In this case, they also claim belonging to the land. After years of repression, the unrestrained congregation and exuberant expression within public spaces rejected Soleimani's ownership and plundering of their lands, whilst endorsing a strong message: *This land is ours.* In shared space of protest, radical

---

23. Bido, "Sayra, Sayra."
24. Flowes, "They All Ate Sweets."
25. Ferzat, "Trump and Soleimani."

FIGURE 1. Cartoon of Soleimani kicked down from the heavens. Used with permission from Ali Ferzat. Shared on Facebook, January 3, 2020, https://www.facebook.com/100000917557614/posts/3634099843297232/?d=n.

subjectivities are impelled not only by the severing of people from their subsistence base and the expropriation of their lands but by drawing divine leadership from the land.

Resistance and Loss

Reactions to Soleimani's assassination were not only revelry; they were steeped with histories of oppression and struggle. This was conveyed most trenchantly with a rhetoric of invective directed at Soleimani as victims laden with the emotional intensity of loss. For instance, internally displaced refugees in Idlib interviewed in makeshift camps channeled and amplified the effect on actual bodies in crisis. With the brute physical reality of harm unmistakable, one man lay down as the camera panned over metal implants protruding out of his injured leg.[26] The visual, with its palpable embodiment of suffering, confronts us as evidence of Soleimani's gratuitous violence and war crimes. The

26. *Euronews,* "Victory."

assassination triggers a carceral recalling of trauma and injustice as the man solemnly places his hand on his heart and grief furrows his face:

> We didn't even know what was happening before a bomb fell on us. My wife died, my son's leg was cut off, and I was hit in both my legs. My brothers were both martyred. We had a lot of casualties. All of this is because of Qasem Soleimani. But, we would have wished that his killing would have been at the hands of our revolutionaries. At the hands of the opposition.

As the video unfolds, another man claims Soleimani's killing a "victory" for Syrians. Rather than attributing the assassination to US intervention, he frames the assassination as rooted in Syrian revolutionary resistance and as poetic justice for Soleimani's relentless violence against them.

Beyond massacres, Soleimani's use of starvation sieges as a military tactic and ethnic cleansing mechanism is recounted—most notably the "starve or bow" sieges which wreaked famine and death in the Damascus suburbs of Ghouta and Yarmouk.[27] This rhetoric interpellates the addressee at the most basic level—the primal need for sustenance. In this context, the language of famine is not metaphoric but an embodied expression of harm undergone. Foregrounding the emotional release triggered by the assassination, Joman Hasan, a Syrian activist and former detainee, elucidated the cathartic moment in which she heard of Soleimani's assassination: "I heard the news of Soleimani's assassination at 1 a.m. I got up, turned the lights on, and wept for all of the kids in Madaya who died of starvation. I wept for the siege of Yarmouk. I wept for the rubble of Aleppo."[28]

Elsewhere, radical subjects directly juxtapose the hypertechnical framing of legality within US American leftist rhetoric—specifically, the argument that Qasem Soleimani's killing was unlawful, privileging procedures, codes, and bureaucratic logic over broader ethical, political, or justice-oriented considerations—with their own discourses of legality and ethical imperatives. For example, one local news article brought attention to Soleimani's sanctioning by the UN and how his movements between Syria and Iraq were in violation of an international travel ban under United Nations Security Council

---

27. *Al-Jumhuriya*, "Soleimani in Syria." The phrase "starve or bow" is a grim encapsulation of a strategy in which populations were forced to either surrender and accept Assad's rule or die of hunger and bombardment. "Starve or bow" sieges have been documented by groups like Amnesty International, Human Rights Watch, and the UN as a war crime—besieging civilians and using hunger as a weapon is explicitly prohibited under international humanitarian law. The sieges were also used in "surrender deals"—where rebels and civilians were forcibly transferred (often to Idlib) in a process of demographic engineering.

28. Huneidi, "Iran's Wars."

Resolution 2231.[29] In the same spirit, the acclaimed Syrian journalist Ahmad Aba Zeid likened Qasem Soleimani to a drug cartel, Daesh, or Nazi leader operating outside of the law:[30]

> [Soleimani acted] not as a state but as a gang . . . the concept of assassination originated in the first place because states do not authorize the killing of leaders of other states . . . he is a symbol of Iran's expansionist project. . . . This is the naked Iranian project, such as Nazism, Zionism and Assadism, just a project of extermination, the dissemination of killing.[31]

Here, Soleimani was not a political statesman but the figurehead of an exterminatory project, whose actions defy any notion of legal or moral legitimacy. In a television report, Syrians on the street describe Soleimani in harsh terms, without the filtering of allegory or illusion, as a "terrorist," "sectarian criminal," "militia man," "najes" (a religious reference to an impure being), and "child murderer."[32] Parallels between Osama bin Laden, perhaps the most infamous terrorist in recent history, and Qasem Soleimani are stressed: "The terrorist actions of Soleimani far outweigh that of Al-Qaeda and Daesh together. The crimes of Iran in Syria alone, are beyond the imagination in terms of the destruction, displacement."[33] Hence, concomitant with the festivity in the streets mentioned earlier is an invitation to consider the assassination as an overdue public reckoning for Soleimani's illegal actions across the region.

Moreover, Soleimani's absence offers restorative hope for relief from the suffocation of everyday life and an opening to imagine otherwise worlds. Journalists such as Fared al-Mahlool and Mohamad Naser retweeted images of billboards and monuments of Soleimani in Lebanon, wondering how one might make these spaces "livable and bearable, to both sides?"[34] Historically, even the regime would permit *tanaffus*—that is "breathing room" or "controlled release"—as a safety valve to release the pent-up pressure of the populace by allowing minimal displays of dissident art, with an eye to prevent

29. Jamal, "Soleimani's Movements."
30. In this book, the term "Daesh" is used as opposed to the more popular "ISIS" or "the Islamic State in Iraq and Syria." The latter lends implicit legitimacy to the narrative of these groups and bolsters them as somehow representing Muslim majority ambitions. Syrians refer to the group as Daesh, the Arabic acronym of the Islamic State in Iraq and Syria, but one which does not have the "sheen" and baggage of the term *ISIS* and which is also phonetically unpleasant in the Arabic language. See al-Haj Saleh, "Dark Path."
31. Aba Zeid, "Soleimani."
32. Orient TV, "Opinions of the Syrian Streets."
33. Alloush, "If Only Syria Had Killed Him!"
34. Safwan, "#Lebanon's Airport Highway."

the explosion of revolution. In an analogous vein, the language of breathing and suffocation speaks to the clashing politics of justice and oppression in the struggle for self-determination: "While his demise is not sufficient retribution—nor does it provide his victims justice—it has nonetheless offered a modicum of breathing space, even cheer, to the survivors of the hellfire, death, and devastation of which he was among the chief architects."[35] Breathing, as a radical conspiratorial practice (from the Latin *conspirare*, "breathing together"), is rooted in life and what Black and Indigenous scholars and activists call "otherwise worlds," that is, a life that unmakes suffocating conditions and builds toward more beautiful worlds.[36] In connecting breathing to the pursuit of justice, there is a discernment of breathing as a fundamental human right that Soleimani abused. The language of breathing advances material and symbolic meaning similar to "a breathing-centered conception of responsibility for justice" in the Black and Indigenous context in the US.[37] In Soleimani's death, the capacity for breath, and for justice, however short-lived, is created.

Heterarchical Structures of Colonization

Finally, radical subjects lay the groundwork for the workings of the "colonial" and the persistence of the colonial dystopic. Speaking to heterarchical structures of colonization, they delineate the intricate linkages among a network of actors—each made up of one or more hierarchies—that facilitate and enable colonization to occur. The Greek word *heteros* means "other," while *achein* means "to rule." Hence, "heterarchical structures of colonization" refers to colonial systems made up of multiple interdependent units characterized by linkages that create circular paths rather than rigid hierarchical ones that dominate all others. American philosopher James A. Ogilvy defined heterarchy in the 1980s using the game of rock-paper-scissors, in which rock beats scissors, which beats paper, which then beats rock. No single element is universally dominant; instead, the elements have a circular relationship of influence and power, each with their own hierarchies. Each element holds a degree of power over others but is also vulnerable to being influenced by them. In this way, hierarchy within a heterarchical system becomes fluid and situational, allowing for shifts in power based on context, time, and space. This means that while individual actors—be they states, organizations, or social

---

35. *Al-Jumhuriya*, "Soleimani in Syria."

36. King, Navarro, and Smith, *Otherwise Worlds*.

37. Houdek, "Recontextualizing Responsibility"; and Houdek and Ore, "Cultivating Otherwise Worlds."

movements—may have their own internal hierarchies, they exist within a broader network of interconnected relationships that allow for influence and power to flow in multiple directions.

Primarily, there is a precise argument for viewing Soleimani as a colonial figure in his own right. One news report considers Soleimani's legacy as a colonial figure through his "constant presence . . . on the ground" in Syria.[38] Soleimani is chronicled strutting seamlessly about Indigenous Syrian lands, water, and air. A spatial and temporal analysis of his movements enumerates the cities and dates in which he was present in Syria, including photographs of him in Daraa, Deir ez-Zour, Hama, and Aleppo. Perhaps the most pertinent is one of Soleimani assuredly strolling the streets of eastern Aleppo in the wake of the displacement of its people after a four-month siege by the regime and Iranian-backed militias. The photograph, which went viral among Syrians, has a traumatizing affect for those in exile: Hundreds of thousands of Aleppans had been killed or forcibly displaced from the city, after four years and five months of battle, before the city fell to government forces due in no small part to Iranian bombardment campaigns.[39] Here as well, the writer brings attention to Iran's altering of "the city's demography" in a rising awareness of the intentional nature of the mass forced displacement of Syrians, mostly Sunni Arabs, from large swathes of the country. The strategic depopulation of Syrians, be it through massacre, detention, siege, starvation, or targeted bombing of civilians, may be more carefully termed demographic engineering. "Demographic engineering" describes the state-directed manipulation of demography, normally of ethnic groups in conflict, for the purpose of control. This engineering of the population is a violent and coercive process, often accompanied by the repopulation of land by non-Indigenous peoples to reshape the ethnic and religious composition of a region.[40] Some important context here is that initially Iran's involvement in Syria was to preserve Bashar al-Assad's hold on power, with the Quds Force at one point deploying nearly eighty thousand militiamen to fight Syrians. However, after Aleppo fell to the Quds Force and Assad regime forces in December 2016, Iran did not evacuate but began to establish permanent command and control and intelligence centers across the country, in addition to using military bases to house personnel, weapons, and installations.[41] As such, as Syrians fled their homes under duress, it was more than just a passing consequence of the conflict (i.e., collateral damage) but an active strategy of depopulation in tandem with the repopulation of these

38. *Al-Jumhuriya*, "Soleimani in Syria."
39. Azizi, *Shadow Commander.*
40. Morland, *Demographic Engineering.*
41. For more, read Karam, "Iran's Role"; and Uskowi, "Evolving Iranian Strategy."

areas by non-Indigenous populations (such as Iraqi and Lebanese Shia). This repopulation of the land was aided by the regime's expropriation of properties belonging to Syrian refugees and the imprisonment of refugees who returned.[42]

In this light, the injustice experienced by radical subjects reaches its apex in the desire to rewrite his death to avenge the violence he wrought on Indigenous lands: "I wish he had died in Aleppo or Deir ez-Zour, where he had desecrated its soil."[43] In the same article, an opposition figure sharpens this indictment with a piercing metaphor, describing him as "a massacre walking on legs!" Inhered within this is Soleimani as a colonizer who abused inhabited memories and not just the tenancy of Syrians on their land.

Soleimani as a colonial figure is also juxtaposed with the lionizing perception of him as an anti-imperial statesman faithful to the Palestinian cause. The perception of him as a champion of anti-imperialism was a calculated construct rooted in Iran's broader geopolitical strategy: Iran named the IRGC's army the Quds ("Jerusalem") Force, purportedly, because it was to be the vanguard for liberating Jerusalem. Along with the Assad regime and Hezbollah, Palestine has been a rhetorical tool for the creation of an "axis of resistance" ostensibly dedicated to confronting the US and Israel. This dominant portrayal of Soleimani as an anti-imperial figure in leftist discourse conceals the enduring structures of colonial domination he produced in Syria. Osama Abu Zayd, a Syrian opposition spokesperson and former detainee, challenges the portrayal of Soleimani as an anti-imperial figure resisting Israeli occupation:

> If support [for Palestine] is the standard on which our values stand, then the Syrian people are ahead of Soleimani and his country. This people have offered solidarity to Palestinians, and this is only their duty. It would have been more befitting if you had thought of the displaced Syrians who had to leave their destroyed cities. The blood of their sons from the rockets of "shahed al quds" ["the martyr of the Quds," i.e., Soleimani] has still not dried . . . they forget that this "martyr," in his quest to "liberate" Palestine, displaced hundreds of thousands of the children of the Syrian people who were true supporters of the Palestinian cause.[44]

---

42. Demographic engineering deliberately alters the balance of power between oppositional groups and has long-term cultural and socioeconomic implications on the future of the country. For more on demographic engineering in Syria, read Bakkour, "Emergence"; PAX and the Syria Institute, *No Return*; and Gardner, "Syria Is Witnessing," among others.

43. Alloush, "If Only Syria Had Killed Him!"

44. Abu Zayd, "If Support for Palestine." Iran justified its support of the Assad regime based on its anti-Israel and anti-American credentials. See Bishara, *Invisible Arab*.

Here, the language of blood and displacement are not "negative affects" so much as positive expressions of grassroots solidarity and anticolonial resistance attesting that Soleimani's rhetoric of anti-imperialism is just a smoke screen. In pulling the rug of "anti-imperialism" from under Soleimani's feet, the "anti-imperial" title is claimed for the Syrian Revolution and its radical subjects.

Indigenous sovereignty is also systematically threatened by the mutually constitutive role of external colonialism (foreign powers or entities that invade or colonize a territory, often resulting in the extraction of resources and imposition of foreign governance) with internal colonialism (local elites that manage nation-states, align with external colonial powers, and undermine the rights of Indigenous communities). In other words, local authoritarian regimes necessarily demand international imperial and colonial powers to sustain control. Soleimani epitomizes this entanglement, as both a foreign invader and key ally of the Assad regime. Local news outlets trace Iran's clandestine suppression of the Syrian uprising from its very early days, long before Iran's presence became "openly visible" in 2013.[45] Soleimani's alliance with the Assad regime is evidenced through the photographs of him with its soldiers, or with Lieutenant Colonel Duraid Awad, the artillery commander of the Assad regime's infamous Tiger Forces militia.[46] These images testify to Soleimani's close coordination with the Assad regime and his direct role in training regime fighters in the butchering of their own people. Adding a layer of symbolic resonance, a final detail is revealed: On the day of his death in Iraq, not only did Soleimani arrive in Baghdad Airport on a Cham Wings airline plane owned by Rami Makhlouf (a vilified regime figure and first cousin of Bashar al-Assad), but he had Syrian currency in his pocket.[47]

The heterarchical nature of the colonial is evident in the "quid pro quo" between external colonizers to further the aims of authoritarian power. Media narratives explicate how external colonizers (such as Russia, Iran, and the United States) work together in the service of maintaining authoritarian domination. For example, it is suggested that it was only after Soleimani traveled to Moscow in 2015 that "the map of Syria [was put] on the table" and Putin was convinced to intervene with airpower to save the Assad regime from collapse.[48] The same article wagers that Iranian imperialism in Iraq was "permitted" in exchange for silence on US imperialism in the region. In these articulations, various colonizers are diachronically, spatially, and conceptually

---

45. *Al-Jumhuriya,* "Soleimani in Syria."
46. Jamal, "Soleimani's Movements."
47. Alloush, "If Only Syria had Killed Him!"
48. *Al-Jumhuriya,* "Soleimani in Syria."

connected. Soleimani was not just a foreign invader undertaking colonial expeditions but an enabler of the colonization of Syrians by the Assad regime and a host of others.

On the whole, these critiques complicate standardly deployed theorizations of the colonial order. As radical subjects unravel the layers of colonialism, the multitude of macropolitical, structural, historical contexts, events, and circumstances that mark the colonial playing field are drawn. Rather than viewing colonization as a unidirectional force imposed by a singular authority, heterarchical analysis uncovers a complex network of influences where colonial actors interact in ways that are both confrontational and cooperative, existing within multiple temporalities and spatialities of the modern/colonial world-system. Radical subjects expose the interlocking systems of colonization that must be dismantled to achieve universal emancipation. The mechanisms of internal and external colonizers operate as global systems rooted in racist ideologies that work synergistically with one another. By bringing to bear the links between colonial logics and the endurance of authoritarian rule, liberatory struggle is situated as an existential struggle at odds with all oppressors, across time and space. In evoking the colonial as global, there is an implicit repudiation of the dominant conception of colonialism as a uniquely white settler project of domination and exploitation. Revealing the heterarchical nature of colonization underscores how decolonial strategies disrupt the conventional view of colonization as a one-way power dialectic between the colonizer and the colonized, instead emphasizing the modes of colonialism that overlap, reinforce, and even contradict one another.

The Perspective of the US American Left

In what follows, I present the response from the other side of the line, so to speak, contemplating the framing of Soleimani's assassination by the US American left. This includes media coverage from leading leftist news outlets, such as *Jacobin* and *Current Affairs,* as well as statements by democratic political representatives and opinion leaders from the US American left. As Syrians rejoiced, the US American left foregrounded competing concerns for making meaning of the assassination. First is the evocation of the US nation-state as a rogue aggressor. This rhetoric shows the US as an unprecedented imperial nation-state and outlier to other nation-states in its propensity to colonize other nations. Second, a narrative of apologia, mired with convictions of guilt, marks Soleimani as an apolitical victim. All nonwhite state actors are seen as inherently colonized, and by extension, colonial brown actors emerge as apolitical victims. Third, and as a consequence of the above, an affective closure to radical subjects and their nonnormative articulations of liberation occurs. The analysis invites consideration on the dialectical relationship between a hyperbolic identification with one's imperial nation ("I") and the alienation of radical subjects, who become at once nonapprehendable and nongrievable.

The Rogue Aggressor

First, a narrative of apologia by the US American left expresses regrets over US actions and its responsibility for the tragedies that have befallen the region. While contesting the US as an exceptional moral actor, exceptionalism still permeates throughout. It myopically, simplistically, and egotistically positions the West, or the white colonial power of the US, as a singular source of evil in the region. For instance, one article articulates the US as responsible for all the "instability that's gripped that region."[49] Another directly compares Iran and the US to suggest Iran is morally superior given its lack of colonial acts:

> Iran hasn't overthrown what passes for American democracy, forced a dictatorship on it, aided an invasion of the country, participated in chemical warfare against the US or destroyed the US economy. The American military has fifty-three military bases; . . . Iran has no bases or soldiers in Canada or Mexico.[50]

Of course, from the Syrian vantage point, the above statement is incredible to read, precisely because it effaces the violence committed by Iran as a colonial actor that forced a dictatorship on the Syrian people. A colonial actor that disrupted Indigenous relationships to land, water, air, and earth. Iran *has* invaded Syria, in what could be called an "annexationist, predatory, plunderous" manner.[51] At the time, Iran retained multiple military bases across Syria,[52] even if it had none in Canada or Mexico. For the colonized, the histories of oppression are embodied, tangible, and not forgettable. The suppression of the brown radical subject under the white gaze is unmistakable in the text.

---

49. Davison, "Donald Trump."
50. Shupak, "Stop the War."
51. Lenin, *Imperialism*, 9.
52. *MEMRI*, "Studies by Arab Researchers."

Narratives of apologia are remorseful for the "profound harm" and "war-mongering" of US imperial aggression,[53] with no concomitant allusion to the quotidian realities in the region, which are arguably far more complex than the unitary assumption of US American guilt. As Syrian activist Leila al-Shami states, "Everything that happens is viewed through the prism of what it means for westerners—only white men have the power to make history."[54] When the US is the only "rogue state" worthy of reference, and dichotomies of innocence and aggression are employed,[55] we foreclose a recognition of "complex political victims" such as Soleimani. "Complex political victims," as defined by Erica Bouris, encourages us to think of the uncertain moral terrain that challenges easily identifiable conceptions of victims and perpetrators and fosters a more refined analysis of political violence and responsibility.[56]

In merely deliberating US empire, undivided allegiance to the US body politic remains intact. Cartesian either-or logics allow for US military force and abuse of power to be the axes around which blame galvanizes. This narrow focus risks perpetuating a worldview where the West is the sole actor capable of exerting supremacy over others. The ever-prescient Edward Said aptly describes the problem that occurs when only the West is seen as able to exert supremacy on others (though in reference to the Orientalist Joseph Conrad):

> All Conrad can see is a world totally dominated by the Atlantic West. . . .
> He could neither understand that India, Africa, and South America also
> had lives and cultures with integrities not totally controlled by the gringo
> imperialists and reformers of the world, nor allow himself to believe that
> anti-imperialist independence movements were not all corrupt and in the
> pay of the puppet masters in London or Washington.[57]

In some ways, the US American left's acknowledgment of itself as an imperial power is admirable and situationally appropriate considering the US has been embroiled in the regions' histories of imperialism and colonial domination. The US continues to demonstrate a willingness to enforce dominance globally—sometimes through violent means—and has vested interests in framing certain groups as terrorists and others as not. I am not in any way denying this. However, in this instance, a narrow-minded centeredness on

53. Lazare and Arria, "Trump Is Pushing War"; and Allen, "How to Revive."
54. Al-Shami, "Syria and the 'Anti-Imperialism' of Idiots."
55. Davison, "Rogue State."
56. Bouris, *Complex Political Victims*.
57. Said, *Culture and Imperialism*, xviii.

the US produces a diminished understanding of the lived experiences and the affective intrusions endured by a range of regional actors.

This perspective also exemplifies the limits of critical race analysis when it functions not as a tool for understanding events but as a catechism. When whiteness is only understood in racially provincial terms, it distorts our understanding of transnational and interracial dynamics. Whiteness shifts from a well-deserved critique to an anticolonial logic that contradictorily justifies oppressive regimes and actors. To say it differently, the US as a uniquely evil force in world affairs evokes a form of white privilege that masks its erasure of others through the metanarrative of anticoloniality. When the US occupies the full space-time of imperial aggression, it is always and already in "a criminal act."[58] Reverse moral exceptionalism becomes rotten with its own perfection, cloaking the operations of others who might share the United States' ideology of imperialism. An apocalyptic occupation with US aggression in the region that simultaneously does not attribute agency (or accountability) to brown actors for aggressions on other brown bodies encourages a superficial discernment of the realities in the region. As Smith and coauthors state, "not all settlers are white."[59] In the passivity toward nonwhite colonizers and authoritarian regimes, the US American left becomes inadvertently complicit in a system it theoretically opposes.

At this juncture, I draw an analogy to how reverse moral exceptionalism functions as mise en abyme, a technique of placing copies of an image within the image itself in an infinitely recurring sequence. Deriving from the phrase "put in the abyss," it refers to the artistic or literary technique of embedding a smaller version of a work within itself—creating a recursive or self-reflective structure. While often celebrated as a gesture of self-awareness or aesthetic sophistication, it can also signal a kind of monological textual reproduction, in which self-reflexivity risks becoming ahistorical and fundamentally asocial. Mise en abyme makes the narrator "an enemy of himself," one who is "blind to the discursive decentering" of others.[60] Reverse moral exceptionalism mirrors this logic. Through overidentification with the weight of US imperialism, global events are reduced to a single explanatory framework. The United States' sins are so all-encompassing that no one can escape them. In the inability to perceive of "alternative(s) to [its own] cruel tautology,"[61] representing the US as an exceptional evil actor is just another form of colonialist elitism. The US American left is no exception in its obsession with itself as a totalitarian

---

58. Shupak, "Stop the War."
59. Smith, Tuck, and Yang, *Indigenous and Decolonizing Studies*, 31.
60. Silk, "When the Writer Comes Home," 234.
61. Said, *Culture and Imperialism*, xvii.

marauder on the world stage. In denying the possibility of multiple exigencies, Soleimani's crimes are a discursive impossibility.

Oppressors as Apolitical Victims

Second, Soleimani is constituted as a victim through a negation of his notorious reputation in the region. This ethos rehabilitation occurs through prolepsis, a rhetorical or literary device where potentially objectionable facts are not conferred or they are passed over to caution the reader against them before they are raised. In the incomplete crafting of Soleimani's character is a preference for testimony that fits stable configurations of meaning. Instead of acknowledging Soleimani as an agent of historical violence in his own right, he is manipulated into the form of a victim within a narrative of US exceptional aggression. Soleimani becomes a moral fulcrum under attack, freed of responsibility or volition, and removed from politics. This rhetoric employs a reductive closure on Soleimani's character, absolving him of responsibility, to accomplish ideological and political ends.

For example, Michael Moore, the Oscar-winning documentary filmmaker on capitalism and social justice issues, in several tweets apologizes to the state of Iran and Ayatollah Khamenei, expressing admiration for the thousands who came to Soleimani's funeral. He warns against being "trained to hate him" and sarcastically asked if anyone knew him or remembered what this "bad guy" had done.[62] Likewise, in a CNN interview, Democratic Senator Bernie Sanders makes an analogy between the assassination of Soleimani and Russia's assassinations of political dissidents.[63] Soleimani is hailed a "martyr to US bullying." Without Soleimani, the audience is notified that the region is "certainly . . . less safe."[64] Soleimani may have "lost some of this sheen" but endures as "one of the most popular" figures and a "war hero" in Iran.[65] Terms such as "dissident," "martyr," and "hero" constitute praise of Soleimani as a good otherworldly character.

The meaning of the event is controlled by anticipating objections and entreating the reader not to consider certain facts and to discount certain truths. In a string of articles published by the political magazine *Jacobin* in the days after the assassination, none mention Iranian imperialism in Iraq, Syria,

---

62. Moore, "Hello Fellow Americans"; Moore, "I Know It's Bothersome"; and Moore, "Just Wondering."
63. CNN, "Bernie Sanders."
64. Davison, "Donald Trump."
65. Marcetic, "Imperial Presidency."

or Yemen.[66] In *Current Affairs,* the public is cautioned that acknowledging Soleimani as a murderer is a "needless concession."[67] Another article notes that "some things are better left unsaid" related to concerns of Soleimani's wrongdoings in the region.[68] Further, one article gestures to Soleimani's popularity as an indication of the questionability of US actions. Raising doubts as to whether Soleimani's death was greeted with "elation" (quotation marks in article), the reader is informed that "most other news outlets reported that tens of thousands of mourners filled the streets of Tehran, many demanding vengeance."[69] Notwithstanding the outpouring of mourning at Soleimani's death, in all these discourses is a maximization of precariousness of the aggressor whilst disregarding his many victims. Altogether, there is a deliberate downplaying of Iranian aggression and a refusal to lay bare Iran's colonialism in several countries in the region. Narratives of Soleimani's aggression do not fit neatly into hegemonic anti-imperialist epistemologies, nor within the boundaries of "antiwar" activism.

Underlying these accounts is a plain subtext: the simmering anxiety that a more complete admission of the full measure of Soleimani's character contaminates neutrality or one's intellectual asepticism to the illegality of the United States' actions. Prominent social justice activist National Football League quarterback Colin Kaepernick objected to the killing of Soleimani, tweeting, "There is nothing new about American terrorist attacks against Black and Brown people for the expansion of American imperialism."[70] In this depiction, all brown subjects are homogenous victims of US American imperialism in a single sphere of vulnerability. The assassination is a "US-engineered calamity for the Middle East,"[71] as if Syria were not already in a precarious situation because of the intervention of a wide variety of nation-state and non-state actors long before the assassination. These forms of reverse moral exceptionalism exhibit the tendency to decline recognition of the agency of other evil actors in a blithe predetermination of meaning. As Syrian activist Sarah Huneidi writes in the title of her op-ed: "Iran's Wars Kill Innocents Just Like America's Do."[72] By excluding aspects of Soleimani's character, exceptionalism erases and renders (the persecution of) radical subjects unintelligible. When

---

66. See Davison, "Donald Trump"; Davison, "Rogue State"; Marcetic, "Imperial Presidency"; Uetricht and Day, "US Cannot Retaliate"; and Shupak, "Stop the War."
67. Robinson, "How to Avoid Swallowing War Propaganda."
68. Fernández, "Mainstream Media."
69. Featherstone, "Neocons Don't Regret."
70. Kaepernick, "There Is Nothing New."
71. Marcetic, "Imperial Presidency."
72. Huneidi, "Iran's Wars."

radical subjects' lives exceed recognizable frames, they trouble our established sense of things. We become "oblivious to the fact that people in other parts of the world have agency too, and that they can exercise it both to oppress others and to fight against oppression."[73]

Absent Radical Subjects

Finally, when the lines between victim and perpetrator are blurred, Soleimani is "present" as a victim at the expense of the presence of *his* victims. Political theorists Judith Butler and Athena Athanasiou describe this double bind as a dialectic of presence/absence in which "presence is constantly haunted by its spectral absence."[74] To be truly present for the other, they suggest, requires a form of dispossession—a relinquishing of one's own full presence. In this case, the radical subject fighting colonial disruption and displacement disappears entirely, obscured by the macropolitical rhetoric of nation-states and nation-state leaders. In the words of the French Jewish philosopher Emmanuel Levinas, there is not even the impersonality of the anonymous "there is"—there is *no* "there is."[75] The radical subject is by and large not invoked, not a part of the scenery, let alone a compelling subject of pivotal concern. Radical subjects, many of them Soleimani's victims, are not constituted, and as a result, their agency is evacuated. In stifling the radical subject, there is a withdrawal from the intimacy of their testimony and the micropolitics of their resistance as a meaningful site of struggle—a testimony deemed hollow in the face of the righteous cause of "anti-imperialism" and the martyrdom of Soleimani.

An attachment to the mythos of US exceptionalism divorces one from the material struggles of radical subjects. Trump's "imperial presidency" is mobilized to absolve Soleimani of his colonial sins.[76] This pardoning rests on a Manichaean refusal to consider that which threatens one's own ideas about how the world is ordered. One of the ramifications of this Manichaeanism— a dualistic either-or mindset that categorizes the world into binary opposites, like good versus evil, or colonizer versus colonized—is an avoidance of the narrative of the radical subject. Edward Said called this a "surreptitious mixing in of hierarchies, doctrines, and unadmitted prejudices in the text" that shape how we interpret the world.[77] The lives of radical subjects are left

---

73. Hensman, *Indefensible*.
74. Butler and Athanasiou, *Dispossession*, 17.
75. Levinas, *Existence and Existents*.
76. Marcetic, "Imperial Presidency."
77. Said, *World*, 193.

out—for fear of the unanticipated results of this recognition. When all brown subjects are victims of US white supremacy, the radical subject's experience is impermissible. They can *only* be a victim of the US, and if not, then we should conveniently not hear from them. US imperiality and the realities of suffering at the hands of another become impossible to reconcile. From this epistemological simplicity, there is an unwillingness "to take [one's] imagination" where others demand it go.[78] The inability to entertain complexity means anything outside of preestablished knowledge, in this case, US imperialism, has no place to go.

In tandem with the above, orientalist notions of weak individuality position radical subjects as agents of the outside world, "mindless fighters" manipulated by various regional and global powers. In the case of Syria, this narrative finds a home in the anxiety over Western-led regime change, due to the perception that the Assad regime was an anti-imperialist state and friend of the Palestinians against Israel. These depictions situate Syria, as a nation-state, instead of the Syrian people, as an underdog and victim of the UN and NATO's attempts at regime change. Within such narratives, the revolution is a foreign imperialist conspiracy against a "resistance regime"—in one fell swoop, denying the agency of millions of Syrians presumed to be susceptible to the whims of the West and incapable of a genuine popular uprising.

Lauren Berlant warns of the risk of overt focus on the US as a nation-state in their writings, observing that when "the nation form . . . [is] at the center of the history of the present tense. . . . [we] underdescribe the experiences and political struggles of persons across the globe."[79] One falls back on already completed meanings instead of becoming open to unexpected insights. In the adherence to nationalistic dualisms of right and wrong, this tendency takes on a predictive quality in political analysis. In its rigor, it usurps the space that might accommodate the affect of radical subjects, and from there, a de facto dismissal of others and their truths is accomplished.

Conclusion

This chapter brings to the fore the uncanny ways in which radical subjects of seemingly distant liberatory struggles are crushed within nationalistic ideologies of those who purport to stand with others in struggles against their oppressors. By looking at a cross-section of texts dealing with responses to

---

78. Power, *Problem from Hell*, 113.
79. Berlant, *Queen of America*, 13.

the same event, we observe the uneasy tensions and competing narratives between radical subjects and the US American left. On the one hand, the grassroots gaiety, sorrows, and anticolonial discourse of Syrian testimony foster a remembering of the oppressor from the perspective of radical subjects. On the other hand, exceptionalist logics articulate narratives of apologia that remember the oppressor as a victim. The juxtaposition of these two rememberings reveals the closure on radical subjects and the affective coolness with which the sanctity of their testimony is met. We recognize the truth of the words of Martin Luther King Jr. from early in this chapter: "In the end, we will remember not the words of our enemies, but the silence of our friends." It is my hope that by illuminating practices of "negative solidarity" (a term from the Combahee River Collective to describe those who acquiesce to power),[80] we become sensitive to the universalizing tendencies of ideology but also how we imagine ourselves, our role(s) in the world, and, ultimately, others. We inculcate an orientation, a "towardness," to those who disclose the world differently.

"We" here is for the readers of this book who might become invested in a collective (re)orientation toward radical subjects. A self-reflexive grasp of one's implication in the erasure of others is necessary before we can become alert to the affective power of radical subjects. Although this chapter has focused on the US American left, those on "both sides of the aisle" are implicated in nationalistic ideologies of self-congratulatory solidarity that are injurious and personally devastating to others. In this respect, the borders between those on the right and those on the left are becoming harder to discern. Whereas Western leftist orthodoxy is oriented toward or "around" itself and the imperialism of Western nation-states, the far right is also spellbound by Islamist violence, which leads to its positioning of Assad as a modern-day hero effectively fighting extremist groups in the region.[81] The nation-state continues to regulate our ethics and solidarities, allowing us to inadvertently support some imperialisms against others or support some oppressors over the oppressed. Our capacity to stand in solidarity is conditioned, or rendered more or less likely, based on the configurations under which we live.

Yes, these configurations are entrenched, but they are not inevitable. In thinking about the points from which we consciously stand, we orientate ourselves toward others and penetrate the nation-state's grip on all of our lives. Judith Butler talks about this as resistance that few can take, resistance to a "part of the self that seeks to join with what is wrong, an internal check against

80. Combahee River Collective, "Combahee River Collective Statement."
81. Al-Shami and Meckfessel, "Why the US Far Right."

complicity."[82] Practices of solidarity require a degree of self-doubt toward one's knowingness and ability to access the totality of knowledge. This requires cultivating an affective estrangement from one's position of privilege, engaging in a process of knowing "to the other . . . by the other," where distance becomes a practice of humility and ethical connection.[83]

A lack of intentionality in how we position ourselves vis-à-vis radical subjects therefore entails a major risk: a compliance with the status quo and its seemingly indisputable assumptions. When we center our own identities and histories, radical subjects become at once nonapprehendable and nongrievable. As political scientist Michael Warner observes, "the direction of our glance can constitute our social world."[84] To be sure, being intentional demands a conscious location of the actors, processes, ideologies, and master narratives that make one incapable of apprehending others. Without this reckoning, we chafe at the distinction between the victim and aggressor, between the freedom struggle of the oppressed and the tyranny of their oppressor. One person's terrorist becomes another's hero. Harms are unaddressed and color affective relations not only between the oppressed and the oppressor but between the oppressed and those who care deeply about justice. As such, this chapter teaches us what it might mean to purposefully orient oneself toward radical subjects and their sense-making activities and affective charge.

In the chapters to come, the affective registers of this emergent figure of the radical subject are to be unpacked more fully. Next, I explore the nature of the radical subject's testimony, lived knowledge, and embodiments of resistance and how they carry the potential to counter the invisible processes through which radical social movements are racialized and obscured and their histories overwritten.

---

82. Butler, *Senses of the Subject*, 216–17.
83. Butler and Athnasiou, *Dispossession*, 94.
84. Warner, *Publics and Counterpublics*, 89.

CHAPTER 2

On Testimony

Reclaiming Affective Politics

Listen, listen oh sniper, this is my neck and this is my head.

—Abdul al-Sarout to the forces posted around the clock
tower in Homs during early protests, "Syria Feature"

When the most credible voices become the most negligible, how might we position ourselves to recognize those with messages of truth? How might we anchor ourselves to solidarity with those in liberatory struggle in the face of the "centrifugal dynamic of discourses"?[1] Insofar as we do not allow these subjects to be seen or heard, we reproduce cultural domination and limit our ability to arrive at transformative outcomes that bring "two worlds" into relation and make encounter possible. In this chapter, I explore the possibilities of the radical subject's affect, an affect that exists at the intersection of testimony, ethics, and lived knowledge.

While a brief overview of the figure of the radical subject appears in the introduction, in this chapter, I further define the characteristics of this new figure in critical theory. After, I expand on the radical subject's testimony as a form of affect gleaned from their ways of doing and being within the political and social order. This testimony is not just a recounting of events but a specific kind of knowledge born of visions of one's own utopia and the experiential registers brought forth when the "impossible" is made possible. Hence, I theorize the radical subject's testimony as an affective force born of the embodied, embedded, and situated character of their resistance. Their testimony is a form of knowledge bridging the cognitive realm with the embodied, that

---

1. Fiumara, *Other Side of Language.*

is, the mind with emotion and sensation. The radical subject, through the very fact of their sacrificial ethos, dissolves the binary opposition between "informing" and "affect" so often observed in rational discursive practice, defying the notion that they are merely irrational actors led by passions or libidinal investments.

In the second half of the chapter, I address the limits of current critical sensibilities toward radical subjects and how they hamper our ability to discern the significance of extreme political acts under existing critical paradigms. This critique identifies an attendant conditionality placed on the radical subject within a capitalist/modern/colonial world-system that prevents a shift of master narratives on radical subjects and props up structures of inequality. Fundamentally, the terms under which progressive "inclusionary" efforts operate actively obfuscate the radical subject, a subject whose agency is already circumscribed and subverted by hegemonic forces. Even those on a well-intentioned quest to inhibit deterministic understandings of history are susceptible to a peculiar moral ambiguity retaining the privilege of those in power. Within this conception, an exhaustive inclusion of a kaleidoscope of discursive formations of variously positioned subjects is not a sign of maturity but rather a case of magnetic interference deflecting the compass away from the material reality inherent in the condition of marginality. It propels us to sit comfortably as "ironic spectators of vulnerable others," open to helping but cynical and ambivalent toward moral attachments.[2]

In the conclusion, I consider what it might mean to place the radical subject as the starting point in inquiry. As the influential anticolonial thinker Frantz Fanon puts it, "The last shall be the first."[3] This is the minimum demand: a movement away from projects of inclusion in a "mass sensorium" of discourses from variously situated subjects that do not rupture oppressive structures. Without privileging the radical subject's knowledge, we will never intuit their material realities. Without centering them as active knowers, as subjects whose embodied experiences and bodily affect determine, as opposed to have bearing on, meaning, we obviate a recovery of the totality of their lived experience. The radical subject is the affective ground out of which emerges knowledge that is existential, complex, and at times inaccessible to those removed from revolutionary struggle.

---

2. Chouliaraki, *Ironic Spectator*, 2.

3. Fanon, *Wretched of the Earth*, 2. Fanon's use of the phrase "the last shall be the first" is a deliberate echo of a biblical reference. In its biblical context, it refers to divine justice and the reversal of worldly hierarchies, but Fanon recontextualizes the phrase in a revolutionary, decolonial register. He uses it to signal the upending of colonial hierarchies, where the colonized— "the wretched"—rise to claim power and agency, reversing the global social order.

The Radical Subject

The "radical subject" is a specific category of subject who dreams of self-determination. Above all, they are autonomous subjects capable of discerning the exigencies of oppressive situations and acting with agency to alleviate these oppressions. I restrict considerations of the radical subject to those who hail from historically oppressed communities, are in crisis, and are revolting against repressive hegemonic forces. As a subject-in-revolution, the radical subject risks injury, imprisonment, and even death to create liberatory social change in society. Their agency is not illusionary or fantastical but has an intentional corporeality arising from purposeful political action in the face of formidable constraints. This assertion does not disregard intention, or even dreams, as a factor of analysis—indeed, intention is central to the radical subject's actions. Though there is a materiality to their resistance, this does not elide their interior striving. Their felt resistance is rooted in optimism defiant of deterministic conceptions of oppressive power.

The term *radical* (from the Latin *radic* or *radicalis*), though now taken as describing an extreme deviation from the norm, originally referred to the fundamental roots of a system. The word *grassroots* is apt here—from Old English, *root* refers to the underground part of a plant, which anchors the body. From this etymology, I derive "radical subject" as a term for non-elite subjects who become engines of social production. They are subjects precisely because they have acquired agency. I avoid referring to these subjects as definitively "oppressed" or "subaltern," in that they themselves have shifted into otherwise worlds where they are no longer (only) victims. This can be deciphered in the rejoinder of Abdul Baset al-Sarout (the national football player turned rebel fighter) to a question about why the regime wanted to kill him: "I don't know how I should answer this question. Should I answer it as an individual who has been oppressed, or should I answer it with the spirit of the revolution?"[4] I also use the term in defiance of those who have co-opted and weaponized the term to evoke associations with extremism, volatility, and an absolutist approach to politics.

In the documentary *Streets of Freedom,* an activist describes the ethos of sacrifice of radical subjects: "Chants emerged spontaneously, and we kept on marching. People were saying, 'God, these people must be suicidal, crazy, why are they doing this?' At the same time, they were dreaming of joining us, but they were too cowardly to join."[5] In a similar vein, the writer Samar Yazbek

---

4. Al-Sarout, "Syria Feature."
5. Shehadeh, *Streets of Freedom.*

describes how she is unburdened by fear of sacrificing her life: "We breathe it in. I wait for it, calm with my cigarette and coffee. I imagine I could stare into the eye of a sniper on a rooftop, stare at him without blinking. As I head out into the street, I walk confidently, peering at the rooftops."[6] Abdul Baset al-Sarout embodied this spirit when he famously decided to put his life on the line to break the siege of Homs to deliver food to those starving in the city: "I decided that I would return, in solidarity with those under siege, that we would starve and even die with each other and if God granted us liberation then we would all be liberated together."[7]

Radical subjects are not born such, nor is this an inherent state of their being. They exist at a moment in time, emerging out of extraordinary, revolutionary events in history amid lived positionalities, but critically, one becomes a radical subject by how one reacts to external events to which they are subject. In the documentary *Our Memory Belongs to Us*, Odai, a Syrian activist who is now a refugee in Europe, articulates the pivotal moment when he transitioned from neutral observation of the revolution to armed resistance, and the harrowing realities that catalyzed his decision:

> There was a border control checkpoint thirty minutes away from my house in Daraa. They would detain a girl and broadcast her rape over the speakers. We would hear the woman screaming, i.e., "Oh people, save me!" What do you want of me? That I come holding a flower? What do you expect when the whole international community is watching and doing nothing? And now they want to hold me accountable for holding a weapon?[8]

Emancipatory possibilities are found when the controlled world we inhabit falters and radical subjects find an opening in the ambiguities of political domination of regimes that are never able to occupy an omnipotent commitment of the populace. In the moment of rupture, we become privy to ways of sense-making and doing arising from those in otherwise worlds. Omar Aziz—an anarchist who lead the move toward self-governance in Syria away from control of the state—defines the juncture from which the radical subject emerges as "an exceptional event that will alter the history of societies, while changing humanity itself. It is a rupture in time and space, where humans live between two periods: the period of power and the period of

---

6. Yazbek, *Woman in the Crossfire*, 4.
7. Al-Sarout, "Syria Feature."
8. Farah, "Our Memory."

revolution."[9] Between these two periods, a critical consciousness crystallizes and a transition in affective states occurs. As M. Jacqui Alexander describes it, rupture is "transgressing, disrupting, displacing, and inverting inherited concepts and practices."[10] As a liberatory social explosion, rupture instigates an inner renewal or awakening that alters the social contract with those in power.

Others point to "affawyit al thawra"—the natural, unaffected, and unpremeditated nature of revolution that comes about without any introduction after the congestion and suffocation of everyday life. In the documentary *Streets of Freedom,* one activist explicates how, "truly, we were all taken by storm."[11] This rupture might be akin to something hidden coming out into the open, or what Frantz Fanon refers to as reaching the "boiling point."[12] As one protester chanted "freedom, freedom," he could not otherwise put his emotions into words: "I can't describe it. . . . It was like letting all the energy out of you, all the things you'd kept hidden for so many years. You felt like you're not on this earth. Like your soul is just flying somewhere else."[13] During the massive uprisings of the Ecuadorian population in the 1990s, rupture was the "awakening of the sleeping lion"—where Indigenous peoples and the descendants of enslaved Africans proposed Ecuador as a plurinational state committed to *sumak kawsay,* a plentiful life in harmony with nature.

In the collective conceptualization of themselves as a social force reorganizing the distribution of power in society, a transformation of common sense takes place. Social movements, due to their very nature, often provoke new identities and cultural meanings in a dramatic breakdown or reassembly of social networks. Razan Ghazzawi testifies to an experiential dimension of revolutionary fervor that is rarely articulated so fully:[14]

This revolution is starting to build a consciousness for Syrians. We did not have that before. We did not even have this word "Syria." Like for example, if

---

9. The translator of this text from the original Arabic is unknown. Omar Aziz left his comfortable life in France at the age of sixty-two to join the revolution, telling his wife, "I will not respect myself, nor will you respect me, if I stay away from my country at a time when I have so much to offer." He believed revolution should permeate all aspects of life and advocated for radical changes even in social relationships. He died of heart failure in Adra prison in 2013. See Hassan, "Radical Lives"; and Aziz, "Discussion Paper on Local Councils."

10. Alexander, *Pedagogies of Crossing,* 22.

11. Shehadeh, *Streets of Freedom.*

12. Fanon, *Wretched of the Earth,* 84.

13. Pearlman, *We Crossed a Bridge,* 55.

14. Razan Ghazzawi is a Syrian blogger who worked at the Syrian Center for Freedom of Expression in Damascus. She was arrested by the regime for her activism multiple times. Amnesty International declared her a "prisoner of conscience." Amnesty International, "Syrian Blogger Arrested."

someone wanted to leave Syria, we would say he wanted to leave the *balad*—the country. We relate differently to the country [now].[15]

Such statements capture the ways in which land is experienced in revolutionary time and the generative capacities that materialize from Indigenous people's embodied experiences. Time after time, radical social movements are occluded from public view because they do not have traditional leadership structures. They might present as "leaderless"—either community-oriented, with liberation being the accomplishment of everyone and no special merit owed to anyone, or headed by local leaders not known outside of certain political and intellectual circles. Or they might be land-led in that their power emerges from coalitional bonds with the land and the spaces where the threat of dispossession looms. In the case of Syria, amid sieges and land-burning as a form of necropolitics inflicted by the regime, radical subjects dismantled the need for state apparatuses. They smuggled seeds and initiated grassroots farming initiatives in the middle of ruined fields, in garbage dumps, and on the rooftops of bombed homes, resisting alongside the land in defiance of traditional forms of authority and state control.[16] In cities such as Daraya, they created secret underground libraries, gathered from burning homes and offices in the most harrowing of circumstances, during the terrifying siege of the city.[17] An extensive grassroots network of dissidents named the Local Coordination Committees organized protests and collected eyewitness testimony to counter the regime's narrative attempting to distort the beauty of their rebellion. These committees were self-sustaining entities crafted in the very process of rebellion—a "mobilizing from scratch" reversing normative temporal logics of social movements as transitioning from organization to protest.[18] Valorizing the radical subject in this way in no way repudiates the power-laden character of social relations; rather, it foregrounds how the radical subject asserts their own forms of autonomy and organizational logics, even in the face of coercion and in continuous negotiation with the constraints of their social habitus.[19]

---

15. Frontline Defenders, "Interview."
16. Social movements described as leaderless often draw direction from a relationship to place, in a phenomenon of land-led politics impelled not only by the severing of people from their subsistence base and the expropriation of their lands but by an ontological relation that draws leadership from the land. See Ghazal Aswad and Lechuga, "Led by the Land"; Rizk and al-Shami, "Land, Revolutions and Lessons"; Ghazal Aswad, "Cultivating Radical Care"; and Ghazal Aswad and Houdek, "Radical Rhetorics at/and the World's End."
17. For more on these secret libraries, read Thomson, *Syria's Secret Libraries*.
18. Pearlman, "Mobilizing from Scratch."
19. Habitus is "the set of dispositions which incline agents to act and react in certain ways," or the ways we are structured by our social surroundings to act in certain ways. Bourdieu, *Language and Symbolic Power*, 12.

In this paradigm-changing event, people emerge from their silence, developing their own languages and slogans. In a society told, "Whisper! The walls have ears," radical subjects find their voice and began to experiment with it as a tool of resistance. In his interviews, Riad al-Turk, a renowned Syrian opposition leader, orients us toward revolution as struggle over meaning, complete with new idioms and advances in discourse, the reappropriation of old vocabularies, and the renegotiation of old attachments to everyday conventions.[20] Radical subjects are not unshackled from the coercion of language or social practice, but they have *ibda'*—human creativity—in the bold disconnection from power structures. In short, semantic forms of expression are immersed within the traditional practices from which they emerge and innovate. Though the language of the dominated is conditioned by the dominant, for radical subjects, this conditioning is no longer a defining condition of their existence. For example, lexical changes may be introduced into traditional songs to contest their original meanings. While the first line of the regime's song "Sūriyā yā Ḥabībatī" (Syria, My Beloved) is "Oh, Syria, you gave me back my dignity and freedom," the revolutionary cover song says, "Oh, Syria, give me back my dignity and freedom." Instead of "the bullet of the rifle is the factory of freedom," the lyric becomes "the bullet of the rifle will not kill freedom."

At other times, there is a brave casting aside of the ideological terms of the state, for example, replacing the lyrics "Now I am an Arab" with "Now I long for my tomorrow with freedom in my hand," rejecting the regime's pan-Arab nationalist ideology. In a complete subversion of the power dialectic, popular revolutionary songs composed and released during the revolution, such as Samih Choukair's "Ya Hif" (Alas, What a Shame), were co-opted by the regime into several patriotic pro-regime versions.[21] Sometimes radical subjects reach back further into their histories, creating protest songs from old folk songs and traditional music (*aradah*) as tools of resistance, or as I show later, Iraqi love songs are reappropriated into revolutionary odes to those in resistance. Radical subjects destroy the torpidity of those in power in ways that bear an indelible mark on the linguistic fabric of their lives. Yet language is just one facet of radical politics. Beyond the invention of revolutionary language, radical subjects open us to a plethora of embodied knowledge born in the struggle, a theme we explore next.

---

20. Extensive interviews with Riad al-Turk were captured in two films made by Mohammad Ali Atassi about al-Turk's life: *Ibn al-Amm* [The Cousin] (2001) and *Ibn al-Amm Online* [The Cousin Online] (2012).

21. For more, see Bader Eddin, *Translating*.

Testimony as Lived Knowledge

Not all who witness the revolutionary moment are radical subjects, only those who exercise agency through choice and in creative imagination with the world. In questioning the possible, their rhetoric is necessarily liberatory. They see no other choice but to manifest their will, asking, "How could I be silent, when the volcano of revolution was erupting within me?"[22] Though radical subjects are responsive to the dominant ideology, they purposefully work for power removal and social change rather than gravitating toward power maintenance. They may be dominated, but they are not domesticated or convinced of their inferiority.[23] They are not empty vessels whose actions are wholly attributable to their subjectivation by his society and culture. Resistance cannot be both against oppressive power and also completely a dependent function of it.[24] Here, I lean on Edward Said's more solid concept of power in opposition to a Foucauldian imagination of power as fluid and everywhere.[25] The latter sticks us within a circle, dissolving the subject into a whirlwind of power that is impossible to resist. When we are intent on seeing power everywhere,[26] the radical subject's agency is annihilated.

Thus, though the radical subject exists in situ and not in vacuo, they act in a politically resistive manner to hegemonic norms. Their subject formation

---

22. Al-Abdallah, "Needy and the Trend."

23. I borrow here from Frantz Fanon's description of the colonized subject. Fanon, *Wretched of the Earth,* 16.

24. Said, *World.*

25. In Foucault's book *Discipline and Punish: The Birth of the Prison,* power is not just exercised from the top down (by the state, rulers, etc.) but is pervasive and operates through everyday interactions and institutions "from below." Individuals internalize societal norms and expectations to the extent that they regulate their own behavior as docile and compliant citizens. He argued that this self-discipline means we act in ways that conform to societal standards without needing direct supervision or threats of punishment. This understanding of power is arguably different from a solid understanding of the use of repressive power to produce obedience and of how power operates in authoritarian contexts. Although Edward Said initially drew on Foucault's theorization of power in his book *Orientalism,* with time he distanced himself from him due to his perception of the pacifying impact of Foucauldian understanding of power. In his words, "Foucault's imagination of power is largely with rather than against it. . . . I wouldn't go as far as saying that Foucault rationalized power, or that he legitimized its dominion and its ravages by declaring them inevitable, but I would say that his interest in domination was critical but not finally as contestatory or as oppositional as on the surface it seems to be." Said, *Reflections on Exile,* 242–43. In short, Said felt Foucault's theorizations of power (as fluid and coming from everywhere) were uninterested in oppositional movements and the dialectics of struggle. Importantly, Foucault derived his theories of power from Eurocentric models of prison reforms and not from colonial and authoritarian contexts. The radical subject is offered as a way of conceiving of how some subjects are able to escape totalizing power.

26. Foucault, *Discipline and Punish*; and Foucault, *History of Sexuality.*

is fundamentally initiated and sustained by power, but simultaneously, they are able to alienate themselves from power. As subjects experiencing self-renewal, they can escape, however momentarily or in limited fashion, hegemonic expectations. It is a subjectivity overfilling with political urgency and the refusal to "accept an assigned position within the amelioratory schemes proposed by the dominant discourse."[27]

Importantly, their agency has an embodied apparatus that brings about superior forms of lived knowledge in existential situations. This notion of agency is born of an ontological positioning—a mode of being in the world anchored in historical, political, and social location. In this acknowledgment is an unmasking of their authority as the originators of meaning. Certainly not exclusively, but perhaps judiciously, their authority matters. The Latin American philosopher Linda Alcoff argues that certain kinds of testimony have an epistemic realism that simultaneously disauthorizes other voices. A speaker's social location is "epistemically salient" for the truth and content of what is said.[28] By "truth," I mean not the philosophical a priori knowledge independent of experience—truth without parentheses—but truth that resides within empirical propositions.

My argument here compels us to theorize the radical subject in intersectional ways—as situated, communal, agentic, and engaging in practices that are constitutive of their knowledge. The radical subject does not "bear" on meaning but "determines" meaning (to switch the wording of Alcoff).[29] In other words, their affect has a relevance born of the boundedness of knowledge and relevance of place. This boundedness arises from firsthand exposure to revolution infused with latent credibility (a historic dimension of affect explored later in the book). Their latent credibility, built on the authority of intergenerational memories, saturates revolutionary practice and enriches their epistemic salience. Such subjects therefore exist at an ecology of various temporal, historical, and lived fluxes that augment their affective power.[30]

Often, they are the only trusted sources when nation-states deny independent media access and suppress the freedom to report on events. In Syria, international journalists and foreign NGOs faced insurmountable barriers entering the country, imposing a "stranglehold" over the country.[31] Many

27. Radhakrishnan, *Theory in an Uneven World,* 97.

28. Alcoff, "Problem of Speaking for Others," 7.

29. Alcoff, "Problem of Speaking for Others," 16.

30. The radical subject's autonomy exists despite and notwithstanding their existence as historicized social actors. They are not unshackled from contingent cultural contexts and (neo)colonial histories. Their testimony affords a critical understanding of the vast social, political, and economic issues that are at the heart of their resistance.

31. Cooke, *Dancing in Damascus,* 43.

citizen journalists and foreign reporters with the audacity to report what was happening died while attempting to communicate Syrian horrors.[32] For months at a time, there was no sign of "an NGO, not the Red Cross, not a Doctor Without Borders; no one."[33] This made international coverage of the revolution extremely limited, with many locals feeling "forced to report,"[34] because if they did not tell their truths, no one else would, or could. Trad al-Zahori, a regional boxing champion and cameraman from Homs who diligently covered events, from Al-Qalamoun to Eastern Ghouta and eventually Yabroud, discloses how the radical subject is at times the sole source of testimony, even to their own suffering:

> If I don't film this video, who will? And send it to people? But with my brother, when I first started filming, I took the video, the first body was my brother, but I didn't realize it. I started filming the others, suddenly I realized that was my brother. This is my brother! Guys, this is my brother! Oh God, Oh God.[35]

Perhaps it is only fitting that Trad al-Zahori would later inadvertently film his own death. With a camera clutched tightly in his hand, he is struck by shrapnel from a mortar explosion, his voice trembling behind the lens as he takes his last breath.[36] Other times, amid the echoes of gunfire and the cries of battle, radical subjects bore both cameras and weapons, shuttling between the two in a seamless dance. Ziad Homsi, a Free Syrian Army fighter and photojournalist, explains this dual existence: "We are fighters, and at the same time we are journalists. When you are holding a camera, and you are on the field holding weapon, often you have to put down your camera, turn around, and pick up your weapon."[37] Molhem Barakat, a daring citizen journalist who worked for the prorevolution Aleppo Media Centre and later for Reuters, took risks that would send shivers down the spine of most veteran journalists. At one point, in the midst of covering a story, Barakat darts to aid a wounded rebel fighter, ducking behind debris for cover while other fighters warn him to be careful as the ominous growl of an approaching tank reverberates through

---

32. Many of these foreign reporters had to break their visa conditions to visit areas beyond regime control or remain within regime territory with a regime minder.
33. Borri, *Syrian Dust*, 13.
34. Al-Ghazzi, "Forced to Report."
35. Pletts, "Revolution."
36. *Al Jazeera*, "Killing."
37. Atassi and Homsi, *Our Terrible Country*.

the air. He would die at eighteen years old, in his final moments covering the battle over Aleppo's Al-Kindi Hospital.[38]

The affective proximity of radical subjects frequently means navigating a labyrinth of revolutionary tasks and emotional labor. As explained by Khaled al-Issa, a media activist and photographer who would later meet his own tragic end in 2016, they would at once be protest planners cleaning the square and gathering people, photographers, audio experts, journalists, human rights documenters, medics, and so on:

> We are in a revolution. No one had a specific job. It is not like someone was a photographer or editor. We all did everything . . . When I was asked to shoot my first protest, I was asked to clean the square and plan things, locate where I will shoot, where the microphones would be placed . . . Sometimes I gathered people. Sometimes I had to take pictures of a martyr (for documentation purposes). I was tasked with going to hospitals and gather[ing] information about the injured. Sometimes I had to take care of the logistics of how to transport the injured to Turkey.[39]

Yassin al-Haj Saleh, the once imprisoned political dissident and towering intellectual figure, reflects on the moment he realized the awesome nature of his own testimony. Apprehensive about his own ability to write about the revolutionary moment, he grappled with an uneasiness about his own "naïve consciousness." He was only able to overcome this hesitancy through the recognition of the power of his *shahadah* (testimony):

> Writing from within a great upheaval, I was worried about my own naivety. It is possible that I carried the seeds of this apprehension from Hegel, some of whose work I had read during my years in prison. This German philosopher said that we live the present with a naive consciousness. This naivety stands in opposition to absolute knowledge, a Hegelian concept that entered Marxist thought under the rubric of "science" and scientific socialism. The Syrian revolution released me from such Hegelianisms. For me, naivety has come to mean the shahada of a witness, my own shahada about what I was part of, and my sense of things when the seemingly impossible erupted into vivid existence in my country. The impossible was a revolution.[40]

38. Tube True, "Rural Aleppo."
39. Al-Ghazzi, "'Forced to Report'"; ellipses in original.
40. Al-Haj Saleh, *Impossible Revolution*, ix.

Here, one can see how the imminent naivety of testimony is directly implicated in the superiority of knowledge. For the radical subject, testimony is not just a retelling of events but forms a specific kind of knowledge born of visions of one's own utopia. At its zenith, such testimony is incapable of transitioning into a "discursive formation"—human language collapses due to the impossibility of bearing witness to that which has no language. Affect is sometimes untranslatable into "discourse," existing instead in the realm of private moments with those held in trust, and articulated through whispers, images, objects, sounds, and silences, which come to the tongue and cannot be expressed. These emanations are abstract but perceptible, not necessarily literal but always rhetorical. This is the pretheoretical, uninterpreted, experiential state of cognition of the radical subject who has not been given a single day of reprieve. They are not distant observers of these events. They are enmeshed within them so profoundly that "we have not had time to catch our breath and look around, to check on ourselves and on our neighbors, to think about where we are and ponder the path that has taken us to where we are today."[41]

At moments, the cameras lay abandoned, a conscious choice born out of concern that the camera would diminish the very essence of their sincerity, or *ikhlas*. For instance, it was difficult to get the Free Syrian Army fighter Abdul Qadir al-Saleh (Haji Mari) to consent to be on camera. He once confided in the journalist Hadi al-Abdallah that "the camera kills our sincerity."[42] This reluctance is likely out of concern for *riya'* (the moral vice of insincerity and hypocrisy). In Islamic theology, narcissism and self-admiration in front of others might seep into the heart and take away from one's good intentions. At times, even the cameras could not document the atrocities witnessed and would be lowered out of reverence for those suffering: "We cannot always raise our camera to transmit the suffering of a child. Sometimes, we try to raise our cameras, but the camera comes down of its own accord, in humility and shame over what has become of these children and these families."[43]

For the radical subject, affective politics is capacitated by their direct immersion, coordination, and invention in concerted liberatory action. Their imaginary of a new world is inseparable from their embodied knowledge and truth. As one radical subject put it, "Anyone who wanted to shed light on what is happening is inevitably supporting the revolution. Conveying truth meant working for the interests of the revolution." [44] Here, not only does revolution

---

41. Al-Haj Saleh, *Impossible Revolution*, 2.
42. Al-Abdallah, "Needy and the Trend."
43. Al-Abdallah, "Needy and the Trend."
44. Al-Ghazzi, "Forced to Report."

mean a quest for truth, truth becomes a force affectively manifested in revolutionary activity.

Within this realm is the now mythic story of the origins of the revolution in the rural province of Daraa. It was there that five schoolboys boldly spray-painted the words "You are next, doctor," in allusion to Bashar al-Assad, on their school walls, innocently hopeful at the wave of protests in the region. The next day, the schoolboys, along with twenty others ranging from eleven to sixteen years old, were taken by security forces to the regional *mukhabarat* (security) headquarters.[45] The elders of the city pleaded for the boys' release. Instead, the head of the local mukhabarat, Atef Najib, told the parents, "Forget you have children. And if you want new children in their place, send your wives over and we'll impregnate them for you." The affront spread like wildfire in the conservative society of Daraa. Local protests exploded seemingly out of the earth itself. Hamza al-Khatib, a pudgy thirteen-year-old who participated with his father in these antiregime protests, was detained. Frantic, his family begged the authorities to release him. In response, his dead body was delivered to his family a month later, peppered in burn marks and gunshot wounds puncturing the skin, his jaw and kneecaps shattered, and his genitals severed. Syrian state TV denied responsibility, claiming the tale was nothing but lies and false reporting. In response, al-Khatib's family distributed a video of his battered purple body with the realities of his torture evident. The violent affectivity of his dead body built up in its circulation across social media, thrusting the protests from an abyss of potentiality to the actuality of revolution.

Aside from the body's ability to spur revolutionary affect, these stories signify privileged testimonies as holding "truth," the unhidden, unconcealed, nonperspectival *Alethia*. The irreducible bodily and autonomous affect of such subjects exists independent of our consciousness of it. The body's somatically sensed truth operates outside the realm of structures of language and discourse, what Alexander Weheliye calls the "prophetic traces of the hieroglyphics of the flesh."[46] One wonders, if the scars on little Hamza's body were not discursively recounted and reproduced, were they real? Is there another set of facts which vitiate the material reality of a dead boy's body and his family's intimate knowledge of the culprit? Are we all in a position to adjudicate the truth or falsity of their testimony? If the radical subject's text is only a fragment of the truth, what other form is more entitled to hold that mantle?

45. The mukhabarat are the regime's sprawling and intricate system of Syrian intelligence agencies, which keep files on the population. Modeled after the Stasi, the German Democratic Republic's state security apparatus, the mukhabarat monitor every aspect of life in Syria. They are above the law and exempt from any form of judicial oversight.

46. Weheliye, *Habeas Viscus*, 125.

These questions prompt us to confront the testimony of the radical sub-ject, as well as the unsettling reality of our perceptual and interpretive limita-tions. Assertions that the subject alone cannot be a truth-teller, but that truth is arrived at from a convergence of voices, fragments, and critics, often results in skewed half-truths or semi-truths.[47] I warrant that in moments such as the death of Hamza al-Khatib, the radical subject is an "active knower" who owns the totality of lived experience.[48] Chouliaraki and al-Ghazzi title this phe-nomenon "flesh witnessing" with "truth-telling authority," which is to say, no omniscient perspective is needed to ascertain the whole truth.[49]

Last but not least, the power of those mobilizing in defense of their dig-nity, lands, and modes of existing lies not only in their truth-telling capac-ity but also in their "ethical affect." Ethical affect, for Judith Butler, is a more nuanced understanding of affect—one that remains attuned to the uncondi-tional nature of ethical demands, while also staying fluidly responsive to the world around us.[50] This is perhaps the most provocative argument for embrac-ing the radical subject as the epicenter of affect, even when their testimony troubles us or resists easy incorporation into dominant narratives. As articu-lated by Edward Said, "If power oppresses and controls and manipulates, then everything that resists it is not morally equal to power, is not neutrally and simply a weapon against that power."[51] When conceptions of power travel too far, even resistance and the pursuit of justice are inventions of power. When we forsake the human as always within the reach of dominating systems, the human is reduced to a reactionary machine produced by the various whims and strategies of those in power. Those protesting on the streets and in univer-sities, chanting "peaceful, peaceful" against the sclerotic Assad regime as they were being shot in cold blood, are not insane rhetors but surely heroes. Their words are not simply words, not even just truths, but are imbued with affec-tive dedication to another world, another possible, with the power to detach us from their distant struggles. In harnessing their affective potential, we lean into their affective power—letting them speak into contested spaces where negotiation over meaning is ongoing.

Next, I tease out paradoxes in understanding radical subjects. This is a critical part of understanding how and why projects of "inclusion" are insuf-ficient to capturing the emancipatory qualities of this genus of revolutionary struggle.

---

47. Badiou, *On a Finally Objectless Subject.*
48. Wood and Cox, "Rethinking Critical Voice."
49. Chouliaraki and al-Ghazzi, "Beyond Verification," 649.
50. Butler, *Notes Toward a Performative Theory.*
51. Said, *World,* 246.

Navigating Perceptions:
The Complexities of Radical Subjecthood

Radical subjects often face incongruities or paradoxes in prevailing public understandings of who they are. As subjects who navigate the world with the most friction and the least favor, they are perpetually embroiled in what Wafa Mustafa—an activist campaigning for the release of her detained father—speaks of as a "competing war of narratives" in light of the fundamentally different readings of their liberatory efforts in the public arena.[52] They are named and described in ways that elicit a sense of unease and limit our ability to acknowledge them. Not only do they not receive the responses of international solidarity or recognition they deserve, but when discussed, they are obfuscated and mystified in endless ways.

First, radical subjects are deemed unworthy of revolutionary mobilization and incapable of achieving self-determination. Even at the initial stages of peaceful protest, they are proclaimed exempt from being "good guys,"[53] extremists fueled by sectarian hatred, or proxies of Western imperialism. Such depictions have not been confined to academics and think tanks. Popular culture is replete with them. For instance, the Syrian Revolution was judged to be deficient in Western liberal democratic norms, underscoring shortfalls in organization, in cohesiveness, in women's rights, and even accused of being co-opted by neoliberal logics that compromised all those who participated.

Elsewhere, it is dismissed as absent of revolutionary ideas and intellectual precepts—at most a "refolution."[54] Or it is unenlightened because it "did not come hand in hand with [a] token revolutionary theorist."[55] Another case in point here is Slavoj Žižek, who mounts a critique of the revolution as a "pseudo-struggle" with no "radical-emancipatory" voice.[56] These deficit pronouncements diminish radical subjects and preclude them from being recognized as capable of conjuring a truly radical vision of emancipation.

Second, the very proximity of radical subjects to the revolutionary phenomenon is held against them. The ontological nature of their political existence compromises them—they are reasoned to be too close to the causes in

---

52. Mustafa, "Syrian Revolution 10 Years On."

53. For instance, see Fisk's article "Syria's 'Moderates' Have Disappeared."

54. Bayat, *Revolution Without Revolutionaries*, 11.

55. Bardawil, "Critical Theory," 180. Aside from attributing intellectual thought only to the cultural and political elite, this tendency disregards the many "intellectuals of the book" who contributed to revolutionary activities, such as Yassin al-Haj Saleh, Hanadi Zahlout, Razan Zeitouneh, and Burhan Ghalioun, to name a few.

56. Žižek, "Syria Is a Pseudo-Struggle."

which they are involved and too intemperate to be reliable. Accusations of bias, emotionality, a dismissal of their "objectivity," or even a failing of rigor or preparedness, are propagated. Matthew Shaer, a Western journalist who covered the Syrian Revolution, opens up on how he "smirked" at the parrhesiastic practice of radical subjects and their flanking of danger. Their very alignment with the political currents at play becomes a point of contention:

> I listened to citizen journalists . . . describe carrying both cameras and sidearms; I heard them say they had helped picked out enemy sniper posts with their zoom lenses; I asked one if he considered himself to be an unbiased journalist, and received the following reply: "Yes, but for the side of the revolution." It was easy to smirk at this . . . to forget that while I had elected to write about the conflict in Syria, these journalists felt no such choice. . . . There are debates about biases and standards, and then there is the fear that your job will get you killed, and you do your job anyway, because you can't not.[57]

His words reveal an appraisal of how the prevailing ideals of rationality and detached witnessing, often summoned in a nonsensationalist manner by the objective journalist, are perceived as more relevant than the embodied epistemologies of the radical subject.

Third, radical subjects are habitually occluded by "grand narratives" of geopolitics and its life-destructive forms. One of the reasons for this is that advocacy, scholarship, and even critical coverage of revolutions implicitly prioritizes the perspective of those in power. In the Syrian case, much critical work centers the regime's strategic response in crushing the revolution, the transition toward militarization, and the complexity of geopolitical presence in the region. The overemphasis on structural factors has arguably resulted in radical subjects being objects of study, diced and deconstructed as passive recipients of the powers that be, but not fully engaged as constructors of visions in the intellectual and political realm. Aside from piecemeal efforts, we do not fully ascertain the breathtaking richness of their defiance, their mastery, and their lucidness in expressing grievances. The political subjectivities of these "lower-status" unconventional actors are not recognized in all their richness and collective audacity. We fail to capture the imaginings of radical subjects as a site of worldmaking populated with their intentions, achievements, and revolutionary mood. They are stripped of their agency and

---

57. Shaer, "One of Syria's Brave."

capacity for conceptual reflection, and in the process, we are unable to recognize the temporal polyphony where radical praxis and mutual liberation
already exist.

Last but not least, the very appearance of radical subjects frequently
antagonizes "rational" and "civil" notions of resistance. They are "complex victims" who do not easily cohere to dichotomies of innocence or aggression,[58]
a phenomenon compounded by their racial construction as "Other." A case
in point: Although initially lauded for the peaceful essence of their protests,
Syrians suddenly found themselves thrust in a negative light when they were
compelled to take up arms in response to mass expulsions and the collective punishments imposed upon entire cities. By 2012, faced with the relentless brutality of the state, many reevaluated their commitment to nonviolence
and decided to defend themselves and their communities.[59] The taking up of
arms eased the depiction of Syrian radical subjects as shaggy, bearded Islamic
extremists. State media was quick to capitalize on these misrepresentations,
which were increasingly susceptible to uptake, referring to radical subjects as
"infiltrators," "armed gangs," and "salafi terrorists."[60] In the vacillation between
the dichotomous prism of the Assad regime and zealot Islamist groups is a
complete subversion of revolutionary grassroot actors. In this maneuver, radical subjects are casually conflated with extremists in one hyphenated mon-
strous identity.[61] Noam Chomsky, the distinguished linguist and intellectual,

---

58. Bouris, *Complex Political Victims*.

59. Sustained repression against unarmed resistance has historically served as the instiga-
tor of armed mobilization, not only cultivating the desire for revenge but leaving many feeling
there is no other way to defend their families and communities.

60. The performative nature of the "bourgeois" Ba'ath party under Assad, within a politics
of whiteness and hypersecularism, similarly served to whitewash the regime's atrocities against
Syrians and present the "secular regime" as a more acceptable option. This allowed the Assad
regime to be perceived within an aesthetic framework where Bashar al-Assad is presented as
young, Western-educated, and polished. The cosmopolitan signification of the mild-mannered
former ophthalmologist Bashar al-Assad, in his tailored suits and ties, along with his elegant
British-born investment banker wife, positioned them as modernizers and a stable presence in
the region, granting him legitimacy to govern over irrational fanatics and "black" Syrians with
beards.

61. Yassin al-Haj Saleh writes: "It is not true that the majority of believers are the natural social base for the extremist groups. I made six profiles of fighters in Eastern Ghouta in
the spring of 2013. Five of them were believers, but none was a fundamentalist." Al-Haj Saleh,
"Syria, Iran, ISIS." Elsewhere, the journalist Hassan Hassan nuances these designations: "Syria
is no longer witnessing a struggle of moderates versus extremists, but of extremists versus both
moderates and religious moderates." Fighting groups were not ideologically homogenous in
terms of religion, with a few joining groups because of effectiveness and discipline on the battle-
field, rather than religious ideology. Hassan, "Army of Islam." Indeed, within the Free Syrian
Army, for instance, fighters "differ so widely in the extent they adhere to the moral principles
of the revolution . . . the vast disparity they embody are a carbon copy of real life in all its
diversity." Yazbek, *Woman in the Crossfire*, 15.

repeatedly disregards Syrian radical subjects by insisting their revolution is indistinguishable from atrocities committed by Daesh, a narrative Syrians have repeatedly denounced.[62] Of note here is that Chomsky's admitted source on Syria is the Irish journalist Patrick Cockburn,[63] resulting in a phenomenon that Syrian writer Leila al-Shami has called "old white men who rely on each other for their news about Syria, rather than actually talking to Syrians."[64] One might even call it a form of "epistemic coloniality" advancing a liberal universalist worldview couched in the vacuum of an echo chamber.[65] These kinds of dialectical practices increasingly rely on mythical constructions of "those-who-are-not-us" to describe worlds beyond us as threatening.[66]

Among the most egregious of claims in this vein is that the White Helmets, a humanitarian organization of search-and-rescue workers who rush to the rubble to salvage civilians, are an Al-Qaeda-linked terrorist organization.[67] Counternarratives by disinformation campaigns seek to disorient, sow doubt, and erode radical subjects as a "hotbed" of terrorists staging chemical

---

62. This is not to deny the presence of colonial actors and counterrevolutionary extremist forces, such as Daesh and the Al-Qaeda affiliate Jabhat al-Nusra, who entered the scene around ten months after the revolution started and contributed to muddying the waters surrounding radical subjects. The entry of extremist factions into the arena allowed for the promulgation of a "war on terror" metanarrative to whitewash the Assad regime by characterizing the entire Syrian opposition as its violent Islamist counterpart. Without denying the disturbing presence of counterrevolutionary extremist groups in Syria, the Assad regime was far more destructively violent against the country's people than any other group in the country. Although media and scholarly debate disproportionately focuses on extremist groups, 94 percent of the victims of the revolution were killed by the Assad regime, with support from its Russian and Iranian allies. See Syrian Network for Human Rights, "6th Anniversary." A "fractional perspective" heightens attention to killings by Daesh over the regime's chemical weapons attacks or aerial bombing. Al-Haj Saleh, "Syria and Western Powers." Neither Daesh nor any rebel factions possessed the attack helicopters or fighter jets that rained death on civilians in the thousands. The truth is that Syrians were victims of two forms of terrorism, that of the Assad regime and of extremist groups.

63. Hamad, "You Want the Truth?"

64. Massey, "Most Important."

65. For all his brilliance, it is often forgotten that Noam Chomsky participated in the denial of the Khmer Rouge's brutality toward Cambodians, dismissing their agency and the veracity of their narratives. In reference to stories shared by Cambodian refugees who escaped the atrocities of the Khmer Rouge regime, he stated that "refugees are frightened and defenseless, at the mercy of alien forces. They naturally tend to report what they believe their interlocuters wish to hear." Chomsky and Herman, *Distortions*. Chomsky's genocide denial has also extended to the Bosnian Muslims killed in the Srebrenica massacre. See Katerji, "West's Leftist"; and Linfield, *Lion's Den*.

66. Singh, *Unthinking Mastery*, 173.

67. *The White Helmets* won Best Documentary (Short Subject) at the 89th Academy Awards. See von Einsiedel, *White Helmets*. For a more detailed analysis of their work and of disinformation campaigns on their activities, listen to the BBC, "Mayday"; *Bellingcat*, "Chemical Weapons and Absurdity"; Solon, "How Syria's White Helmets"; and Atlantic Council, "Russia's Disinformation Campaign."

weapons attacks against themselves. In an analogous vein, President Obama spoke of "ancient sectarian differences" when describing the Syrian Revolution, feeding into parochial stereotypes of the region as mired in blood feuds and primordial hatreds between ethnic groups and religious sects.[68] By giving sectarianism a disproportionate visibility as a factor in the resistance, radical subjects are articulated within the parameters of a sweeping Islamic resistance embedded in Sunni-Alawite strife and not based on a genuine desire for reform.[69]

The vernacular of radical subjects often relies on culturally and socially specific language reflective of their local knowledge, value schemes, and traditions. Hence, the problem of solidarity is also a problem of translation and language, one that becomes pronounced when language is a vessel of identity and faith. To borrow the words of Homi Bhabha in his fiery forward to Frantz Fanon's *Wretched of the Earth,* radical subjects are "culturally clothed" subjects who may not always conform to norms and practices of so-called civil society.[70]

Undeniably, resistance against the Assad regime, though initially worldly and secular, in certain localities became asserted within a rhetoric of religiosity.[71] In numerous ways, this vernacular theology makes radical subjects

68. Obama, "Statement by the President." Though I do not sidestep the presence of sectarianism in the country, the Assad regime was responsible for impelling sectarianism to the surface as a tool of governance to divide the working-class solidarity of the revolution. From the perspective of the Syrian Revolution, the Assad regime, along with Iranian militia, Hezbollah allies, and Alawi *shabiha* (state-sponsored "thugs"), was more intensely sectarian than the resistance has ever been. For more, read al-Haj Saleh, *Impossible Revolution.*

69. Another iteration of this phenomenon is the term *civil war,* a term many radical subjects eschew for its suggestion of an equal playing field between the oppressor and the oppressed, arguing the balance of power is so asymmetrical that it is better characterized as a genocide against civilians and poorly armed revolutionaries. In a discourse fashioned on narratives inherited from colonial powers, the regime cast itself as the protector of racial and ethnic minorities. Alawites are members of a secretive Muslim sect that predominates in the mountainous areas of Lattakia. Only a select few are initiated into their core dogma and rituals. Though they are minorities in Syria, after the Ba'ath party took power, they displaced the Sunni majority for domination of the country. Minorities were tokenized to legitimate the regime's behavior and scorched-earth policy toward the majority–Arab Sunni population. Through recruiting minorities as a social category, both real and imagined dangers of racial and ethnic intolerance were exploited to the regime's benefit. Identity markers once bequeathed by colonial actors in the country were reinvigorated as a shield to camouflage the massacres of the Assad regime.

70. Fanon, *Wretched of the Earth,* xxiv.

71. For example, the chant "Ya Allah Malna Ghairak Ya Allah" (O God, we have nothing but you) became ubiquitous among protestors. Over time, a segment of radical subjects drew justification for their fight against tyranny from their religion. For many, there was a sincere devotedness from which they found succor for their resistance. For them, demands for political and civic freedom were not incongruent with religious piety.

culturally unrecognizable as freedom fighters within hegemonic notions of civil discourse and secularism. By vernacular, I imply the language of the working class, the disempowered, and the marginalized in their everyday communicative exchanges when resisting oppression. Vernacular discourses commonly manifest themselves within religious and cultural formations. The expectation of cultural assimilation here is a tactic of political, racial, and imperial domination pigeonholing radical subjects into mutually exclusive "secular" or "religious" narratives, overlooking that many do not live in either binary.[72] Religion is deemed culturally antidemocratic and intrinsically alien to civil modes of resistance. Within a Christian-centric global religious hierarchy, certain faiths cannot incite, or even coexist with, emancipatory mobilization. This framing also ignores the intersectional grassroots mobilization of radical social movements, which cuts across class, political, religious, ethnic, and gender divisions. It effaces the manifold realities of radical subjects, glossing over their remarkable diversity—Christians, atheists, secularists, and "secular" people of faith—who are all critical in the long-term trajectory of these kinds of movements.

In sum, these narratives are no doubt rooted in acute reservations about those for whom a theological corpus imbues their resistance to oppression.[73] To use the language of Judith Butler, the radical subject's vernacular becomes the "frame differentiat(ing) the lives we can apprehend from those we cannot."[74] This is true of all sorts of ethnic, peasant, and marginal urban groups, whose vernacular(s) is one of the tools harnessed to make terroristic the very forms of political dissent these movements seek to displace.

---

72. The expectation of cultural assimilation can be seen across various communities. See Ghazal Aswad and Partain, "Gift or Gilded Cage?" For example, in the context of Black lives, the pressure to assimilate into white cultural norms has a long history in the United States and beyond. During periods of slavery and Jim Crow segregation, Black individuals were forced to adopt the language, religion, and cultural practices of white society as a means of survival and acceptance. This expectation of assimilation was not only about cultural conformity but also served to justify systems of racial oppression. Black cultural practices, including language, music, and spiritual beliefs, were often denigrated as inferior or threatening to the dominant order.

73. This was evident in early concerns that the majority of early protests came out of mosques (the only place large numbers of people could gather without arousing suspicion). Christians, Alawites, Druze, and atheists attended Friday prayers with the singular intention of joining the protest afterward. Many protestors were also practicing Muslims who headed to protests after prayer. Mosques were institutions highly monitored by the state and were not a place of free congregation or recruitment, but Friday prayers were the rare exception where people could legally gather and organize. Essentially, as forms of indigenous infrastructure, mosques were appropriated as spaces of resistance, as was the case with African American churches in the American Civil Rights Movement.

74. Butler, *Frames of War*, 3.

These are just some of the affective frames that find currency in popular and political discourse and which put a sharper edge on the ways in which radical subjects and their worldmaking projects are invisibilized, maligned, and misunderstood. For other radical subjects, the narratives will not be the same but may be built on similar notions of erasure and negativity that dilute moral outrage at the state's exterminatory tactics of repression.

The radical subject's raced body is excessive and chaotic, to be disciplined, consumed, or decried, particularly in ways that relieve others of responsibility. It is not possible to fantasize these abstractions, "discourses," or "representations" as separable from the (non)political commitment to solidarity. They make apparent the many forms of normativity proliferating in "representations" of the radical subject that must be dismantled to create the possibility for solidarity in revolutionary times. Such frames not only dehumanize the radical subject, they constitute the very terms of our imagination of them. They attest to the need to recalibrate our instrumentarium—our analytical approach and tool kit—in the presence of the radical subject. This will be explored at greater length next.

The Problem with Inclusion: The Radical Subject as the Starting Point in Inquiry

In this section, I advocate a shift away from the equal inclusion of all discourses, a widening of the scope, or an attempt to adopt more voices into consideration. It is crucial for "projects of inclusion" to recognize how some privileged voices stifle radical imagination and unintentionally annihilate, dispossess, and silence radical subjects. We live in an era of epistemic crisis, propaganda, and conspiracy theories in which many different types of social, political, and moral subjects engage in practices of witnessing, which communication scholar Bradford Vivian claims "infuse(s) public discourse."[75] Liberal ideals of inclusion, progress, and reform originate from and thus unintentionally perpetuate the same epistemological foundations and structures that they seek to critique. As Karma Chávez rightly states, "Projects of inclusion don't rupture oppressive structures; instead they uphold and reinforce those structures by showing how they can be kinder and gentler and better without actually changing much at all."[76] Such liberal ideals are dominated by

---

75. Vivian, *Commonplace Witnessing*, 2.
76. Chávez, "Beyond Inclusion," 166.

individualistic, universalistic, and rationalistic frameworks that assume a subjectivity that rejects the ontological and affective nature of radical politics.[77]

Moreover, certain privileged locations may be "discursively dangerous" in that they have the potential to harm or reinforce the oppression of certain peoples.[78] Subjects speaking from such privileged locations are often incapable of reckoning with what Colombian anthropologist Arturo Escobar calls the "pluriversal world," a world where resistant collectivities breach impenetrable systems of power.[79] For example, in the case of Syria, most dismissive readings of the revolution have been by well-respected and renowned experts, intellectuals, journalists, politicians, social media influencers, and academics, including Noam Chomsky, Robert Fisk, Patrick Cockburn, and Seymour Hersh, to name a few. Oftentimes, those removed from conflict are afforded theoretical primacy, positioned within a worshipful lens toward cosmopolitan dispositions, objective observers, institutional bodies and their "discursive formations," and "the transparency of the intellectual."[80] The latter are more often than not dominated by the modernist and rationalist bias of the West, and the prerogatives of those who exhibit hierarchical patterns of epistemic judgment embedded in the judicial and public sphere. Notwithstanding the presence of dissenting voices, these subjects, particularly when situated in states competing for hegemony, have "disproportionate influence and power over how international political space is represented."[81]

Naturally, in conditions of crisis, our allegiances are to those who are "recognizable to us, and who conform to certain culturally specific notions about what the culturally recognizable human is."[82] We are all implicated in the universal constructs of the current dominant systems, including capitalist, patriarchal, neoliberal, colonial, racist, and hierarchical systems, which directly inhibit the ability to listen to the radical subject. Therefore, this chapter is not about singling out or isolating any individual thinker, commentator, or public official but is meant to reflect on the conditions that pervade our contemporary life and dispositions toward radical subjects. None of us are impervious to these trends. Neither do I claim ethical superiority, as much as acknowledge the ways in which we are all complicit and how our actions might perpetuate the problem.

---

77. Mouffe, *Agonistics*.
78. Alcoff, "Problem of Speaking for Others," 7.
79. Escobar, *Pluriversal Politics*.
80. Spivak, *Can the Subaltern Speak*, 75.
81. Tuathail and Agnew, "Geopolitics and Discourse," 195.
82. Butler, *Frames of War*, 42.

Configurations of knowledge forms prevalent in patriarchal, capitalist, and colonial/modern settings decenter radical subjects, delegitimize them, constraining not only what we consider "true" but also our ability to register their affect, and "who can speak and with what force."[83] As discussed in the previous chapter, even those who claim a politics of liberation and a concern for historically marginalized subject matters and populations are inimical to the radical subject. It is therefore no surprise that critical readings of this genus of revolutionary struggle often mirror oppressive hierarchies, denying radical subjects competency in providing determinative analysis of their revolution. Yassin al-Haj Saleh formidably words this sentiment:

> Either there is no value to what we say, or we are confined to lesser domains of knowledge, turned into mere sources for quotations that a Western journalist or scholar can add to the knowledge he produces. They may accept us as sources of some basic information, and may refer to something we, natives, said in order to sound authentic, but rarely do they draw on our analysis. This hierarchy of knowledge is very widespread and remains under-criticized.[84]

Hierarchies of knowledge (in which Anglo- and Eurocentric structures of thought dominate) make it necessary to center the intellectual practice and testimonies of those who insurrect hope in productive opposition to biopolitics and its reductive ontologies of political and material death. This is in line with ongoing conversations among scholars in Indigenous studies, cultural studies, feminist studies, and other disciplines to transition toward embodied, material, and nonhuman forms of meaning-making from the standpoints of those at the margins. For instance, in her writings, Chicana scholar Gloria Anzaldúa refers to *conocimiento*—embodied consciousness—as a form of knowledge deeply rooted in the body, experience, and identity.[85] For Anzaldúa, conocimiento is a way of knowing that comes from one's experiences of living at the intersections of various identities, such as being Chicana, feminist, and queer. Conocimiento is a way to reclaim and honor the wisdom that comes from lived experiences, from the struggles faced by those on the margins of society.

Building on the lived knowledge of radical subjects, as well as the implicit and explicit ways in which their intellectual practice is disrespected and marginalized, I end this chapter with a call to privilege their testimony to build

---

83. Campbell, "Agency," 3.
84. Al-Haj Saleh, "Syrian Cause and Anti-Imperialism."
85. Anzaldúa, *Borderlands / La Frontera*.

affectual bonds of solidarity. Any radical alternative to dominant ethics of making meaning, I propose, must start by reclaiming the testimonies of the radical subject, setting them apart as entitled to veneration. By positing the radical subject as the principal locus of suasive conception or as the responsible means of creating meaning, we brace ourselves for affective attunement, sensitively listening to their truths as opposed to hiding them under philological bushels or viewing them with critical suspicion. The invitation enacts a "stance of openness" where one "stands under" them listening not for what one can agree or disagree with but rather "for the exiled excess."[86] In other words, listening not for what one can agree with or challenge but practicing an undivided attentiveness which intends to understand.

As critical scholar Homi Bhabha notes, "The affective experience of social marginality—as it emerges in noncanonical cultural forms—transforms our critical strategies."[87] This is not to say that the radical subject should not be answerable to critical contemplation, but that they might be approached with the same privilege furnished to mainstream orders of knowledge. As explained earlier, the radical subject's emancipatory rhetoric rarely aligns with normative scripts of resistance, thus triggering anxieties that lie at the heart of Euro-American reason, whether by rule or convention. As "disturbers," their rhetoric is illegible, offending, ill-suited, and inappropriate. The innumerable tensions they evoke act as a repelling force impinging on the willingness to apprehend them. When we subject them to the same suspicion afforded to the hegemonic discourse of those with "superior" rationality, we preemptively prevent a dwelling with the radical subject.

Hegemonic perspectives are always and already afforded a privileged space within the field of the social. Demonstrably, an "excess of information" has allowed for an environment that allows "ambiguity, contingency, and competing views to thrive."[88] Though privileging all forms of rationality echoes an ethos of inclusivity, in broadening the possibilities of what "counts," we inadvertently relegate to lower dominion those with intimate knowledge of crises. When radical subjects are just one reading within a constellation of other readings, we prevent an intentional dwelling within their affective milieus. This "inclusive" ethos hovers too close to the institutional standards that demonstrably marginalize the radical subject time and time again. The "aggregation of talking heads"[89] does not enhance our capacity to create or produce solidarity but makes invisible or secondary the affective dimensions of radical

86. Ratcliffe, Rhetorical Listening, 25.
87. Bhabha, Location of Culture, 172.
88. Wedeen, Ideology, 82.
89. Fiumara, Other Side of Language, 167.

subjects. In a similar vein, rhetorical scholar Bradford Vivian describes the phenomenon of "commonplace witnessing," in which a wide variety of citizens, politicians, and civic institutions adopt idioms of witnessing to serve a variety of social, political, and moral ends, although many of these subjects do not possess any intimate or historical experiences of injustice or tragedy.[90] In warning, the French philosopher Emmanuel Levinas argues that a multiplicity of perspectives is not necessary to arrive at absolute truth, because, as he words it, it is not as though "each person, through his uniqueness, ensured the revelation of a unique aspect of the truth, and that certain sides of it would never reveal themselves if certain people were missing from mankind."[91]

In the tendency to designate the radical subject's discursive formations doxastic—just a matter of opinion and not knowledge-based—we find that ambiguity enters into interpretations of radical epistemologies. Without privileging the radical subjects' testimonies, one slips into a sea of epistemic misrepresentations that make "obvious issues mysterious and complex issues even more complex."[92] Otherwise, even if we carefully open ourselves to a labyrinth of knowledge and perspectives, if we were to "unroll" this labyrinth, "we would find a single thread in our hands."[93] As such, a kaleidoscope of viewpoints is not always a sign of health or maturity but rather serves a gatekeeping function deflecting from the material reality detected solely on conditions of radicality. Counteracting by not constraining those who require higher orders of hearing, response, and theorization allows for radical subjects to be on a level playing field with those in elevated positions in hierarchies of civilizations (i.e., where white Euro-Americans land squarely on top). In essence, failing to distinguish between that which must be esteemed and that which must be disparaged suppresses the affective power of the radical subject.

My logic here is akin to those who problematize the rhetoric of "All Lives Matter" as inviting a color blindness to those whose voices are not heard in the struggle for social justice. Those already implicated in the dominant rhetorics and who are detached from the historied nature of conflict are given equal considerations of credibility. This results in a "standard total academic view"[94] far removed from what the radical subject has experienced. Due to the imposing nature of hegemony, entrusting many different subjects with the authority to disseminate knowledge compounds the negation of radical subjects and retains the inherent precarity of these subjects even among those who

90. Vivian, *Commonplace Witnessing*.
91. Levinas, *Beyond the Verse*, 133.
92. Al-Haj Saleh, "Syria and Western Powers."
93. Fiumara, *Other Side of Language*, 160.
94. Ear, "Khmer Rouge."

theoretically stand in solidarity. Hegemonic perspectives attuned to those in power within the capitalist/modern/colonial world-system ignore or misrepresent their insights while placing themselves as chief informants. The onslaught of perspectives within a fragile political economy of attention leaves audiences alienated, disempowered, and worse, apathetic and even adverse to the struggles of others.

It is important to therefore draw this distinction: The radical subject as the starting point in inquiry is the means through which we open ourselves to their affective essence. They disclose a cradle of affectability at the locus of knowing, truth, agency, and the body, each integral to the other. In awaiting the abundance of the radical subject's affect, in venerating their testimonies and lived knowledges, one might not necessarily negate the adverse norms of recognition mentioned earlier, but we certainly open the possibility of escaping its fissures.

Conclusion

Although the radical subject emerges from liminal spaces, in the wake of their embodied and embedded revolutionary practice, they become the leaders of affective politics. Their affective power arises out of ways of feeling, ways of thinking, and ways of behaving in the world. Put differently, the radical subject destabilizes our sense of the dualisms between reason and emotion, power and ethics, the body and knowledge. Their testimony is affectively infused with the power both to inform and to elicit affect, beckoning us onto the sensual routes that might lead to solidarity. Actions of solidarity are the meaningful conclusion of a process that purposively values the radical subject's testimony as knowledge. Through acknowledging the mobilizing potential of the radical subject, their affective pull, we are agitated toward a space where we might all become "cognitive revolutionaries," a term by Black feminist philosopher Sylvia Wynter to refer to the expansion of our thought that enables us to forge relationships with one another.[95]

This chapter has asked the reader to be mindful of their starting points. We cannot place the testimonies of those in liberatory struggle on the same plane of suspicion as mainstream discourses and hope to transformatively inculcate the imperative for action on their behalf within dominant ideological schemes. Riad al-Turk, a prominent Syrian opposition leader nicknamed "Syria's Mandela," beautifully captures the hermeneutics of decolonial love

---

95. McKittrick, *On Being Human*, 179.

with which to approach the radical subject: "Now we face a people emerging from their silence. . . . Let us listen to them carefully, walk with them and not ahead of them and forbid ourselves to hijack their voices to our benefit."[96] Solidarity cannot be grounded in notions of neutrality, impartiality, and independence if it hopes to intervene in structures of power. By placing the radical subject as the leading point of inquiry, the world is revealed differently. Such hermeneutic efforts recognize the affective authority of subjects of liberation struggles and how we might engender consciousness of their vibrant intensities of truth. Though privileging all forms of rationality evokes an ethos of inclusivity, in narrowing the possibilities for what matters, rather than impoverishing meaning, we attune ourselves to its fullest potential.

But the radical subject's affectivity is not found only at the cornerstone of their lived testimonies and bounded knowledge in the revolutionary moment. In the next chapter, the historicity of the radical subject comes into view, in particular the ways postmemory compels us to look to histories far longer and more inclusive than those we have to date. As will be shown, memory not only brings the radical subject into effect, it is a constitutive element of their affective life and their capacity to induce solidarity.

---

96. Atassi, *Ibn al-Amm Online*. This reorientation requires strict discipline, an attitude of rigor, to unblock the affectively limiting habitual modes of meaning-making, and a willingness to believe radical subjects. This will be addressed extensively in chapter 5.

CHAPTER 3

On Postmemory

Our Hearts Haven't Been Quenched Yet

Oh stories, take us out of your mind
And in the heart of the present keep us
What do you want from the past?
We weren't created for our history
Our nights, our nights
The prisoners of yesterday don't leave us.
—Julia Boutros, "Oh Stories"

When I first heard that Kenda had participated in a women's protest in 1979, I was on a cloud for a few days. Kenda, the woman who had a hand in raising me, the epitome of propriety and gentility, was, in her own way, revolutionary. Her stance of civil disobedience was instrumental to how I understood my stance against the regime.[1] The affective fabric of her memories, as one of her daughters, Maya, words it, "come out of the heart and fall into the heart (of others)." When I asked Kenda about the protest over the phone, she told me, "We did nothing, close the topic." I could imagine her lifting her eyebrows to signal she could not talk. In spite of Kenda's denial, and the undisputed waning of memory, she did not suffer from amnesia. Remembering is not always a choice. The past cannot be exorcised.

While she kept her stories to herself during phone conversations, ever fearful of the regime tapping her communications, over her kitchen table she would share memories which had survived the ravages of time. Despite the state's frequent infringement of her private space, we bore witness to her trauma. We were her community, providing succor, if not resolution, to her melancholy. By keeping the past in the present, she was able to tolerate the unbearable contingencies of living. We were enchanted by her memories. Every time we visited her, Kenda would "repeat the whole story, in all its

---

1. All the quotes from family in this chapter were translated by the author from the original colloquial Arabic. The names of family members, as well as the precise familial relationships I have with them, have been anonymized.

details. Every time, it's the same story. But she needs to tell it. And we listen" (Maya). She would remember, then repress, speak in broken refrains, then fall silent. When she was alone, she would take out the decades-old newspaper with her son's image on it, falling apart with holes and curling at the edges but somehow still intact, one of the few remaining relics of her son.

When the 2011 revolution erupted into vivid existence in Syria, the elderly were cautious. The activist Najlaa al-Sheikh describes how our elders warned her: "This movement will lead to your end. And they were right."[2] Others were optimistic, such as a family friend who lost all her family to the regime: "We will be victorious, it is impossible for it to happen again and for us to not be victorious. It *will* happen means it *will* happen." Even with the knowledge of past traumas, the revolutionary Syrian spirit endured. This time, it was not into the unknown or with innocent gullibility but with knowledge inherited from confessional ancestors. Syrians had an ethic of sacrifice, innately aware of the incalculable risks they were assuming. As expected, those that chanted "the army and the people, hand in hand" were detained, imprisoned, tortured, mutilated, and as a courtesy, left at their family's doorstep.

This chapter engages the historic dimensions of the radical subject's affect, their postmemory, to describe how their affect accumulates, temporally and spatially, beyond the public sphere. Postmemory, that is, second-generation memories, impacts the latent credibility of radical subjects. Latent credibility is an avenue from which we might understand the formation of their affect and its intensification over time. It indexes their affect as infinitely more complex than and therefore uncontainable in a single discourse of affect, while also pointing to the ways the past, present, and future intertwine with legacies of authoritarian and colonial violence.

For Marianne Hirsch, postmemory is how the generation after the Holocaust has experienced the personal, collective, and cultural trauma of their ancestors by German leadership, crimes that reached an end point and were prosecuted in the Nuremberg trials.[3] In the case of Syria, postmemory operates at various registers of spatiotemporality given that the Assad regime (with the father, Hafez al-Assad, and then the succession of his son Bashar al-Assad) remained in power for over fifty years, persisting for generations in oppression, arbitrary detention, summary executions, torture, and enforced disappearance of Syrians as tools of repression and control.[4] The trauma was at

2. Kadi, *Little Gandhi.*
3. Hirsch, *Generation of Postmemory.*
4. During the revolution, it is estimated that the Assad regime and their militias arbitrarily detained around a hundred thousand individuals, denying them due process, legal representation, and communication with their families. There was also weekly incineration of bodies. See International Center for Transitional Justice, "Gone Without a Trace."

once inherited and contemporaneously experienced. Even with the fall of the Assad regime, as yet there have not been comprehensive trials or reparations that could mark an attempt at accountability or atonement toward closure for Syrians.

With this intention, this chapter visits the Events, a resonant event in modern Syrian history and a multivalent knot of memory. *The Events* is a euphemism for the rebellion by the Muslim Brotherhood and the ensuing violence and massacres that occurred during late 1970s and early 1980s.[5] In February 1982, Hama was leveled to the ground with infantry, armor, air assault, and artillery. It was a deliberate decision by Hafez al-Assad to make an example of the rebellious city and signal to the populace how the regime deals with dissent. In disproportionate revenge, ten to forty thousand people were slaughtered and buried in mass graves.[6] In the aftermath of the Events, organized political opposition weakened and civil society was quiescent—i.e., the Assad

---

5. There was a protracted and bitter history between the Ba'ath Party and the Muslim Brotherhood in Syria. For some context, the Muslim Brotherhood was founded in Syria in 1942 as an extension of the main branch in Egypt. At one stage, they ran for elections and had four member representatives in parliament. They did not call for sharia law in the country, but rather their rhetoric centered around freeing Syrians from colonization. The founder of the Syrian Brotherhood, Mustafa al-Sibai, who lead the organization from 1945 to 1961, authored the canonical book *The Socialism of Islam*, which argues that Islam is compatible with socialism. The Brotherhood's activities came to a halt when they were outlawed, once by Gamal Abdel Nasser in 1958 and subsequently by the Ba'ath Party in 1963, after which they operated in secret. The organization went through evolutionary cycles and had a "deeply heterogeneous geographical, cultural and ideological composition." Lefevre, *Ashes of Hama*, 82. Initially, the organization was opposed to armed militancy and focused their energies on educational reform. However, in 1979 there was an acute ideological shift toward armed struggle, with the conviction that it would be impossible to achieve their objectives of emancipating Syrians otherwise. In a Majlis al Shura (advisory or consultative council) meeting in Amman, the leaders created a military branch and endorsed violence as a legitimate response to state repression. This caused a fracture in the leadership, but the decision was justified as appropriate self-defense in the face of Ba'athist provocations: "We did not begin our jihad until . . . after having received the broken bodies of our brothers who had died under torture." Lefevre, *Ashes of Hama*, 110. Like other political movements, Islamism does not exist in a vacuum and draws on the peculiarities of time and space. The endorsement of violence was as an option of last resort in light of the regime's military warfare, rather than a result of core beliefs in its ideological documents. Some claim the brotherhood split from the Fighting Vanguard, while others claim this never formally happened. In any case, there was a crossover of membership. This chapter centers the Syrian Muslim Brotherhood (considered the Syrian right), arguably the opposition group that mounted the largest resistance to the regime. The Syrian left never "had the preparedness and capabilities to possess power and confront the regime's violence [that the Syrian right had]." Shabo, "Exile." Admittedly, this focus risks minimizing the role of other currents of resistance, all representing diverse constituents in the political fabric of Syria. For more, read al-Romoh, "MB in Syria"; Batatu, *Syria's Peasantry*; Conduit, *Muslim Brotherhood in Syria*; Kilani, "Introduction to Syrian Political Life"; Zakaria, "Traditional Opposition Parties in Syria"; and Zollner, *Muslim Brotherhood*.

6. Sardar and Yassin-Kassab, *Syria*.

FIGURE 2. Poster of the Norias of Hama with the phrase
"It will not be repeated." Used with permission from The
Syrian People Know Their Way. Shared on Facebook,
January 30, 2012, https://www.facebook.com/Syrian.
Intifada/photos/a.148885538508914/284149684982498.

family was by and large uncontested for power. In the words of the leftist dissident Riad al-Turk, Syria became "a kingdom of silence." But, determinations
of Syrians as politically dead obscured much. Indeed, the memories of *the
Events* are so scorched into the minds of Syrians that in the initial protests of
2011, Syrians chanted "we will not let the massacres of 1982 be repeated!" (see
figure 2).[7]

Unlike the 9/11 Twin Towers memorial, there is no public iconography or
memorial for the Events, nor is it taught in school history books. There was
no back-and-forth civic discourse and deliberation among those in the public
arena about what happened. Instead, the memory of the Events was systematically erased: Entire urban districts were bulldozed and the rubble of the dead
steamrolled over as if it were a parking lot. In Al-Kilaniyya, the place where
the Hama Massacre occurred, the Afamia Cham Hotel, a vegetable market in
the Hamidiyeh neighborhood, and a garden near Bakr al-Sadiq mosque were

---

7. The waterwheels are the landmark symbol of the city of Hama, where the Hama Massacre took place in 1982.

built. When the authoritarian state suppresses genocidal memory, the legacies of resistance perdure in the private domain. As banished histories, there is a "gap in narratives. . . . The puzzle of silence. . . . it is as if Hama was forgotten," but on closer inspection, the memories are infused with an amalgam of meanings and feelings in Syrian life.[8] In this sense, I diverge from "the public" as the central realm of action and immortality and instead consider the private domain as a realm of visceral affect for radical subjects.

In the first part of this chapter, I share a vignette from oral family histories to probe how unresolved grief in the authoritarian context informs radical subjectivity. It reads and feels differently than the other chapters in the book, situating the reader with a story I grew up with, one that precedes and supersedes my life. Rafi's story is a sufferer's lament, a story of embodied resistance, armed opposition, and murder by the state. It is relayed in narrative form, without critical analysis. Under the weight of intense state censorship, venues of remembrance are often constrained. Stories are generative for understanding the embodied experiences of others, especially those that go against official narratives and are frequently muted or distrusted.[9] Before now, most of these stories have been absent from the historical archive, not written on paper, stone, or brick.

In the second part of the chapter, I excavate the autobiographical dimensions and affective workings of Rafi's revolutionary resistance in my own life. His story serves as departure points for my own subjectivity as a writer and scholar. Reflecting on his story, I glean the ways in which generational memories are passed down from those with ancestral power and how those in radical liberatory struggle are anchored in historical, political, and social location. I unpack how second-generation memories, or postmemory, act in my own life, and influence my burgeoning awareness of the affective force of the radical subject and its accumulation across and through time.

Specifically, I outline how latent credibility, a form of etho-affect inherited from those with ancestral power, is characterized by both resistive and intellectual bearings.[10] Memories of immemorial struggle instigate fantasy

---

8. Ismail, *Rule of Violence*, viii. Though the Ba'ath army suppressed several uprisings across the years, Hama was the "most traumatizing" of these repressions, at least until the revolution. Yassin-Kassab and al-Shami, *Burning Country*, 13–14.

9. The four foundational principles of cultural rhetorics practice include: story as theory; actively engaging with decoloniality and its practices; employing constellative practices to foster community and comprehension; and embracing relationality, which involves honoring our relatives through acts of reciprocity. See Bratta and Powell, "Entering the Cultural Rhetorics."

10. The prefix "etho-" signals how ethos extends beyond the radical subject's individual character to include inherited, affective forms of credibility. In rhetorical theory, Aristotle conceptualized ethos as the perceived character, credibility, and authority of the speaker or writer, which serves as a key means of persuasion.

investment in resistance long before revolution is ignited. Postmemory "bites" radical subjects with historically uncirculated knowledge, inculcating a unique intimacy with historical problems related to systems of power and resistance. Though lived experiences do not extend backward in time, radical subjects carry with them the heritage of previous eras. Intergenerational acts of witnessing become resonant for their affectability and ability to affect.

Rafi's Story

I never met Rafi, the son of Kenda, though I have revered him since childhood. A cynic might say there is a naivety and sentimentalism in this remembrance. I share this story with trepidation about mischaracterization, and even more so, an acknowledgment that there is a danger of oversimplifying his story to that of uncomplicated heroic resistance. He is a far from "ideal victim" within normative scripts of resistance. But what can be said with certitude is that he had a vision for resistance and liberation. The mechanisms by which he sought to achieve this liberation can certainly be critiqued, but here, I reclaim his story and proceed with the conviction that it is conducive to fathoming the legacies of resistance to the regime in the current day.

I have only seen a handful of photographs of him, but I can picture Rafi clearly: He was tall and slender, olive-skinned, with straight brown hair and hazel-green eyes. Kenda tells me how beautiful his lashes were, long and luscious. I do not know why this detail is important to her, but it is. Much of how we remember him fixates on his love for his mother. He was *murdi,* a child who was kind to his parents, so much so that they would say Rafi was like a butterfly around his mother, always in her service. She would be behind with housework, when, out of nowhere, he would appear, telling her class had been canceled and he had left early, knowing she would need help: "Mama, what can I do for you? What can I get you? Should I take things to the attic? Should I carry that large pot for you?"

Rafi was born in 1962 in Aleppo, inside the family home, as were all five of his siblings. He was given a Kurdish name that his father had taken a fancy to, though Rafi never liked his name. By 1963 the Arab Socialist Ba'ath Party took power after a coup d'état led by Hafez al-Assad and his comrades. From then on, it would function as the only officially recognized political party in the country. Assad became the de facto head of the Syrian Air Force, though he would not become the president of Syria until an intraparty coup in 1971. Hailing from the mountains of the coast, Assad came from a simple Alawite family, a Shia minority that for many years faced poverty and degradation.

Assad forced himself into the presidency and drafted a new constitution placing all executive, legislative, and judicial powers in his hands. His "Corrective Movement" preached a leftist manifesto based on Arab nationalism, but
his rule was authoritarian, implementing intense restrictions on media, free
speech, and trade.

Rafi came from an eminent Aleppan family of high religious standing. His
father's cousin was a local venerable Islamic scholar, Sheikh Abd Allah Siraj
al-Din al-Husayni, a direct descendant of the Prophet Mohamad known for
his *karamat*, supernatural saintly miracles performed by Muslim saints. The
family took great pride in the reclusive sheikh's visits to their home, one of
the few in the family who had had the honor. Unlike other prominent Sunni
scholars (*ulama*) who acquiesced to the regime, such as Sheikh Ahmad Kuf-
taro (the Mufti of Syria) and Sheikh Mohamad Said Ramadan al-Bouti, Sheikh
Abd Allah refused to partake with the regime, preferring to leave the country rather than succumb to pressure to submit a state-facilitated Islam to the
masses. When he returned for a visit to Syria ten years later, the regime sent a
limousine to pick him up at the airport and offered to have him stay at their
expense in one of the luxury hotels in Aleppo. It was an attempt to gain his
goodwill, but he declined.

In line with the family legacy, Rafi was genuinely devout as a child, completing his morning prayers in the mosque and spending hours huddled in
a corner reading the Quran. He would wake before dawn, and tiptoe out of
the house in pitch darkness. His mother would hear the scrape of his slippers
on the floor. After the door clicked shut, she would wake up and watch him
from the balcony till he reached their neighborhood mosque. Ever vigilant
for his safety, she would wait for him to return, listening for the front door
to latch before she went back to bed. He committed al-Nawawi's Forty Hadith to memory, a collection of the prophet's hadith valued over the centuries
for being the foundations of Islamic sacred law. When he won third place in
a local hadith competition, he was awarded a cutlery set, which is in Kenda's
kitchen cabinets till this day. Kenda swears, "I can't find contentment in any
meal except with those spoons." We were raised hearing stories about Rafi,
and my cousins and I would write them in our diaries. Much of my writing is
flushed with the rosiness of Kenda's remembrance of him.

It was around this time that Hafez al-Assad was taking steps to engender
loyalty and fear of the regime in the youth. To this end, the Ba'ath Vanguard
Organization was created to provide elementary students with a nationalist
education that derived its intellectual and ideological materials from the Ba'ath
Party. As such, when Rafi went to Al Fateh, an all-boy public school, he had to
wear a khaki military-style jacket, a cap, and a scarf around the neck. Students

would sing the national anthem every morning, write essays about the 8th of March "Revolution," the military coup in which the Ba'ath party took over, and take *Qawmiyyeh* (nationalism) classes. In a chain of filial piety and paternal authority, students were taught to love Baba Hafez (Father Hafez), memorize his sayings and life story, and emulate his pioneering achievements. Rafi's sister Maya recalled how her existence as a child teetered between the molding from those with coercive power and the protective envelope of family. The glorification of the eternal leader, Hafez al-Assad, permeated their childhood and was for a time internalized by her and her siblings:

> In school, all day they would teach us, Al-Assad! Al-Assad! I reached a stage in fifth or sixth grade when I started to love him. In summer, they would take all the students outside of Aleppo for a week of military camp teaching us how to be "good citizens." Students would live outdoors and camp overnight. I cried because I desperately wanted to go, but my parents wouldn't let me. We began to love Hafez in earnest. I feel pity, sorry for myself, when I look back—they brainwashed us. If it wasn't for my family, and the people around me, I might not have woken up.

By 1978 Rafi was fifteen, but he was far from an aimless teenager. Despite efforts to cultivate an emotional bond between the people and their leader, coercive practices of social control were only capable of making him act "as if," not of evoking heartfelt commitment. At home, he would overhear snippets of conversations by his parents in response to the news, "Hafez, that criminal!" He began attending classes with university students and young scholars at his local mosque. He became a student of Sheikh Taher Kheirallah, with whom he was greatly taken. Sheikh Taher, with his charismatic persona and eloquent sermons about the state of the Ummah (the global community of Muslims around the world) and possibilities for reform, became so popular so as to attract students from all over Aleppo. Rafi also grew close to Sheikh Mujahed Shaaban, a highly esteemed Islamic scholar in Aleppo. The family was unaware of this connection, when, to their astonishment, their young son was invited to Sheikh Mujahed's *talbeesa*, a folkloric tradition where the groom's closest male friends undress and re-dress him in his wedding attire before he accompanies his bride to the wedding. These scholars were dissidents of the regime, and their ideas resonated with Rafi, awakening his political consciousness to the regime's corruption and suppression of personal freedoms. The seeds of discord were planted.

The main party stirring opposition to the regime was the Muslim Brotherhood. The Brotherhood was intent on waking people from their "deep

slumber," calling for the freedom to assemble, protest, and form political parties and trade unions.[11] They condemned the arbitrary decrees and inhuman
police practices of the regime, stressing that "the need of the nation to regain
its freedom is as vital as its need for air, water and food."[12] Membership in the
Brotherhood drastically expanded. Numbers in the Aleppo branch ballooned
from eight hundred in 1975 to between five and seven thousand members by
1978.[13] And so, Rafi became a member of the Brotherhood when he was barely
sixteen years old and still in high school.[14] Though most members had relatives or friends who recruited them into the movement, Rafi joined of his own
volition. Years later, Rafi's mentor Waleed al-Attar would tell all the young
men gathered around him: "All of you had someone who brought you here (to
the Brotherhood). You had your brother, *ibn khaltak* [your cousin from your
mother's side], *ibn ammak* [your cousin from your father's side]. Except Rafi.
He came to us alone, with his own two feet." Rafi's membership became official
when a Brotherhood leader visited his family's house to ask their permission.
After they departed, his father had a stern talk with Rafi, crudely warning his
son of his concerns: "I have no objections. I am happy if my son is religious
and diligent in prayer, but don't hold religion from its ass."

The details of Rafi's political activity are sparse, as his goings-about were
mostly clandestine.[15] Though I do not know this for certain, there are indica-
tions that he was one of the armed insurgents against the regime, a member
of the Fighting Vanguard (al Tali'a al-Muqatila).[16] The Fighting Vanguard was
the only armed faction of the Brotherhood, made up primarily of its youngest
members. Rafi was discernably preparing for an insurgent role within their
nationwide network: at one point, he was sent to a training camp in the mountains and forests of Ras al-Bassit near the coastal city of Latakia. In these
camps, members learned crucial combat skills, such as how to throw grenades

---

11. Shurbaji, "Diary of a Vanguard Combatant."

12. Batatu, "Syria's Muslim Brethren."

13. Batatu, *Syria's Peasantry*.

14. Most members tended to be university undergraduates (mostly from medical or engineering backgrounds), members of the professions, and generally from the middle class or old
bourgeoisie. The majority of those arrested by the regime from 1976 to 1981 were students. See
Lefevre, *Ashes of Hama*; and Shurbaji, "Diary of a Vanguard Combatant."

15. There has been much internal debate around the Brotherhood, their leadership, and
their ideologies, even from those supportive of the revolution. Many have been critical of the
Brotherhood's leadership, suggesting leaders left the country for safety when they knew matters
were falling apart and abandoned younger members on the front lines. Some argue that critique
of members in combat is unfair, given they took on the main burden of fighting against the
regime and paid the highest price for their resistance. See Lefevre, *Ashes of Hama*.

16. This is my educated guess through piecing together events in family memory with the
literature.

and operate light machine guns.[17] Each camp was constituted of thirty to forty insurgents from Aleppo, Damascus, and Hama, led by a handful of leaders. Rafi would cook for the members of his team, making them *mamounia*, a semolina pudding breakfast, topped with cinnamon, cream, and string cheese. Rafi also took two jars of his mother's homemade apricot jam with him to share. They must have enjoyed the jam, as he returned to her with empty jars, telling her, "They flew!"

In 1976 the Brotherhood carried out a campaign of sporadic assassinations of key Ba'athist figures. Political figures with decision-making power in the regime apparatus were targeted, including members of the military and the mukhabarat, as well as individuals like Deputy Prison Director Hamed Abbas, who tortured Brotherhood members in prison. The Brotherhood's rebelliousness toward the authorities emboldened others to follow their lead. In 1979, a major escalation took place with an armed assault in the Aleppo Artillery School, in which eighty-three Alawite cadets in training were killed.[18] Unlike the assassination attempts of key Ba'athist figures, the cadets were considered innocent, and their killing had a sectarian flare. The Brotherhood denied involvement and accused the regime of fabricating the incident to tarnish their image. The Brotherhood leader, Issam al-Attar, called it a "barefaced lie unsupported by any fact or proof."[19] Some believe the Brotherhood were infiltrated by Ba'athist members, that is, co-opted, or as Maya claims, "It was fixed." It remains a controversial matter to this day. There is evidence that the regime knew the Brotherhood was not responsible, but it is also conceivable that Adnan Uglah, the leader of the Fighting Vanguard, acted independently from the Muslim Brotherhood's leadership. In any case, the event was a pretext for a brutal crackdown on the organization. Just days after the massacre, eight thousand of the Brotherhood were detained in Aleppo,[20] and the regime slayed, in quick succession, the leaders of the Fighting Vanguard.

In March 1980, antiregime demonstrations took place in the major cities of Aleppo, Hama, and Homs, as well as in Idlib and Deir ez-Zour. These were organized by a medley of dissident organizations, including the Muslim Brotherhood, labor unions, communists, and socialists. A women's protest demanded the release of several scholars and intellectuals who had been disappeared by the regime, including Sheikh Taher Khairallah and his brother,

---

17. Shurbaji, "Diary of a Vanguard Combatant."
18. Batatu, "Syria's Muslim Brethren"; Conduit, *Muslim Brotherhood in Syria*; and Lefevre, *Ashes of Hama*.
19. Batatu, *Syria's Peasantry*, 266.
20. Mansel, *Aleppo*.

the prominent dissident Dr. Zein Al Deen Khairallah, the general secretary of the Arab Medical Association.[21] Rafi's mom, Kenda, participated, after confronting her husband to let him know with a "humph" that she would be going. He didn't like it, shrugging his shoulders in disapproval, but he did not prevent her.

A turning point for the family was Rafi's arrest during these protests. In an unforgiving offensive, army units were dispatched to quell the protests, and hundreds of those participating were forcibly collected and thrown in prison. Rafi was one of those incarcerated. His father scrambled to find a *wasta*—an informal political connection—to get him out. Eid came, and Rafi was still in prison. The family was distraught. As was the ritual on Eid, Rafi's father visited his own father's grave. When he arrived at the tombstone, he crumbled on the grave, calling out, "My son [*ibni*]!" in anguish. For a stony man who never revealed his emotions, this scene is engraved in Maya's head: "My father was a harsh man. His words were orders. He wouldn't say things twice. It was hard to see a strong man cry. As they would say, he was *rejaal*, a man. But Rafi knew what he wanted and there was no convincing him otherwise." A month later, Rafi was released. Maya describes the moment Rafi returned home and the merriment that ensued:

> I remember when he opened the door and came in. Mama was sitting on a rug near the window in the living room. She was folding the laundry. I hadn't slept yet. We didn't even notice, until we heard the click of the door, and Rafi came in. *Yey, yey, yey* [a sound expressing the magnitude of joy]. It was a wedding! Rafi came! Rafi came! We enveloped him, kissed him, embraced him. My mom called her parents, and they came. We opened the formal guest room, put the lights on, and we were all together. We served each other rice pudding. Rafi sat there happy. Jeddo [his grandfather] told them, "Oh people, get the boy some food! He was inside [prison], oh people, feed the boy! Get up and feed the boy."

Kenda was so happy her son returned, she couldn't sleep. She lay awake till the morning. Once things settled, she asked him, "*Habebi*, my sweetheart, what did they do to you?" He was reluctant to share details: "A hit, a prod, something like that." His refusal to detail what happened to him may have been to avoid causing his mother anguish, or possibly, the indignity of what

---

21. I have not seen this protest referred to in the literature and cannot place its exact timing. It was conveyed to me by Syrian activists from that time as well as by Maya.

happened to him was too much to put in words.[22] The euphoria of his release did not last long. He persisted in his political activities, notwithstanding pressure from the family to cease. But now, he was on the regime's radar. One day, when they were alone at home, his father had a tête-à-tête with Rafi, pleading with him to reconsider his political activities: "Listen, I don't have it in me to endure this misery. I am worried about your sisters and what the mukhabarat might do to them. I can't tolerate the repercussions of what might happen." Maya was the only one who observed the interaction between her father and brother. She knew it was a half-hearted attempt to goad Rafi into leaving the Brotherhood, but there was air of resignation and lack of force in the request. Rafi was unswerving, telling him, "That's it. This is the path I have chosen, I won't go back. It is done, I am committed." He was ardently attached, to the point of foolhardiness, to the cause of resistance.

A few months later, their father died unexpectedly, under mysterious circumstances that are unclear to this day. There was hope his death might change Rafi's calculations. Rafi's brother Najm quit his university studies to work abroad and take over as breadwinner for the family. The family was left without a male protector in the home, but even then, Rafi was resolute: "All he could see was the *ghayah*—the greater purpose of the struggle. He was ready to sacrifice himself for it. It is not that he wanted to harm the family, but all he could see was that the corruption, that the injustice, needed to stop" (Maya).

The Fighting Vanguard took their activities up a notch, carrying out attacks on government buildings, army units, and police stations. In June 1980, an attempt to assassinate Hafez al-Assad almost succeeded.[23] The day

---

22. The prisons of the Assad regime are more aptly named human slaughterhouses. The regime was notorious for its techniques of protracted torture to annihilate political dissidence. Inmates were forced to strip naked, had their nails ripped out, had their flesh plucked with scissors and pincers, or were beaten with Kalashnikovs or tank belts (improvised tools made of leather from a tire tread and attached to a wooden handle). The mechanisms of torture have nicknames, such as the "Black Slave"—in which the inmate is strapped into a metal chair (with a hole in it) to sit while a hot metal skewer is shoved up the anus until it reaches the intestines; the "Flying Carpet," where the inmate is strapped to a foldable board that is closed in half into them; the "Wheel," where the inmate is forced into a vehicle tire and beaten; the "German Chair," in which the inmate is tied to a flexible chair with hinges and the back of the chair is bent to stretch the spine and neck; and the "The Crucifixion," in which the inmate is tied to a cross while their reproductive organs are beaten, among others. There are other forms of torture, such as forcing prisoners to rape each other. See Baker and Üngör's *Syrian Gulag* for a comprehensive account of Syrian prisons and Faraj Bayraqdar's poetic prison memoir, *Khiyanat al Lugha Wa l Samt* [The Betrayals of Language and Silence].

23. Two grenades were thrown at Hafez al-Assad while he awaited an African diplomat in the presidential palace. He kicked away one that landed at his feet, and his bodyguard threw himself onto the second grenade and was killed in the explosion. See Seale, *Asad of Syria*.

after the botched assassination attempt, Hafez's brother Rifaat al-Assad gave orders for the killing of Brotherhood inmates in Tadmor Prison. Rifaat was the head of Saraya al-Difa (the Defense Companies)—an elite, heavily armed guard dominated by Alawites whose only responsibility was to protect the Assad regime from domestic enemies. In the space of half an hour, around a thousand inmates were machine-gunned to death in their cells in what is known as the Tadmor Prison Massacre. Detainees were defenseless. None had been arrested or charged on any legal basis. A month later, Law No. 49 passed, which declared membership in the Brotherhood a crime punishable by death. The mukhabarat received decrees that they had impunity in dealing with all "suspects."[24]

The environment of suspicion was at an all-time high. Newspapers covering the conflict waged a campaign against the Brotherhood, calling them vermin threatening to contaminate the national fabric. Not even innocent children were spared the regime's scrutiny. One day Maya and Rafi's little cousin, a boy of seven years, was walking in front of his parents' house. A military officer stationed in a kiosk below, tasked with guarding a regime figure living nearby, seized him by the arm. "Come here, lad. I have a question for you," the officer said. "When your father watches the TV and the President comes on, what does your father do? Does he close the TV or does he listen?" It was a ruse of course, and the boy, not comprehending what was being asked, responded honestly: "Oh, he shuts the TV."

The mukhabarat intensified "cleansing raids" of homes, entering into each and every home in the neighborhood, one after the other, breaking in by force. The family home became a site of contestation with the authorities. Maya vividly remembers one of many such visits:

> We were at home. May your eyes never see such a thing. Thugs, from the streets, they come in like they own the place, shouting "Go here! Come here! Check here." Cursing, swearing. My mother was still in *iddeh* [religious practice of isolation after a woman's husband dies]. My grandfather was worried about us—we were women alone in the house and the mukhabarat would rape girls or take them, so he started sleeping in our house at night. When they came in, he told them not to enter, to respect his daughter's iddeh, to which the military officer responded with a sarcastic drawl: "What iddeh, *khityar al jinn* [crazy old man]! Go from here! What a joke." They opened and went to see her.

24. Armanazi, *Story of Syria*.

Arrests by the mukhabarat skyrocketed. Because most visits by the mukhabarat were at night, as a measure of safety, Maya and her sisters began to leave the house after dusk to sleep at their grandmother's house and would return the following morning. The private realm of the home became a site of struggle:

> We were living in terror, we were afraid to sleep at night. Imagine you are in your home and at any moment they could fall upon you, open the door and take you. *Ihsas raheeb* [it is an unimaginable feeling]. For a while, we would sit dressed and ready, with our socks and clothes and scarves on, waiting. They could come in and say, "We want that girl, give her here," and no one could say a word of no to them. We were expecting someone at any second. That feeling of security, the lack of it, no matter what you write about it . . . it was terrifying. Especially when you hear what they did to that girl, and that girl. A friend of ours had the most beautiful mane of long hair. When she heard what they were doing to girls, she went and shaved it just like a boy to zero, like a garçon. Her mom told her, "What have you done to yourself?" She told her, "You want them to take me?"

Anyone could be arrested, even on a whiff of suspicion of being adjacently connected to the Brotherhood. Several of Rafi's friends were killed, and in a matter of days, the regime increased surveillance of public spaces and those in the movement. His best friend, Waleed, an engineering student, was murdered. Rafi was heartbroken. On learning the news, he came home with bloodshot eyes, got into bed, covered himself under the bed sheets, and cried and cried for days. When his siblings asked him what had happened, their mother shooed them away, "Leave him, leave him be." His heartbreak over his friend steeled his resolve to persevere in the resistance:

> The death of his friend made him more adamant on his path. He loved him to death; he was so attached. There was not a single [bad] word you could say about Waleed. [He had] beautiful character, manners, and knowledge. He was the one mentoring him, his teacher. But they hunted him down and shot him. (Maya)

The regime began to ask about the friends of those who had been killed, and it became clear to Rafi that he was being surveilled. With the atmosphere saturated with dread, Rafi stopped sleeping in the family home. When he was not hiding, he took sanctuary at family members' houses and the basements of friends. He would knock at their door and ask, "Can I sleep here tonight?" A few refused him shelter, such as his own grandmother from his father's side, who rebuffed his request to stay at her house out of fear for her other sons. Kenda was in disbelief and never forgave her mother-in-law for this, cynically telling her daughters, "This is supposed to be *ibn al ghali* [the son of her precious son]?" Others took him in at considerable risk to themselves and their families, fed him and took care of him for long stretches, treating him like one of their own. He shared the same bed with their own sons, their legs side by side—if the mukhabarat had entered, both would have been killed.

They were expecting the regime to visit them at any moment. Tensions were so high that when Rafi's elder brother, Najm, came home to Aleppo, visiting from abroad, he didn't dare stay at the family home, out of fear it was being surveilled by the regime. Instead, he headed directly to his grandparents' house, where unbeknownst to him, Rafi was hiding there that very night. It was the crack of dawn when Najm knocked on the door. Rafi was fast asleep but was jolted awake by the knock. Panicked, he leapt from the window into the garden, believing it was a *kabseh,* an unexpected raid by the mukhabarat. The family, equally on edge, feared Rafi would be snatched from his bed. One relative, hurrying to open the front door in terror, slammed it into his own forehead and bled. To their relief, it was Najm standing there.

Rafi was in a blaze of hiding and hairsbreadth escapes, on the run for a period that lasted about a year. He would pass by intermittently to see his mother for fleeting unannounced visits. Sometimes, those sheltering him called his mother to come visit her son. On one of these visits, Rafi led them in prayer:

> They told me he came, "He is here, come." I couldn't see him for more than half an hour. These visits were stolen from time, *khatef.* I went, and the time for prayer came. He was our imam and I prayed behind him. I remember he read a verse I hadn't heard before. He was reading with *tajweed,* the rules of recitation, so deeply and so intently. From my pride in him, I cried and cried as we prayed. That is what I remember. (Kenda)

After that visit, she would not hear from her son again for a long time. Kenda was consumed with worry, her anxiety simmering just beneath the surface. She was distraught without news of him. All she could think of was where he might be hiding: "Is he hiding here? Is he hiding there? *Akh ya albe*—Oh my poor heart!"

One day after this long absence, Maya was walking by the mosque near their house when she saw Rafi. She was stunned. He was in costume, almost unrecognizable. The image of this encounter is lodged sharply in her mind:

I was going up, returning from school or my grandparents' house, I can't remember which. He was on the opposite side of the street, going down. I saw him—my brother, of course I knew him. He was in disguise as a "don juan"—looking "cool" with fashionable shades. I know he doesn't dress like that, and his hair was brushed differently too. Our eyes met. He saw me but he didn't talk to me. Someone was following him.

Maya ran home to let her mother know she saw Rafi. Little did she know that would be the last time any of them saw him alive.

In November of 1981, Rafi's youngest brother, Fadi, who was just ten years old at the time, was playing with his friend in the neighborhood. His friend asked, "Is your brother dead? We saw his picture in the newspaper. Isn't this him?" Fadi grabbed the newspaper and ran upstairs to his mother, screaming, "Mama, mama, this is my brother! Rafi *maat,* Rafi *maat,* Rafi died, Rafi died!" Kenda was startled, trying to make sense of his words: "Son, I don't understand. What happened?" She looked again at the paper in his hand. Her voice caught in her throat. She tried to speak, but the words would not come.

On the front page of the paper was a photograph of eighteen-year-old Rafi, lifeless, his eyes open and unblinking, his mouth gaping ever so slightly, on the slab of a house in al-Jamiliyeh. He was with three or four others, and the heading celebrated, in black-and-white terms, the capturing of "armed terror-ists" and "criminals" who formed a threat to the state. Kenda called her sister, Ibtisam, gasping for air, from the landline in the living room. Their phone lines were being surveilled, and they were certain they were being watched. She spoke in coded refrains, terrified of even saying Rafi's name over the phone and unsure how to tell her sister the news. She called her, breathless, her words stumbling over each other: "Ibtisam, my son . . . my son . . . my son . . . Ibtisam, my son!" But she couldn't say he had died over the phone. Ibtisam listened silently, already knowing Rafi had died. Ibtisam hung up the phone, looked to the family gathered around her, "Kenda found out . . . *oomo, oomo,* get up, get up." They all knew he had died, but no one wanted to be the one to break the news to her. It wasn't till the shock settled that Kenda noticed the date on the newspaper—it was from two months prior.

She summoned the strength to make the ritual washing before prayer and stood to perform two *rukas* in the living room (the *ruka* is a step of prayer where someone bows down and then drops their forehead on the ground). Every fiber of her being was shaking, but she disciplined her body to stay still. She prostrated, and then, rivulets of tears released themselves. It was in that moment that she submitted to the fact of her son's death, the finality of it, finding solace in the idea that perhaps this was his destiny. What was planned for him. In a way, his death was a relief from the painful extremes of forever worrying about what would happen to him, whether the regime would seize him or her other children in his stead, and when and whether he might unexpectedly return.

The sorrow of his death and the repercussions on the family have been long-lasting and immeasurable. Rafi was the dearest of her children. Kenda would tell us, "I felt sad when my husband died, but Rafi, he seared my heart. I feel something burning in my heart, burning, burning, burning." Her heart was attached to his.

Decades after his death, Maya confided in me how raw the hurt still felt: "Sometimes, I look at my mother and I see her laughing. And I wonder, how can she laugh? You know, it has been thirty years, and I still wonder how she can laugh. I think I would have lost my mind if I were her. I probably wouldn't smile all my life." At this point in relaying the story to me, Maya could not move her tongue. The silences between her words stretched longer. Her body was tense. Some details about those last days were unspeakable: "You are reminding me of situations I don't want to remember, Noor. You don't know how much it takes from me. I don't want to be sadder than I already am." The enormity of affect within her left her incapable of speech. Even though Rafi died so many years ago, this is the enduring affect of his death. I felt cruel for opening the story, yet each retelling, woven together in fragmented pieces, unveiled new haunting details.

For years after Rafi's death, the security forces would visit the family home to ask about his whereabouts and why he had not signed up for military service. Our family could not make sense of the visits, and they would terrify them to the core. Did they not know they had killed him? Was the regime trying to test them? Was it a trick? Had they not documented that he had died? But they must have known. Kenda became skilled at appeasing the mukhabarat during these visits. She would pretend her son was alive, airily telling them, "Oh, we don't know where he is! He went to Lebanon and never came back. We haven't heard from him!" For these random visits, she kept a fine bone-china plate with Hafez al-Assad's picture on it. Whenever she felt them coming, she would take it out to show her allegiance and love for Hafez. The plate operated talismanically to shield her from further recrimination and gave her the strength to brave their visits.

The family never recovered Rafi's body. Family members of the executed did not receive remains and were rarely informed of their deaths,[25] and they

---

25. Victims of executions were not recorded in death certificates by the state, though they were secretly documented. Other times, death sentences were signed after the death had already taken place, as official cover. See Amnesty International, "Human Slaughterhouse."

did not dare to ask. Later, Kenda met the mothers of the young men who had died with Rafi. From them, she learned the bodies were dragged, thrown in a mass grave, and covered with dirt, but they could not pinpoint where exactly. Another rumor was that his body was thrown from a five-story building after his death. They never found his name published in lists of the dead, neither in regime accounts nor those of the Muslim Brotherhood. It is as if he never existed. Except of course he had. Tens of thousands of Brotherhood members fled the country,[26] but Kenda still sees Rafi in her dreams. My cousins and I used to always say that if any of us had a son one day, we would name him after Rafi, but none of us ever did. His name was too large, and too doomed, to bring to life again.

In what follows, I examine how Rafi's story acts as a form of postmemory in my own life. Unfolding these family histories, I show how they have seeped into my own recognition of the radical subject and how *post*memory and *living* memory together infuse the affective offerings of the radical subject.

Toward a Conception of Radical Postmemory

Years before the revolution, I was a teenager walking along a stretch of smooth pavement between both of my grandmothers' houses in Aleppo. It was a pleasantly sunny summer day, and the streets were bustling with traffic. I looked up to the right of me to see two columns flanking the outdoor entryway of a building. On one was a poster of Bashar al-Assad, and on the other, his father, Hafez. My chest tightened, and in a rush of adrenaline mixed with wrath, I ripped one of the posters from the nail holding it and threw it on the street. I rushed home, proudly relaying to my mother the rebellious moment. I knew she would be proud. But instead of applauding me, she was furious at my idiotic act of transgression. She told me I was lucky no one saw me and never to contemplate such a thing again.

It was a silly gesture. As I write, I contemplate the memories of Rafi that fueled a reverie of resistance within me. I was young and instinctively oppositional, but I had yet much to learn about how to transgress boundaries of the permissible. I was a "second person," an heir defined and formed in relation to their accounts of Rafi. Though I was born in exile, long after the events in my family history had "ended," I was interpellated by their memories of Rafi

---

26. After this squelching of the unrest, the rebellion did not spread further. Other leftist opponents and rival Ba'athist comrades were also neutralized. See Halasa, Omareen, and Mahfoud, *Syria Speaks*.

and of my father, whose story of exile I leave for another time.[27] I was captive to the past.

Around the same time, in the summer of 2007, I was diligently writing in my diary. Amid school squabbles and teenage angst, I was also evidently eager for revolution, though I did not have words for it yet:

> I have the utmost distrust and hate of the Syrian government, which sadly has not changed since those days [the massacre in Hama]. They rule by force and abuse not only the common rights of their fellow citizens but launder the country's money into the bank accounts of a few rich supposedly elite men in power. They all work for the president. Syria is poor and ravished. One man once told me the Syrian soul has died, they no longer fight, just complain. Bashar, the former president's son and who somehow inherited the title, is lauded not because he has achieved any tangible change or improvement in the economy or given people their rightful due, but simply because he has not yet ordered any large-scale massacres as his father did.

Looking back today, I am intrigued at my own premonition of the massacres Bashar would one day order, his capacity for violence, and the "yet" to come. I am careful here not to position myself as a radical subject as I have defined them in this book. I recoil at any indulgence in my own work as a form of embodied resistance, rejecting the tendency of the "knowledgeable researcher" to position themselves above the subjects of study. I look *up* to radical subjects, learning *from* and theorizing *with* them. Indeed, it is my own postmemory that has humbled me with regards to the reverie of grandiosity

---

27. Nevertheless, at times, memories act as lessons in preservation rather than resistance. Within a dominant ecology of fear, not everyone actively resists violence, and at times, rebellion is prophylactically nipped in the bud. Some understand their place within or contra to particular histories—in other words, either with relationality or rejection. Maya explained to me why her other siblings did not join the revolution, despite the legacy of their brother's resistance:

> The one who has been scalded, it is hard for them to take even a 1 percent chance that they would be burned again. We learnt our lesson. It was enough for us. Our brother was in and out of jail. We had two to three of the most strenuous years. We were afraid to sleep at night, that they would come knocking at our door. It was to that degree. So, anyone can come and posture that [family members] should have done more—but they haven't tasted what we have tasted.

These relatives of mine are not *ramadiyyin* [gray people], the ambivalent middle vacillating between desire for reform and attachment to order (see Wedeen, *Ideology*). Rather, they are "burned" by previous eras of resistance and opt for self-preservation, "a curling in on oneself to protect one's body from harm." Al-Haj Saleh, *Impossible Revolution*, 227. Sometimes, postmemory subdues the rebellious spirit.

we unwittingly slip into when superimposing theory onto ethnographic evidence. Nevertheless, through my own postmemory, I am an active witness to the radical subject, with connective historical, ancestral, relational tissue to their lives and beings. I am summoned and obligated by their power in my own life. I sift through the traces of their memory that comprise me.

Through their affective intensities, generational memories interpellate (to borrow the Marxist philosopher Louis Althusser's term) subjects into resistance in various ways, in a slow and delicate manner—"hailing" them into opposition from a position of power. Althusser introduced the concept of "hailing" as the unconscious process by which ideology addresses or calls out to individuals. Individuals become interpellated when they respond and are transformed into subjects.[28] Though "interpellation" as presented by Althusser tends to be by "state apparatuses" (such as mass media, schools, churches, the judicial system, police, and government), in this book, interpellation is contextualized as emanating from those with custodianship or ancestral authority. In this sense, I diverge from Hannah Arendt's understanding of the public as the realm of action and immortality and instead present the private domain as the realm of action.[29] The recipient exists a priori—they are "already there" and constituted by togetherness with those with whom they have organic bonds, rather than by coercive state power. Organic bonds exist with one's family, tribe, or sect, but here, I narrow this to intimate family members, spouses, siblings, children, and grandchildren with whom duties of memory are present. These are "thick relationships" with which one has a shared history, as opposed to "thin" relationships one might have strangers with whom one has no binds aside from a shared humanity.[30] In the former, there is an obligation to remember the event the memory is about. The uptake of ideology is secured intersubjectively, not within the genre of the dramatic event or memories that have been institutionalized in places, buildings, monuments,

---

28. Althusser uses a simple example to explain this concept: imagine a police officer calling out, "Hey, you there!" on the street. When an individual turns around in response, they recognize that the call is directed at them, thus acknowledging the authority of the police officer. This act of turning around is what Althusser refers to as hailing. Interpellation is the broader process that follows hailing and the mechanism by which ideology constitutes individuals as subjects. When an individual responds to hailing, they accept and internalize the roles and identities imposed by ideology.

29. In *The Human Condition*, Hannah Arendt distinguishes between two realms of human life: the private and the public. For Arendt, the private is the domain of necessity—where biological needs (like eating, reproducing, working to survive) dominate. The public is the domain of freedom, speech, and action. It is where individuals disclose themselves to others through deeds and words, striving for immortality—meaning that great actions and words can be remembered beyond one's lifespan.

30. Margalit, *Ethics of Memory*.

and books, but between those who are the only audiences that can be trusted to listen to what has been endured.

Despite attempts to interpellate radical subjects into the dominant ideology, the spatiality of the family circle, as worded by Maya, "wakes them up." This is the subtle operation of ideological interpellation within the family circle when one teeters between those holding coercive power and the protective envelope of family (indeed Maya was at the precipice of *starting* to "love" Hafez al-Assad). Affective family investments pry radical subjects from this clasp, making the landscape fertile for later transgression and resistance at the opportune moment.

All too often, our conceptualizations of revolution are framed in narrow terms of sound after years of blanket silence, of grievance expressed in exterior spaces, be it neighborhoods, mosques, public parks, city squares, back alleys, or streets. A case in point is the extraordinary juncture at which schoolboys in Daraa graffitied the walls of their school with calls for the end of a dictator, or the scenes in which the revolutionary icon Abdul Baset al-Sarout led thousands in protest and dance with his signature tender and stirring voice "longing, longing for Freedom," forever captivating the heart of millions of Syrians. In these performances of public theatricality, the political street becomes the ultimate arena to communicate discontent. These moments are the immediate triggers for revolution, speaking to its abruptness and explosive essence—a tornado undeterred by the mythology of a powerful state. The awakening of those in slumber. Undoubtedly, revolution marks a rupture in time and space—revolutionary grassroots rhetoric speaks to a radical shift in critical consciousness of the masses. While I do not negate these interpretative frames, there is much truth to them, they valorize public resistance in implacable opposition to "power" in areas under the observation of the oppressor, while displacing subversive forms of resistance which occur in the intimate spaces where radical subjectivities are provoked. Without going beyond the purview of the public resistance paradigm, we deny the forms of familial resistance that are not "watershed" or "floodgates bursting" events, occurring in spaces such as Kenda's kitchen, or an apartment in London where family recapitulated their stories to me. Postmemory has none of the exhilaration of protest or the devastating violence that follows, but it is a potent catalyst for what is to come. We do not capture forms of affect, which due to their inconspicuousness and inchoate nature are deemed irrelevant to our conceptions of liberatory social movements.

A pivotal dimension of the radical subject's postmemory is its "biting" with historically uncirculated knowledge—inculcating a unique awareness of a set of historical problems related to systems of disciplinary power.

"Bite" depicts the involuntary nature of affect transfer and knowledge acquisition when certain subjects are chosen as "designated carriers of awesome knowledge."[31] Knowledge, to borrow a gory phrase of Hirsch, "bleeds" over from one generation to the next.[32] As containers of a historical legacy, radical subjects inherit knowledge that is secretive and bounded in nature. This knowledge is existential, complex, and at times, intransmutable to those outside the struggle. This is where their testimony acquires its *ça-a-été*, or having-been-there quality, reminiscent of Roland Barthes's depiction of the affect of the photographic image.[33] Although we are told nobody knows the number of the dead, as the keepers of knowledge bequeathed to us as descendants and next of kin, we know. We were the target for this knowledge, who were bitten with the trauma of what happened. Such knowledge comes about by way of memories transferred inter- and transgenerationally in which the intersecting and conflicting structures of power are understood:

> The same people who lived in the eighties, they are still here now. We tasted
> the bitterness of loss, the bitterness of deprivation, the bitterness of oppres-
> sion. It wasn't the first time the regime engaged in this kind of behavior; it
> wasn't the first time the regime was oppressing us. We know the situation,
> we know what they do, how they behave, how they go into homes, how they
> take women. We know their injustice. People had tested them—they have
> priors with the regime. (Maya)

The radical subject is privy to the concreteness of the lived pain of family, what political scholar Salwa Ismail calls "memory-marking incidents," which are relayed to descendants to manage the threats posed to them within menacing atmospheres.[34] They are singularly positioned to grasp their meanings. Through living connection with the past, they know the ways of their oppressor, where others might only apprehend irrationality and experience bewilderment. They know the intricacies of domination, the symbolic and instrumental, the ideological and behavioral tendencies. They know the *patterns and repertoire of domination,* be it the gradations in politics of repression, the spatial strategies of the regime to control the population (e.g., intrusions into the integrity of the home), the unmaking and remaking of subjects in political prisons, circumscribed mobility across borders, or mechanisms of

---

31. Hoffman, *After Such Knowledge.*
32. Hirsch, *Generation of Postmemory,* 34.
33. Barthes, *Rhetoric of the Image.*
34. Ismail, *Rule of Violence,* 118.

societally embedded surveillance—all of which might be termed the "scales of death," or politics of killing, against intransigence.[35]

Simultaneously, radical subjects are familiar with *patterns and repertoires of resistance,* that is, the spatiotemporalities of safety and danger; the limits for what is thinkable or sayable, and to whom; how one might avoid inspection, conscription, detention, and stoppage at borders; the power of relaying memory to one's descendants, who might be trusted with such knowledge; and the affective charge of the realm of dreams, which guide us to a world before and beyond life as we know it. They learn from their ancestors how to compromise and placate when needed, be it with Hafez al-Assad's plate on their kitchen counters or with the lie that their sons deserted them. They are knowledgeable about the art of disguise, be it in the heat of escape from the regime or, decades later, when determining how to anonymize one's writings to avoid repercussions.

There is not always an originary moment in which knowledge transfer occurs—it is an inchoate process, and the unpacking and decoding transpires at a later stage. A memory of a memory that has always been there. I invariably *knew* the memories related in this chapter, so much so that I cannot recall a time before I knew them. This is the affective charge of memories transmitted from our forebears, which interpellate before one even is aware of it. Eva Hoffman—the child of Polish Jews who survived the Holocaust, with the help of neighbors, but whose whole family perished—describes how the tortuous memories of the Holocaust are received from those who came before us as something "more potent and less lucid; something closer to the enactment of experience, to emanations or sometimes nearly embodiments of psychic matter—of material too awful to be processed and assimilated into the stream of consciousness, or memory, or intelligible feeling."[36]

Memories are transmitted to radical subjects in a myriad of ways. It might be through emanations—perceptible, aural, or sonic. Or it might have a tangible issuance, but one that differs radically from ordinary language conversations in its vulnerability and intensity, where the hidden, the unspoken, and the unspeakable are entrusted. "Emanations," mentioned above, invocate the clandestine and forbidden nature of memories in the realm of private discussions with those held in trust. Affect is more than a spoken word, it is any form of felt relations and the sensuous forms they stir.[37] It is the stories told over the years about family members we lost; it is the closet in the house that no one uses because it contains their belongings; it is dining with the cutlery

35. See Munif's *The Syrian Revolution* for more on the "scales of death" of the regime.
36. Hoffman, *After Such Knowledge,* 7.
37. Massumi, *Politics of Affect.*

gifted by them, so many years after they are gone; and it is the tone of your loved one's voice when they tell you sternly to "close the subject." It is in all the silences and moments that make themselves present and the affective intensities evoked within the ancestral realm.

At its most extreme, affect is incapable of transitioning into any sort of "discursive formation." It resides instead in the lacuna where human language collapses due to the impossibility of bearing witness to that which has no language. This is palpable in the moment when Maya, in relaying the story of her brother's murder, could not move her tongue. The air was heavy, and though my heart willed her to talk, she could not: "You are reminding me of situations I don't want to remember, Noor. You don't know how much it takes from me." The enormity of memory left her incapable of speech. Though untranslatable into "discourse," there is a transference that occurs in the realm of private moments with those held in trust, be it through whispers, objects, sounds, silences, heaving, or the lingering affect filling the air. I was privy to these affective moments, one of the great traumas of her life. It was imprinted into her thinking, her body, her psyche, her very character. And into mine.

These manifestations of postmemory are a threat to power and its governance, as they disrupt the narratives that buoy authority and the mechanisms used to suppress dissent. Ahmad Aba Zeid, a Syrian journalist, voices the regime's attempts to eviscerate the memory of radical subjects: "We are in front of a regime that does not only want to demolish cities and to demolish humans, but also to demolish memory. The memory of Syrians, aside from the fact that it is being disfigured, bit by bit, it is also being re-written."[38] Memory interpellates from positions of interiority, drawing us away from the clasp of power's interpellations and into the sanctity of the private space.

When the rebel fighter Abdul Baset al-Sarout died after wounds sustained from a battle with regime forces, I observed with foreboding awareness the manipulation of his memory that was to come. Just as when Rafi was killed in 1981, when Abdul Baset al-Sarout was killed by the regime in 2019, it again opted for politics of erasure:

[The regime was] obsessed . . . with destroying any and all meaning, memory, and thought outside their fevered accusations of "terrorism." . . . This was not any sort of discussion about the meaning and symbolism of Sarout, nor an examination of any objectionable positions or indefensible remarks he may have uttered here or there. It was a war against every version of

38. Syria TV, "Ahmad Aba Zeid."

history inconsistent with the regime's absolute insistence that all who rose against it were "criminals" and "terrorists."[39]

I could see in the story of Abdul Baset the story of Rafi, the regime's seemingly irrational reaction of extreme violence and continued aggrandizement of the radical subject within the state's apparatus. But what appears senseless to an outsider is just one of the rationalities of rule to which we are accustomed. Abdul Baset and Rafi were woven from a similar, but not identical, fabric. Though Abdul Baset was an irresistibly charismatic figure much revered in revolutionary circles and Rafi's life was short and unknown to those outside the family circle, both their legacies have an affective load that plays out in the life of those they left behind. In temporal reiterations of resistance, echoed in Rafi and Abdul Baset and endless others, comes the contention that knowledge legacies are affective for solidarity-making mechanisms. And so, I end by putting their deaths into conversation with each other. To remember how for those who had lost them, the victims did not recede into oblivion, hardly a cipher or empty number. Rather, they imbue their lives with an amalgam of meanings in the intimate knowledge of what once was, and what is to come. The accumulation of affect in memory inheritance is a threat to a regime rattled to the core from the memory of its own people. This memory finds a release in moments of rupture from the status quo, be it in subversive forms of everyday resistance or in the seismic shifts that unfold into revolution.

Today's media environment is much different than the pre-internet days of the 1970s and early 1980s. In recording the stories of this chapter, I knew they would irretrievably be "out." In the process of collecting the family's oral history, even I at times felt like an intruder into entrusted spaces. Along with my recorder, I became an agitator in my urge to confront the stifled past. In jest, Maya would tell me, "I feel I am being questioned by the mukhabarat," "close this topic, there is no need for it," or "please don't get us into problems! For the sake of God." During this period, in "opening this can of worms" to write this chapter, the interaffectivity of memories in my life was pervasive. I would write, then drive my car with tears streaming down my face from the rawness of the memories. I soon realized that the legacy of my own postmemory was unavoidable. If my weapon is my pen no matter how feeble my voice is in the shadow of exile, I decided that would be my path of resistance. Eventually, we came to an agreement as to the terms through which my family's stories would be relayed. Then, the memories would overflow, articulated with the assurance of a trusted space. Other times, in litanies of sorrow, there

---

39. *Al-Jumhuriya*, "Days of Abd al-Basit."

would be tears, and I couldn't differentiate mine from theirs. The weight of the densely packed affect was at times too much for me. In one snippet from the recordings, I could feel the affective load of the memory transference: "This subject is heavy, I feel it is heavy, heavy, heavy. Especially that we haven't had relief, the people haven't had relief, their hearts haven't been quenched. Until when?" (author).

Generational memories of this nature are affectively potent in inculcating a predisposition to revolution, an animating force for the seemingly impossible. In his writings, the Mexican insurgent and former spokesperson for the Zapatistas, Subcomandante Marcos, talks about the powerful nature of this intimate inheritance: "We looked inside ourselves, and we looked at our history. We saw our eldest fathers suffer and struggle, we saw our grandfathers struggle, we saw our fathers with fury in their hands. . . . Courage and valor came to us through the mouth of our elders, who were dead but lived again in the dignity that they gave to us."[40] As Native American activists, protesting and blocking the highway to prevent the government access to the sacred Black Hills at Mount Rushmore, cry out: "We got this power from our ancestors."[41]

This connection to ancestral memory profoundly shaped my own response when the revolution came about. I was prepped and primed, and immediately aroused by its fervor. Over time it has brought about a reckoning with momentous questions about how I want to proceed with my life and my work. Of course, memories cannot force us down a path of resistance. It puts the path in us, so by the time we learn of it, we are the ones who decide if we will follow it. Memories may be reincarnated as many things. But what they do is create a field of potential—a well of affect drawn on for resistance should that be our route. As Lauren Berlant puts it, "The extraordinary always turns out to be an amplification of something in the works, a labile boundary at best, not a slammed-door departure."[42]

I have always been aware of the pronounced limitations, nay, the impossibility, of conveying the full affect of these oral histories. As Maya, Rafi's sister, testifies, "No matter what you write about al mu'anah—the struggle—we went through, it won't be the same as the truth of what happened, the actuality of it." I say all this to signal the affective force of memories, and the intensity of intergenerational testimonial sharing, which by their very nature cannot be transmitted with the reach of the pen.

---

40. Marcos, *Our Word Is Our Weapon*, 41.
41. Huber and Woodiel, "Protesters in Keystone."
42. Berlant, *Cruel Optimism*, 10.

Conclusion

In the epigraph to this chapter, Julia Boutros's poem "Oh Stories" captures the yearning to break free from the weight of history and the tales that tether us to the past. It reflects the radical subject's groundedness in genealogies of struggle as they wrestle with the memories that shape us and the futures we foresee. Memories that will not release us completely into the present. In February of 2020, the Arabic hashtag #it_will_not_leave_my_mind (#ما_يروح_من_بالي) went viral. Syrians shared memories of what had happened to them at the hands of the regime. One was about a young medical student attending her anatomy class at university to find that the cadaver they were dissecting that day was that of her brother, who had been detained by the regime.[43] Another was the haunting visual of a man holding his two dead young daughters after a chemical weapons attack in Ghouta. He held them to his body, one on each arm, imploring them to wake, "Ya abi, oomo, oomo, mshan Allah, oomo [My girls, rise up, rise up, for the sake of God, rise up]."[44] I could barely watch—their little hands tied in plastic rubber bands, and next to them, a line of lifeless children. His cries of devastation, *oomo, oomo*, evoked the memory of the exact same sound Kenda's sister had, decades earlier, used in response to her sister's coded phone call relaying the death of her son, pleading with those around her to get up: "*Oomo, oomo*, rise up, rise up, she found out about Rafi."

Lina Sergie Attar, under the pen name Amal Hanano, writes about this a priori affectability—the surreal temporality of "knowing well" what has happened and knowing "what would happen"—as the radical subject's sense of time is distorted when the past enters the present:

> We watched the events of March 2011 while in our hearts we were watching the events of February 1982. The YouTube videos projected the present but they also replayed the past. Finally, we had the evidence, the images of what we had never seen but only imagined. Though it happened in another time, in another city, at the hands of the son instead of the father, we watched and remembered. We were split in half, dealing with our past by watching our present. We watched knowing very well what it means for a Syrian city to be sealed, knowing very well that what was happening in Dara'a—and what would happen over the next years in cities across Syria—had already happened before.[45]

---

43. Al-Zayat, "It Will Not Leave My Mind."
44. Idlbi, "Man Who Came."
45. Hanano, "From Hama to Daraya."

The radical subject disavows the separation between the past, the present, and the future of revolution. There is no elision, no caesura or interruption between them—we are "locked in a recurrent curse."[46] Falling through a pocket in time, spinning backward into the past.

With intensified affect inherited from those who came before us comes a strong embeddedness and belonging to struggle, to others, and to place. However, though the past spills into the present, and the present into the past, the radical subject is not a passive inheritor of legacies of their ancestors—the infusion of their *post*memory and *living* memory stands for a unique accumulation of affect. The radical subject's affect is multivalent in its temporality, dealing with the present through making meaning of the past. In this context, I traced the possibilities of what postmemory means for affect and the recognition the radical subject warrants. It speaks to the solidarity potential of their affect, built on knowledge bound at the touchstones of the past, the innovative qualities of their political subjectivity, and iterations of resistance to a historical oppressor. Within them is a multitude of internally fragmented subjectivities and differentiated grounds, which unfolds the power of their affect.

Many radical subjects are still in the throes of their generational battle for freedom. Postmemory offers insight into their affective realm and the embodiments of trauma inherited from those whose actions and deliberations have been historically closest to the oppressor. This chapter shows how there are many more affectively mediated relations in play than a narrow focus on the radical subjects of today would suggest. Their testimony, that is, their acts of generational witnessing, are more persuasive and closer to our hearts than the "logical," affectless state of those bracketed from resistance. We would do well to heighten our sensibility to the radical subject as a historicized social actor with stakes and magnitude in producing affective sensibilities that spur solidarity.

The next chapter forces into view the affective solidarity among the radical subjects of the world. In it, we explore gestures taken to incite visceral collective affect in concert with others. The chapter brings into focus how radical subjects, even while anchored in the peripherality of their locales, are able to join toward others so they might sustain and affirm their being in the world.

---

46. Yassin-Kassab, "Literature of the Syrian Uprising," 144.

CHAPTER 4

On Peripherality

Mobilizing Affective Geographies

I am Palestinian until de-colonisation; Syrian until the triumph
of the revolution; Saharawi until liberation; Kashmiri until
independence; Kurdish until full freedom and equality. I'm a
Darfurian in Sudan, Shi'ite in Bahrain, Ahwazi in Iran, Asian
housemaid in Lebanon, illegal immigrant in the US and aboriginal
in Australia. The cause of every oppressed people, every
indigenous minority and each unprivileged group is my cause.
—Budour Hassan, "Global Voices"

On the night of the 28th of December 2011, after an eventful year of revolutionary awakening, thousands gathered near the clock tower in Homs, their hands
on each other's shoulders in unison. The magnetic football goalkeeper Abdul
Baset al-Sarout, nicknamed the nightingale of the revolution for his beautiful
voice and powerful ballads, was at the helm, singing "Heaven, heaven, heaven,
my homeland is a heaven, sweet-hearted homeland, with sweet soil, even your
fire is heaven."[1] The old Iraqi song took on a new dynamism in al-Sarout's
melodic and soulful voice, becoming a signature of the protests—if not *the*
anthem of the revolution—while its lyrics testified to the revolution's aspirations for self-renewal and social change. Originally sung with valences of joy
and optimism, it was a fixture in the early days of large-scale peaceful protests.
With time, the song took on macabre overtones, sung with *istimata*, an Arabic
word denoting an ethic of sacrifice where one risks their life for their struggle. Al-Sarout would sing it with the melancholy of mourning to suture the
wounds of protesters pining for those killed. Soon, the song became a siren
warning to those attending protests, cautioning them that they might soon be
attending their own funerals.[2]

---

1. Al-Khalidiya District Coordination in Homs, "Heaven, Heaven."
2. *Dom Tak,* "Janna, Janna, Janna."

The Iraqi artist Rida al-Khayat first performed the folkloric song, with lyrics by Karim al-Iraqi, a songwriter famous for his poems encouraging Iraqi soldiers to fight in the Iran-Iraq war. This song, with its simple and repetitive lyrics, was never intended as a revolutionary song. Yet, Syrians reclaimed it, reshaping the song into multiple variations, each rooted in the lived realities of resistance. In one version, "Revolt, revolt Daraa, in our eyes, you are a torch." Elsewhere, "Homs is calling *faz'aa* [stand up], oh the stance that has our back," to generate a sense of collective struggle between the cities and towns of Syria. After al-Sarout's assassination, the song became associated with his martyrdom and took on a life of its own.

Three years after his death, protests erupted in Palestine over the expulsion of families from their homes in Sheikh Jarrah by Israeli police forces. Protesters waved Palestinian flags as they sang their own version of "heaven, heaven, our homeland is a heaven." Amid the forced evictions of Palestinians, demonstrations took place in front of the Damascus Gate, one of the gates of the Old City of Jerusalem. One Palestinian protester held a hand-written letter of solidarity from Syrians describing the intimate relationality between the two liberatory struggles. It is a beautiful letter. I copy part of it here:[3]

> Borders kill us and our diaspora kills us, as they stand in the way of our actual presence with you. That is why we are writing to you, in the hope that it will convey the slightest hint of the feelings of pain, anger, and burning, that rage in our hearts because of your great suffering and pain.
>
> In your revolution, we saw our revolution, and in your steadfastness our steadfastness, and in your displacement our displacement. We know, like you, the meaning of oppression. We faced it at the hands of the Assad regime, as you faced it at the hands of Israel. . . .
>
> In your liberation from the occupation, we see our liberation from tyranny, and in your chants, we hear the chants of our martyrs, and in "heaven, heaven," we remember our voices and our revolution. . . .
>
> Greetings to you from the revolution of freedom and dignity,
> The undersigned, the Sons and Daughters of Syria

---

3. The letter was never formally published and is no longer available online. I have a copy of the letter, which I translated from Arabic. The full letter is in the appendix.

On the Elastic Peripheral

This is not the first time resonances between the two struggles surface in a manner outlining what I term the "elastic peripheral." The elastic peripheral emphasizes not only the imposed peripherality radical subjects face—whether in Syria, the United States, or Palestine—but also how those on the periphery stretch themselves in inventive and powerful ways to exercise resistance and agency. Notwithstanding the complexity and internal diversity of struggles, radical subjects construct a spatiality in which they, and others like them around the world, are central to a global revolutionary project. In this formation, those in resistance work to subvert dominant political geographies of power. Alliances are secured through leaning into the "peripherality" of those under various forms of oppression, be it settler colonialism, colonialism, authoritarianism, or white supremacy, reconfiguring the margins as spaces of global resistance.

Without institutional power and access to traditional spaces of oratory, radical subjects must be creative in how they generate attention to their cause. When revolutions are perceived as so particular, so place-specific and local, they can become almost impossible to communicate. As this chapter shows, radical subjects exert significant efforts to instigate translinguistic and transnational affective encounters across borders in response to waning attention to the cause. In their peripherality, they produce affective and politically productive arguments to overcome "negative solidarity" (a term from the Combahee River Collective to describe those who acquiesce to power) and to confront unevenness in the building of political coalitions among differently situated subjects.[4] Rather than simply issuing didactic calls for "help," radical subjects strategically channel tensions and discourses clustered elsewhere to facilitate a coming to consciousness of those from whom solidarity is demanded.

By making their struggles relational in urgent and compelling terms, radical subjects harness global networks of circulation and transmission to overcome a lack of receptiveness to their cause. In contesting constraints of visibility, they do not emphasize a common "enemy" or perpetrator with linkages across states or borders as much as establish relationality between those in liberatory struggle to elicit scaffolding for solidarity.[5] In this revolutionary strategy, a panoply of events and social actors are woven together to exert

---

4. Combahee River Collective, "Combahee River Collective Statement."
5. The intersectionality of struggles (rather than the intersectionality of identities) is an approach that goes beyond a focus on individual perpetrators of oppression to take on larger questions of imperialism, structural racism, and state violence. See Davis, "Freedom Is a Constant Struggle."

affective pressure on those from whom solidarity is requested. Eclipsed possibilities for solidarity are realized through the kairotic placement (i.e., seizing opportune timing) of situations that are often interpreted separately in the same critical geography. It impels energy into utterance by capturing the intensity of audience attention and stretching itself toward where the world's attention is centered. Even as they recognize the vast plurality of worldviews, radical subjects imbibe an affective sociality that resists simplistic notions of "we are all humankind" to forge deeper, more nuanced connections.

Communication scholar Thomas Farrell describes the "weight of rhetoric," or how one might make "things matter," as the affective energy of discourse that creates the potential for audiences to care about and act on an issue.[6] The sensational quality of rhetoric institutes the "response-ability" of the audience to what Lauren Berlant calls the "shapelessness of the present."[7] The adjective "elastic" in "elastic peripheral" thus speaks to bolstering the salience of an issue, its importance, hierarchy, and significance through the provocation of sensation. Elasticity suggests a responsiveness, a capacity to expand and contract in ways that draw attention and heighten the intensity of a cause as one becomes attuned to others also at the periphery. The elastic peripheral, then, does not merely react to marginality; it transforms and amplifies it. In the process, affect is generated by virtue of attentiveness and making present "events" that the audience has been seen to respond to morally. As I will show, because it does not exist in a predefined or settled manner, the elastic peripheral is able to expand multidirectionally from one milieu to another to establish relationality. It is a critical invention that situates the radical subject in relation to human geographies that are more familiar in their operations of domination and oppression. As it is not affixed to any region or geostrategic bloc, it opens up a space of reflection exceeding a sole focus on one's own revolutionary telos, modulating itself at an opportune moment in relation to consequential dynamics on the world stage. As a translational move, it renders the unimportant important, making present that which is outside the "corner of one's eye." This conceptual stretching encompasses one's liberatory struggle within frameworks of other movements (and their attending sensory channels) deemed to fall outside its purview.[8]

---

6. Farrell, "Weight of Rhetoric."

7. Berlant, *Cruel Optimism*, 8.

8. This "stretching" mirrors Fadi Bardawil's reading of Césaire's letter of resignation from the French Communist Party (addressed to the party's secretary general, Maurice Thorez). Césaire proposes that "critical practice should be . . . attuned to the world, by inventing new forms that enable solidarities. This inventive labor of critique can take the form of stretching, a concept to encompass practices that previously fell outside of its purview." Bardawil, "Critical Theory in a Minor Key," 183–84.

Specifically, I consider the following questions: How do radical subjects engage with liberatory struggles of different traditions and genealogies, of different futures and emergences, and of different temporalities of revolutionary time in order to open new spaces for solidarity? What affective labors are produced as they call audiences to (re)consider their revolution amid the tragic predicament of the erasure of their revolutionary teleology? What constitutive imaginings are forged in their instrumental aspiration to raise the visibility of their struggle? How do they negotiate and resolve the tensions of solidarity that our times force upon us in and through their peripherality?

With these questions in mind, this chapter develops over two sections. First, I offer a critical review of the term *the Global South* as affectively limited in its conception of radical subjects. Second, I proffer the rationale for the "elastic peripheral" as spatializing a competing set of affects which eschew hemispheric or geographic logics to solidarity—of "global linear thinking," of "the Global North" helping "the Global South," or of the West helping the non-West—with the aim of remedying injustices of recognition. This is framed in conversation with two reference points exemplifying this pattern of affective practice: (1) Palestinian liberation and (2) the Black Lives Matter movement. I conclude by contemplating the prospects of such translocal calls and the powerful affects they catalyze for solidarity with differently situated radical subjects.

On "the Global South"

The Global South as a Geographic Marker of Inequality

As a mode of framing, *the Global South* enjoys increasing popularity as a transnational space encompassing "darker nations" and continents of Africa, Asia, Latin America, and Oceania. After the collapse of the Soviet Union, it took the place of its pre–Cold War predecessor *the Third World,* though it still retains some of the term's fraught associations with backwardness and underdevelopment. Primarily, the term is employed as a geopolitical marker of inequality for countries negatively impacted by capitalist globalization, where the Global North is the center of the world, and the Global South is the periphery. The Global South was cemented as a category in the 1970s with the formation of groups facing economic disadvantages in the international finance system, such as the Non-Aligned Movement and the Group of 77. These each consisted of a diverse group of nation-states with a common South-South ideology hoping to assert their political independence and collective economic interests. On the other hand, the South Commission established in 1987 used "the South" not only as an economic descriptor, but to highlight their exclusion from international decision-making. Regardless, the term is inextricably tied to what Caroline Levander and Walter D. Mignolo describe as the enduring "consequences of the colonial wound" by the European conquest of the Americas and colonial domination of Africa, parts of Asia, and the Middle East.[9]

The Global South as an Epistemological Marker

A second definition of the Global South understands it as an epistemological marker that challenges the dominance of Global North ways of knowing. Here, the term serves to foreground the histories, experiences, and knowledge production of regions that have been marginalized in mainstream discourse. It offers a counterpoint to *the Global North* as the source of universal, objective knowledge—a claim that often masks its own positionality. This arises in the increased recognition of the uneven weight placed on Northern academic theorizations and the authority conferred to scholars of the Global North. When Northern nations are the main sites of theory production, the Global South is only a superfluous source of ethnographic data. Hence, the Global South creates a geographically distinct source of intellectual production and of "epistemologies of the South" that question Northern epistemologies.[10]

The Global South as a De-territorialized Geography

A third definition of the Global South is as a deterritorialized geography blurring the lines between North and South. Transnational globalization (evident in the emergence of the "Big Four"—Brazil, India, China, and Russia) complicates the ease with which one may refer to an oppressed South and a hegemonic North."[11] Accordingly, some differentiate between the "South from above"—the elite, state-led representation aligned with dominant global institutions—and the "South from below," which centers grassroots social movements and bottom-up resistance that challenge global inequality and envision alternative futures. Another incarnation of the term ambiguously extends to

---

9. Levander and Mignolo, "Global South," 184–85.
10. Santos, *Epistemologies of the South*.
11. Prashad, *Poorer Nations*.

the North's geographic Souths and the Souths in the geographic North. This phenomenon is apparent in the intersectional struggles within the geographic North, such as African American, Indigenous, and Chicano/a/x struggles. By way of illustration, African Belgian protests demanding the removal of statues of King Léopold II (a colonial figure responsible for the death of 10 million Congolese) in Belgium's squares, parks, and university campuses makes tangible the ways in which a Global South / Global North rubric falls short. Global migrations and shifts in economic power also problematize the dichotomous dialectic of the Global South / Global North, though of course the distribution of wealth and power in the global economy remains disproportionately in countries in the geographic North.

Limitations of *the Global South*

In sum, the term *the Global South* carries quite a few conceptual limits. The territorial underpinnings of the term as married to the "South" contribute to its inherent spatial and metaphorical limitations in capturing the transnational dimensions of certain subjectivities. By virtue of the term's origins in histories of Cold War decolonization, it has been ingrained in colonial histories since the Global South / Global North as an organizing principle became popular. Alternate geographies preceding colonialism are not accounted for. Edward Said's classic *Orientalism* traces the significance of counter-geographies and spatial markers and how they express specific intentions about how space is perceived. By way of illustration, the maps of Al-Idrisi, the Moroccan geographer and cartographer of the early twelfth century, in the world of today would be seen as skewed or even upside down—the map is oriented with the south at the top and Mecca as the focal point. Even the term "Bilad of Sham" (the region of Greater Syria) translates to "Land of the Left," pointing to a geography in which a person standing in the center of Arabia facing north had Sham to his left. *The Global South's* attachment to histories of colonization arguably makes it unable to account for other transnational (and local) cartographic imaginings of the globe. In emphasizing a structural subjectivity principally opposed to Europe and its hegemonic forms of knowledge, it reinforces an ethnocentric focus on non-Western peoples subordinated to *the Global North*. Competing collective movements, such as anarchism, which have historically drawn on diverse languages, ethnicities, and local traditions to imagine alternative global orders, are unaccounted for. In its loyalty to old colonial boundaries, decades of local dynamics and Indigenous relations between peoples are neglected, potentially stifling alternative visions to the present order. Another concern is that the term does not differentiate between the people on the ground and the "Global South regimes crushing us."[12]

These critiques of *the Global South* proffer a rationale for the elastic peripheral as a revolutionary conception of global cartographies and political imperatives with the potential for affective collective coherence. As I show, the elastic periphery is not at odds with the varied meanings associated with *the Global South*, but as its conceptual kin, evokes a specific set of spaces, affects, and actors capable of challenging hegemonic frames that cast certain struggles in a deficit. The *elasticity* of the periphery is important, compelling us to resist reifying the center-periphery binary or the borders that divide us, and instead shows how radical subjects disrupt and subvert these dichotomies (whether within "Third World" nations, along "North/South" lines, or in "advanced/underdeveloped" nations) in the pursuit of affective resonance. In what follows, I draw on the Palestinian liberation movement and the Black Lives Matter movement as touchstones illuminating the modus operandi of the elastic peripheral and the affective qualities through which collectives are forged.

"Syrian Palestinians"

On the eve of the Sheikh Jarrah expulsion of residents, I was in an online discussion with a group of Syrian activists when one exclaimed, "Before the revolution, Palestine was our sick child. After the revolution, it is like we have two sick children." The allegory of the child serves as a reminder of the intimate attachments between Palestinian and Syrian liberation. The coupling of the two movements occurs both organically and strategically as an affectivity of belonging to both causes. Though one is primarily a struggle against authoritarianism (Syria) and the other a struggle against settler colonialism, these twin foci envisage and claim a common cause along the periphery. In this section, I explore the ways in which the Syrian Revolution and Palestinian liberation animate shared worldviews and collective fantasies of anticolonial futures.[13]

Of note is the anonymous Syrian collective The Syrian People Know Their Way, comprising fifteen artists both inside and outside of Syria who created political posters to be carried at demonstrations. For one, the collective's Facebook page is provocatively called The Syrian Intifada. The literal translation of

---

12. Ayoub, "On Erasures and 'Discourse.'"

13. It is important to remember that the Golan Heights were seized from Syria by Israel in the 1967 Six-Day War. Although the US recognized Israel's sovereignty over Golan Heights in 2019 during Trump's presidency, reversing years of US policy, the majority of the international community regards the occupation of the territory to be illegal.

the term *intifada* in Arabic is "tremor," but it also relates to the word *nafada*, meaning "to shake off." Today, the term is almost exclusively associated with the armed uprisings of Palestinians against the Israeli occupation of the West Bank and Gaza Strip (the First Intifada of 1987–93 and the Second Intifada of 2000–2005).

In The Syrian People Know Their Way's rich archive of over two hundred posters, one of the central motifs is the conceptual linking of the Syrian Revolution with the Palestinian liberation movement. As an example, one of the collective's posters shows a young man throwing a stone against a pale orange background, under which is penned "the Palestinian spirit is in every revolutionary." The stone-throwing is a nod to the powerful emblem of the first Palestinian intifada, where Palestinian youth, facing disparity in power and military equipment, engaged in the symbolic practice of throwing stones against heavily armed Israeli forces. In the poster, two stone-throwers are hazily echoed onto one another, one presumably Palestinian, the other presumably Syrian (see figure 3). This image draws on an iconography so deeply associated with Palestinian resistance that it has come to dominate media representations of the conflict, receiving more international press attention than many other, often more destructive, forms of violence.[14]

In another poster we see "Zaytoun, the little refugee," a Syrian Palestinian refugee child video-game character forced to flee his home in Yarmouk camp after a siege imposed by the Assad regime. Yarmouk was a refugee camp in the suburbs of Damascus (sometimes called Syria's Gaza), which once housed the largest Palestinian population in Syria before being pulverized and depopulated by the Assad regime in 2018.[15] Zaytoun, originally created by a group of Syrian, Palestinian, and Spanish activists to bring awareness about the life of Palestinian refugees in Yarmouk, is lightly sketched in black and white. Little Zaytoun's slingshot aims at the words "Baba Amr," in reference to the massacre in Baba Amr that took place in Homs in 2012, a city that is symbolic as an enclave of Syrian resistance (see figure 4). The image punctuates the similarities between Syrians and Palestinians in struggle, in particular the unavoidable fact of the immense discrepancies between the Assad regime's military capabilities and the weaponry of Syrians on the ground. At the same time, Zaytoun, in his worn-out clothes, is resilient as he aims his slingshot determinedly.

---

14. Chenoweth and Stephan, *Why Civil Resistance Works*.

15. Yarmouk was established in 1957 to house Palestinian refugees. It grew to become home to the largest Palestinian population in Syria, with over 160,000 residents at its peak. However, starting in 2012, it was besieged by the Assad regime and its allies, who restricted the flow of food, medicine, and humanitarian aid into the camp. By 2018, much of the camp was in ruins and many of its residents displaced.

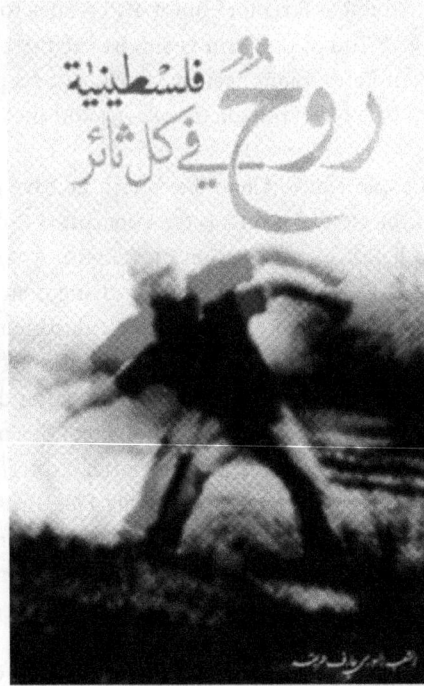

FIGURE 3. "The Palestinian spirit is in every
revolutionary" poster. Used with permission
from The Syrian People Know Their Way.
Shared on Facebook, July 14, 2012, https://
www.facebook.com/Syrian.Intifada/photo
s/a.148885538508914/389147281149404.

Meanwhile, activists from Occupied Kafranbel drew from the Palestinian liberation movement in a unique intersection of political activism and
aesthetic experimentation. Kafranbel, a small town in the Idlib countryside,
the revolution's "musical note," became an international sensation after global
news agencies, such as *The Independent,* the *Huffington Post,* and the *Washington Post,* caught wind of their weekly Friday banners and demonstrations.[16]

---

16. Several exhibitions of the banners were held outside of the country to garner attention and fundraise for the revolution. Eventually, some of the banners were sold in Europe and
profits sent back to fund revolutionary activities in Syria. Raed Fares, Kafranbel's protest leader,
became a "legend of epic banner-making" who traveled the world to talk about what was happening in Syria. Sergie Attar, "Revolutionary Wit." Sometimes, in Boston for example, Americans made banners to send messages of solidarity back to Kafranbel. The protesters dreamed
of one day making a "Museum of Freedom" in Kafranbel, where they would display all their
posters. For more on Raed Fares, read AlRifai, "In Memoriam."

FIGURE 4. Poster of Zaytoun the Little Refugee in Baba Amr. Used with permission from The Syrian People Know Their Way. Shared on Facebook, March 1, 2012, https://www.facebook.com/Syrian.Intifada/photos/a.148885538508914/305716362825830.

The group created witty, irreverent, yet piercing banners to raise awareness about the liberatory struggle in Syria.[17] By pulling on new techniques and vocabularies, the eye-catching banners reversed waning attention to the Syrian Revolution. Instead of only covering events in Syria, the banners showcased an unprecedented level of interaction with world events, from a range of pop culture references and geopolitical analysis, such as the Boston Bombings, the war in Ukraine, UN vetoes, Black Friday sales, and Caitlyn Jenner's coming-out as transgender, to references to a Pink Floyd album cover and even *The Lord of the Rings*.

In what only can be called the embodied process of making solidarity, each banner was hand-made, staged, and authored with the date by the protestors who would stand in dense unison behind and around the banner. Ahmad Jalal was the cartoonist, and a calligrapher and translator would design and translate the texts from Arabic into multiple languages, such as Turkish, English,

17. The archives of the weekly banners are on the Facebook page "The Occupied Kafranbel Banners."

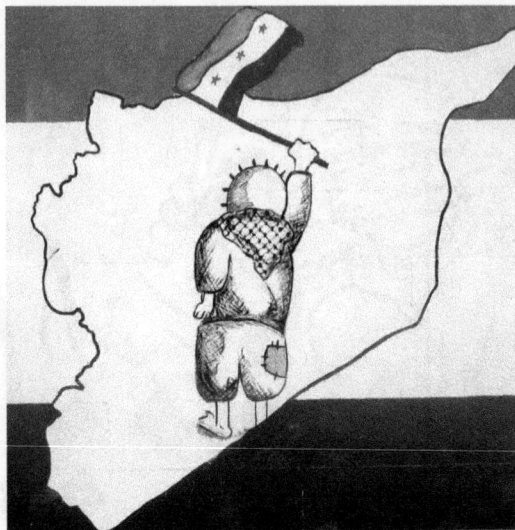

FIGURE 5. Handala with the Syrian Revolution flag.
Used with permission from Occupied Kafranbel Banners.
Shared on Facebook, March 14, 2021, https://www.
facebook.com/kafrnbl/photos/3965409476885796.

Russian, or Chinese. Protestors meticulously planned the locations in which banners would be held, often in public sites or in front of bombed-out buildings. Eventually, when the activists became the target of regime airstrikes and barrel bombs, they protested in inconspicuous side streets. Because of weak internet service, pictures of the banners were taken with a Nokia flip phone and sent to friends living outside of Syria to circulate online. As they began to generate international attention, the people of Kafranbel pled with the activists to stop creating the banners due to the conviction that they were the reason for the regime's intense air raids of the town. The behind-the-scenes machinations of the banner-making reveal a discernable drive to initiate a translinguistic and transnational affective encounter with the world, at great risk to themselves and the people of the town.

In one social media entry, the Occupied Kafranbel group posted an image of "Handala," the refugee child character designed in 1969 by the Palestinian political cartoonist Naji al-Ali. The name Handala comes from *handhal,* a perennial plant local to dry areas of Palestine, which bears a bitter fruit, has thick roots, and grows back quickly when cut. Barefoot in his kaffiyeh and darned clothing, an effect of layering embeds ten-year-old Handala inside the geographic border of Syria, a composition then implanted inside the stripes

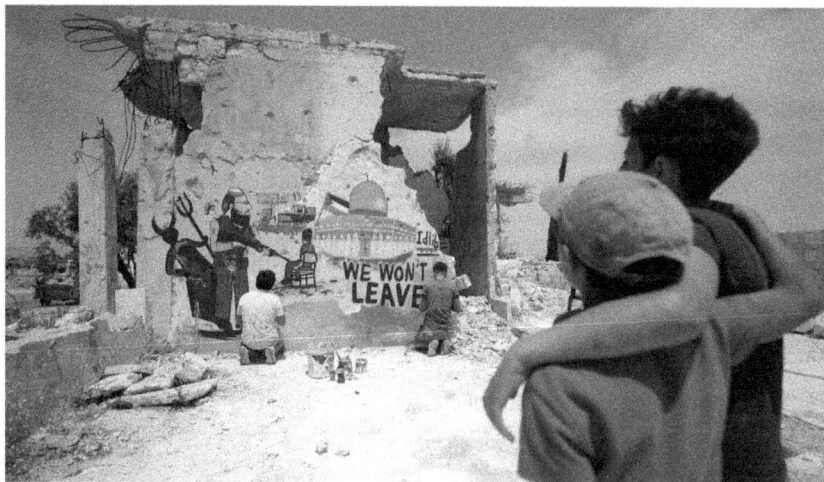

FIGURE 6. "We won't leave" mural. Used with permission of Aziz Asmar.

of green, white, and black of the Syrian Revolution. Handala, a quintessential symbol of Palestinian resistance, turns his back to the viewer in a silent yet powerful gesture—rejecting both the superficial solutions offered to resolve the Palestinian Nakba and a world that has long ignored his people's suffering. In this picture, Handala triumphantly clasps the flag of the Syrian Revolution. Initially symbolizing the affective resistance of Palestinian children who refuse to bow to Israeli might, here, Syrian refugees are also radical subjects in resistance rather than destitute humans depending on the international community for survival (see figure 5).

Invoking a similar vein of resistance to tyranny, the artist Aziz Asmar drew the Dome of the Rock—a historic mosque at the center of the Al-Aqsa compound in the Old City of Jerusalem—on the wall of a destroyed house in Idlib (see figure 6). In the mural, a child sits as an Israeli soldier holds a gun to his knee. The mural itself stands amid rubble, tangled barbed wire, and crumbling buildings. Underneath, Asmar irreverently writes, "We won't leave." In a rhetorical twist, the "right of return" of Palestinians and the "refusal to leave" of Syrians are juxtaposed onto one another. Recounting his motivation for the composition, Asmar contemplates the reciprocity of anguish between Syrians and Palestinians: "The pain of the Syrian & Palestinian people is one."[18] In these emotional registers, the analogous experiences of the loss of Indigenous lands and the forced displacement of Syrians and Palestinians are brought to bear.

---

18. Shweish, "Syrian Artist Aziz Asmar."

فلسطينيون حتى الحرية

FIGURE 7. "Palestinian until freedom" poster. Used with the permission of The Syrian People Know Their Way. Shared on Facebook, August 5, 2012, https://www. facebook.com/Syrian.Intifada/photos/a.148885538508914/396650947065704.

In these examples, there is a deliberate effort to embrace of Syrian revolutionary identity as inherently intertwined with the Palestinian struggle. An affective spatiality emerges—one shaped by fluid understandings of the self as refracted through the gaze toward others and the shared pulse of those engaged in struggles against domination. In a close mimesis of this rhetoric, The Syrian People Know Their Way designed a poster with the profile of a Palestinian revolutionary in a black-and-white fishnet-pattern kaffiyeh (see figure 7). The revolutionary holds a weapon, symbolizing the struggle for freedom. Across the poster the caption reads: "Palestinian until Freedom," arguing for the deterritorialized nature of Palestinian identity as spanning to other human geographies: "Palestine is not a fixed identity or a nationality or a status of belonging to a certain geography, but it is the cause of the liberation of the human, every human."[19] The emphasis shifts away from the ethnic or national category of "Palestinian" and toward the geography of "liberation," a spatial imaginary that transcends borders to encompass the insurgent anticolonialism of all those engaged in struggles for freedom.

Although the kaffiyeh was originally a practical garment worn by rural farmers and peasants (the fellahin) to shield their necks from the sun and sand, it eventually acquired political significance during the Arab Revolt of 1936–39 (a major uprising by Palestinian Arabs against British colonial rule and mass Jewish immigration in Mandatory Palestine), when British authorities banned it because rebels were using it to mask their identities. Since that time, Palestinians wear it en masse as a show of unity with Palestinian resistance. Transposing iconic symbols of Palestinian anticolonial resistance into

---

19. The Syrian People Know Their Way, "Palestinian until Freedom."

the Syrian context not only underscores the inspiration drawn from the Palestinian liberation struggle but also redefines the parameters of the Syrian Revolution. Beyond highlighting the relationality between Syrian and Palestinian struggles, this act controversially advances a political interpretation of the Syrian Revolution that firmly embeds anticolonial politics within its emancipatory framework. Anticolonialism as a subjectivity has been largely borne by and readable in the Palestinian context. As a grand term, *colonization* describes the invasion of foreign countries driven by capitalist and racist ideologies. This historiographic tendency foregrounds the temporal origins of colonialism in the European and American domination of overseas cultures and peoples (that is, locating colonialism's origins in modern Western imperialism, often ignoring older, non-Western forms of conquest and domination). Colonial discourse operates within a paradigm of difference, or what Alexander G. Weheliye calls an "ontological face-off,"[20] that is, a confrontation between white and nonwhite, civilized and savage, Western and non-Western. Settler colonialism, as a variant of colonialism when the colony is converted into a home (and not just pursued for labor and resources), falls into similarly top-down dynamics of racializing Indigenous peoples. Yet, these conceptualizations of colonization, inherited from the dualisms of a Cold War framework, have at times delegitimized or obscured liberation struggles against local oppressors. Anti-imperialism (along with secularism) is among the "theoretical first principles" that ease the exclusion of the certain revolutions as not "properly revolutionary," casting them instead as mere extensions of US or Soviet interests.[21] While colonialism is rightly recognized as a critical force that defines our modern age, authoritarianism is too often localized as a form of Oriental civilization in historically immobile cultural and social contexts. When the "misère of the Arab masses" is only attributable to "evil external forces,"[22] local liberation struggles fall outside the anticolonial orbit and into a political deadlock, which maintains them as marginal, if not squarely in the domain of sectarianism or humanitarian crisis.

On the other hand, the Palestinian resistance has more easily cohered into anticolonial frameworks. While the Syrian Revolution has been mostly isolated from public view, the Palestinian question is "at the heart of anticolonial struggles in the region."[23] As I write in mid-2025, the world's attention is fixated on Gaza and Rafah. Palestinian liberation has become a cause célèbre in the Arab and Islamic world and a vital part of a worldwide project

20. Weheliye, *Habeas Viscus,* 26.
21. Bardawil, "Césaire with Adorno."
22. Postone, "History and Helplessness."
23. Bardawil, *Revolution and Disenchantment,* 36.

of anti-imperialist liberation.[24] Symbolically, the caricature of Handala, originally a metonymic marker of the over 750,000 Palestinians expelled during
the Nakba of 1948, has transcended its origins as a national Arab emblem to
become a symbol for anticolonial resistance around the world.[25]

As such, interlacing the two movements leans into the prominence of the
Palestinian liberation movement and its substantial and immediate anticolonial reverberations in the global arena. Without falling into a banal equation of
histories, the Palestinian movement's standing as an anticolonial revolutionary
movement is careened to refract grand emotions into the low-intensity affectivity of local struggles that do not enact the same constellations of emotion
or political acuity. For Syrians to be in the political with Palestinians in this
fashion is intentional: they realize they have not been the object of sustained
political analysis and attention on the world stage, and in response, they offer
a critical intervention with radical decolonial potential. By diverting Palestinian symbols from their original compositions, contextual clues, a sort of lin-
gua franca, are offered for situations in which audiences may be less certain
and less univocal about making moral judgments.[26]

Within this is an implied rethinking of hegemonic framings of colonization as inevitably tied to the racial hierarchization of human species, considering reverberations of the colonial that might otherwise remain obscured.
Indirectly, it questions dominant assumptions of colonialism as tethered to
"foreignness," "externality," or explicitly racialized forms toward a more elastic conception of anticolonial struggles. The boundaries between "internal"
struggle and anticolonial movements become fluid, attuned to how precarity
is created when tenancy to one's land is in someone else's hand. Thereby, the

24. For more on this, see Üngör, "Screaming"; and Wallet, "Niet Zomaar Een Land."
25. For instance, Handala has become a symbol of the worldwide Boycott, Divestment and
Sanctions movement as well as a mascot for the Iranian Green Movement, among others.
26. As Professor of Holocaust and Genocide Studies Uğur Ümit Üngör words it,

If it is the body count, then next-door Syria or Iraq should be a concern too;
if it is racism, then Darfur should not be forgotten; if it is the urgency, then
Nagorno-Karabagh should not be ignored; if it is settler colonialism, then the
Uyghurs should be included. In fact, to characterize Israel as the "last bastion
of colonialism" turns a blind eye to Turkish-nationalist settlerism in emptied
Armenian villages, or the Arabization policies of Kurdish regions in Iraq and
Syria in the 1970s—which uprooted hundreds of thousands. One could even
ask if there is a colonial gaze in not focusing on the next-door Arab lives
as grievable; in other words, do the Israeli nation-state boundaries ironically
function as a type of moral boundary? If "decolonial" means all human lives
are fundamentally equal, then holding a settler colony's perpetrators to higher
standards of scrutiny, or its victims to more compassion is hardly decolonial.
(Üngör, "Screaming")

elastic peripheral might be said to align with internal (or domestic) colonialism theory, which describes the structural domination and exploitation of marginalized groups within a single nation-state, treating them as if they were colonized peoples. The philosophical and affective articulation of colonialism's heterogeneity is deciphered in how al-Haj Saleh talks about the Palestinization of Syrians by an "internal Israel" (i.e., the Assad regime),[27] and the alienation of shortsighted geopolitical approaches that dismiss their radical revolution as less than or as containable within the scope of "domestic" politics.

The self-conscious implication within discourses of colonization also recognizes the Syrian Revolution as a land revolution committed to territorial integrity. One of the ideographs which appears repeatedly within the rhetoric of Syrian radical subjects is that of *ihtilal,* an Arabic word roughly connoting colonization or occupation. In the *Frontline* documentary "For Sama," as the city of Aleppo teeters on the brink of falling to regime control, the journalist Waad al-Kateab employs the rhetoric of *ihtilal* for the regime's slow encroachment on liberated territories in eastern Aleppo.[28] On the eve of Aleppo's fall to regime forces in 2016, she gazes sorrowfully into the camera as the city slips from their grasp, naming it *Halab al-Muhtalla*—Aleppo the Occupied. Her close friend, Afraa Hashem, an activist in her own right, claims the regime has rendered Syrians *ghurabaa*—strangers in their own land.[29] In many respects, the Assad regime had successfully severed Syrians from their subsistence base and painfully expropriated and dispossessed them of their lands. Land dispossession here is not only a political and humanitarian phenomenon but strikes at the very essence of how we inhabit, experience, and belong on the land. In light of the regime's use of necropolitics on the land, including sieges, the wanton torching of farmland with incendiary weapons, and the confiscation of the lands of Syrians who fled for their lives, the language of colonization clarifies the stakes and impediments of the struggle for self-determination. It is against this backdrop that the jubilant cries of Syrians who proclaim that "our country has returned to us" in the aftermath of the regime's fall takes on full meaning. More than a celebration of political change, it signals the end of an internal colonization—and the reclamation of one's homeland.

This reclamation animates an emancipatory politics in which "Syrianness" is distinct from national state identity and tied to a belongingness to ancestral lands. In this narrative, Surya (Arabic pronunciation of Syria) is the land where Indigenous people live and resist in an embodied act of decolonization. In the *Al Jazeera* documentary *The Revolution Is Being Televised,* about

---

27. Al-Haj Saleh, "Syrian Cause and Anti-Imperialism."
28. Al-Kateab and Watts, "For Sama."
29. Hashem, "Regime's Crimes."

the besieged town of Al-Qusayr in Homs, cameraman Trad al-Zahori confronts questions of the colonial when he corrects himself mid-sentence when describing the national army as Syrian: "Indiscriminate shelling continues on Al-Qusayr and its surrounding fields. . . . God save us, God save us. The Syrian Army, no excuse me, the Assad army, is shelling the town of Al-Qusayr and its surrounding fields."[30] After his slip, he incisively strips "Syrianness" from the Syrian national army. In this context, "Syria" is for those loyal to ancestral lands. May Scaff, the iconic actress renowned for her public stance against the regime in the early days of the revolution, in her last Facebook entry prior to her death in exile, made a similar stylistic choice: "I won't lose hope . . . I won't lose hope . . . It's the great Syria, not Assad's Syria."[31]

These pronouncements provide a moral discourse that condemns Assad as a colonizer. Not to mention, they are a reminder of how the Assad regime, as its grip of power became tenuous, compromised Syria's territorial integrity and allowed for the growing long-term military presence (along with economic and logistical support) of other nation-states, such as Iran and Russia. Coupled with earlier discussion in this book of the radical subject's heterarachical conceptions of the colonial as multiple and entangled, rather than one singular system of colonialism where the domestic is separate from the international, *colonial* becomes a fitting term for those who do not treat the land and its inhabitants as their own.

Taking this point further, the adoption of the Syrian Revolution flag, with its green-white-black tricolor and three red stars, was not just aesthetically motivated to differentiate the opposition from the regime's flag but also tapped into the anticolonial ethos of times past. The Syrian Revolution flag had a previous life as Syria's unofficial flag during the French Mandate and was later adopted as a symbol of Syria's liberation from French colonialism.[32] It was hoisted on government buildings on April 17, 1946, the day after the evacuation of the last French soldier at the conclusion of the French Mandate. This "independence" flag was in use from 1932 to 1963, aside from the period of Syrian-Egyptian unity (1958–61), when Syria and Egypt merged to form the United Arab Republic. It remained in use until a year after the Ba'athist party took power in 1963, after which the Syrian Arab Republic flag took its place (a standard with a red-white-black tricolor and two green stars). In the selection

30. Pletts, "Revolution."

31. Scaff, "I Won't Lose Hope."

32. The Syrian flag has been officially changed nine times since the formation of the state after it gained independence from the Ottomans in 1918. Interestingly, the French enforced several flags for each of the five "states" of Syria, each with a French flag in the canton. The "unofficial" independence flag was used from 1932 to 1946 during the French Mandate by Syrian revolutionaries. It adopted the colors of the Arab Revolt flag of 1918–20 but in a new form. See Sergie, *Recollecting History*.

of the independence flag for the revolution, the decolonial politics of the revolution are impelled by gesturing to the historic severing and expropriation of Syrians from their lands, and the ways they were dispossessed under the Assad regime. It also gestures to how the revolutionary struggle of 2011 is inherited from the age of decolonization.

Promoting the political valence of the land (and its colonization) therefore reflects not only a shared investment in land and place, what sociologist Yassir Munif calls a "politics of life,"[33] but the shaping of an otherwise dissimilar analysis to expand the audience's political and moral obligations to those who are similarly vulnerable. To bring this full circle, these readings must be critically weighed in light of the Assad regime's pro-Palestinian rhetoric and the authentication strategies on which it constituted itself. Part and parcel of this is the smearing of the revolution as an imperialist conspiracy against a stalwart anti-imperialist regime. The regime has historically presented itself as embodying nationalist principles of Arab unity as a state in existential struggle with Israel. In actuality, the regime instrumentalized the Palestinian cause for its own benefit to legitimate its own existence under the guise of protecting the nation from imperialist encroachments.[34] In sum, through the entwinement of the Palestinian and Syrian liberation struggles, the contours of our political imagination are shaped by the intricacies and necessities of day-to-day resistance required to live on one's land in dignity.

"Syrian Blacks"

After watching the footage of George Floyd pleading for his breath while a police officer pinned his neck to the ground in Minneapolis, Aziz Asmar had

---

33. Munif, *Syrian Revolution*.

34. Interestingly, the "Emergency Law," which came into effect when the Ba'ath Party seized power in 1963, was put in place to counter the military threat of Israel. However, it was always used for arbitrary detentions and for repressing any internal dissent. The largest branch of military intelligence in Damascus (Military Intelligence Branch 235, or more infamously known as "the Palestine Branch") purported to collect information for Palestine but was in fact notorious for its torture of Palestinians (and Syrians) who opposed Assad. See Human Rights Watch, "Torture Archipelago." It held the majority of intelligence on Syrians, in addition to the Fedayeen Office, a division within the Syrian intelligence apparatus—under Hafez al-Assad's regime—responsible for overseeing and monitoring Palestinian armed groups (referred to as *fedayeen*, meaning "those who sacrifice themselves") and their organizations on Syrian territory. A case in point is Tal al-Mallouhi, a young woman detained in 2009 and later charged with "disclosing information to a foreign country" for blogging poems about Palestine. See Oweis, "Mother of Young Syrian Blogger." Not to mention the various ways in which the regime's forces, along with its military and affiliated militias, besieged and attacked Palestinian refugees, be it in Yarmouk Camp in Syria or in Tal Zaatar Camp in Lebanon.

FIGURE 8. Aziz Asmar's portrait of George Floyd. Used with permission from Aziz Asmar.

flashbacks of Syrians gasping for breath after sarin gas attacks by the Assad regime in the suburb of Eastern Ghouta. He was inspired to paint George Floyd's likeness on the remains of his family's kitchen wall in the town of Binnish after it had been destroyed by the regime's air strikes. The vividly colored eight-foot mural of Floyd's face is appended alongside his last chilling words, "I can't breathe" (see figure 8). In an interview, Asmar brings to life the scene of George Floyd's murder and how it evoked memories of Syrian suffocation he had witnessed: "In those hospitals, the victims were crying, and they were asking to breathe. I saw George Floyd pleading with the officer to let him breathe and it reminded me of the way they were killed."[35]

Breath, and the lack of it, cannot be easily textualized. As a site of rhetorical invention, painting George Floyd's likeness on the scarred landscape of a ravaged home is significant for the space on which the compass of suffering is mapped. Amid habitual images of extinguished Syrian cities, the theatricality of the canvas creates discord with audience expectations as a razed home in a small town in Syria becomes the literal and ideological backdrop for remembering George Floyd. The location of the painting—in the middle of a destroyed landscape dispossessed of its people—dramatizes bodies in crisis, and the apocalyptic aftermath left after bombing raids. The act of painting is one rife with considerable corporeal costs and existential agitation: "There are

---

35. Hincks, "In Solidarity."

WE STAND IN SOLIDARITY WITH THE
OPPRESSED WHO CANNOT BREATHE
#BLAKLIVESMATTER.

THE SYRIAN REVOLUTION-FROM KAFRANBEL 13 DEC 2014

FIGURE 9. Black Lives Matter banner in Kafranbel. Used with permission
from Occupied Kafranbel Banners. Shared on Facebook, May 26, 2020,
https://www.facebook.com/kafrnbl/photos/3092542220839197.

logistical problems. We draw on walls destroyed by bombs. Because of that, it is difficult to draw on them. Sometimes rocks fall on us, and sometimes planes return to bomb the areas in which we are drawing."[36]

After George Floyd's murder, the Kafranbel activists mentioned earlier were also taking notice. On their official Facebook account, they reposted an image of themselves from a few years prior, when they had stood with their revolutionary flags and held a banner in solidarity with Eric Garner, a Black man killed by two New York police officers after being locked in a choke hold. The banner—designed by community organizer and mastermind of the Kafranbel banners, Raed Fares, in 2014—states in bold letters: "We stand in solidarity with the oppressed who cannot breathe #blacklivesmatter" (see figure 9).

In this case, a new caption brings the assassination of Raed Fares in 2018 and the assassination of George Floyd in 2020 into conversation with one another:[37]

---

36. Aletto, "Aziz Asmar."

37. Raed Fares, a brave Syrian journalist, activist, and civil society leader, was abducted and targeted numerous times. He was gunned down by unknown assailants with fellow activist Hamoud Jneed just before Friday prayers, on November 23, 2018.

Before he was killed, the man was saying, "I cannot breathe." Today, another Black man is killed by Minnesota police, as a policeman put his knee on the neck of the man who was lying on the ground and unable to move, and unable to breathe, and he did not remove his knee until that man had taken his last breath. Our hearts are in solidarity with those in a far-off continent despite our own catastrophes. It burns our hearts and it will not be repeated.[38]

The death of George Floyd presented an optimal moment to illuminate the unexpected yet significant dimensions of relationality of breath with the Syrian liberatory struggle. By coding their liberation struggle into the political discourses of others, they offer an interpretive assessment of the relationality of the two movements. Through this juxtaposition, Syrian radical subjects seek meaning in the African American struggle and construe its relevance within the tapestry of theirs. Though the political heritage and trajectories of the Syrian Revolution and Black Lives Matter could not be further apart, the disinterested spectator is asked to recognize a diffuse and heterogenous set of subjects based on a shared experience of suffocation. In the absence of obvious racial, ethnic, or geographic kinship, the emotional registers of death are channeled to indicate the ways in which Raed Fares's and George Floyd's killings are bound by a common ontology of dispossession and structural violence. The narrative estrangement of the two assassinations is evident in the sentient admission of frontiers and distance from those in a "far off continent." Nevertheless, there is the imperative of transcending this space, "despite our own catastrophes." In this narrative, analogous experiences of suffocation, their pervasiveness and persistence, are intertwined with the recognition that breathing is a fundamental human right inherent to our existence.[39]

The existential experiences of suffocation are stretched to name a manifold experience uniting these subjects at a site of peripherality. In this effort of transnational solidarity, the specificity of one's struggle is jettisoned amid the potential for political mobilization. Radical subjects weave their experiences together without resorting to the flattening tendencies of a universalizing liberal humanism—"we are all humankind"—or a singular narrative of shared humanity.

---

38. Occupied Kafranbel Banners, "We stand in solidarity. . . ."

39. The theme of suffocation has inspired several public awareness campaigns in Syria, such as the Do Not Suffocate the Truth campaign on the anniversary of the Ghouta chemical attacks, which stresses the simultaneous denial of breath and memory of those who suffered these attacks.

While this mobilization centered on the tragic killing of George Floyd, there is indisputably a diachronic dimension in which the historical moorings of racism and slavery beyond Floyd's killing are signaled. The signifier "black" situates Floyd's death within its historical, racial, and cultural contexts, prompting the audience to reconsider the faraway Syrian radical subject within the larger narrative of racial subjugation. This framework fosters a connection between Syrians and African Americans through a shared affect of solidarity, even as it grapples with the inherent tension in drawing comparisons. Yassin al-Haj Saleh articulates this tension forthrightly and does not mince his words: "Ours is a struggle against racism, though without races."[40] This seemingly oxymoronic statement reveals the divergent categorizations of race in the US and Syria, as well as varying orientations toward race itself. In the same article, al-Haj Saleh makes this analogy explicit: the sovereign state is "busying itself killing Syrian blacks."

Though Black Lives Matter does not lend itself to a facile translation to the Syrian context, the rhetoric ventures beyond a shared humanitarian concern with the suffering of others toward an implication of oneself within the narrative of others. A critical affect is manifested *in and through,* rather than over and against, constructions of race and racism. "Syrian blacks" implicates Syrians within the hierarchical racialization of the planet and its people, in particular the construction of "race" within the dialectic of white supremacy and its colonized "other." The divergent "phenomena" of Floyd's murder by a white police officer in Minneapolis and Fares's murder by extremists are foregrounded to establish racialized significance for a public that might make meaning of the events in relation to each other. The importance of the question of Blackness also pays heed to Achille Mbembe's argument about a veritable "becoming black of the world" over and beyond the Atlantic slave trade,[41] and the extent to which we are all embedded in global systems of racial stratification. Race here is enunciated as a fluid construct attached to biopolitical apparatus rather than shaped by ethnic clashes between civilizations or colonial difference. This framing of race provides a lens through which to understand the dynamics of power and oppression within Syria, where tyranny is exercised not only against racialized minorities but also against the majority population. Syria is marked by tyranny toward "the majority"—by and large, Sunni Muslims, who form the majority of the population and are not known for their "otherness," are oppressed by a regime from the Alawite minority sect. Added to this, ethnic racism exists against Kurdish Syrians, who have

---

40. Naprushkina, "Surviving Monstrosities."
41. Mbembe, *Critique of Black Reason,* 6.

been historically exiled from the public space and systematically discrimi-
nated against by the regime and by other Syrians.[42] Racism emerges as a critical and adaptable factor within the Syrian struggle for emancipation, albeit in
less overt ways than might be deciphered at first glance.[43]

In harnessing the affective energies of certain social movements, namely
those with an identifiable racial element and relative situational privilege,
radical subjects are able to destabilize spatial economies of affect. Relating
struggles in this way is a precarious endeavor but has the political potential
to extend conceptual contiguity in a manner conducive to solidarity building.
To illustrate this, I draw on Weheliye, who considers how the colonial outpost,
the slave plantation, and the concentration camp are "neither exceptional nor
comparable, but simply relational."[44] Weheliye argues that to the public, racial
slavery does not "seem as great an abnormality both in its historical context
and in the way it is retroactively narrativized" as the Holocaust. In essence,
various modes of extreme brutality and directed killings are weighted differently among audiences, producing uneven affective and political responses
and conjuring divergent forms of bare life.[45] Lamenting the fact that slavery is
not included in "conceptualizations of this category" in scholarly discourse or
by the United Nations,[46] he is wary of the Third Reich as being the "paradig-
matic example" of the full reach of biopower, preferring the conceptual contiguity between Nazi racism and other forms of biopolitics, such as colonialism,
Indigenous genocide, and racial slavery.[47] In a similar vein, the anticolonial
Martinican poet and politician Aimé Césaire observes that class struggle often

---

42. As a minority, the Kurds were "the primary scapegoats of rising Arab nationalism in
Syria." Daher, *Syria After the Uprisings*, 149. Aside from the 120,000 Syrian Kurds stripped of
citizenship in 1962, even Kurds with Syrian citizenship face institutional racism. They could
not publish in their language, have cultural festivals, or teach in their language. Ethnic tension
between Arabs and Kurds eventually resulted in a splitting from Syrian (Arab) revolutionary
groups and an increased marginalization from the wider uprising.

43. Admittedly, there is room for reflexivity on the color-blind minimization of racism
that might occur in the attempt to explore the personal and communal commonalities needed
to produce effective coalitions.

44. Weheliye, *Habeas Viscus*, 37.

45. "Bare life" refers to basic biological existence, devoid of rights, agency, or recognition
within society. The term was popularized by the Italian philosopher Giorgio Agamben in his
book *Homo Sacer: Sovereign Power and Bare Life*. Agamben draws on ancient Roman law to
describe "bare life" as that which can be killed but not sacrificed, excluded from political life
and the protections of the law and yet still subject to sovereign power. Agamben's concept of
"bare life" has been influential in critical theory and political philosophy, particularly in discussions of sovereignty, biopolitics, and the state of exception.

46. Agamben, *Homo Sacer*, 38.

47. Weheliye, *Habeas Viscus*, 59.

robs the colonial question of its singularity and renders it subordinate within broader Marxist or Eurocentric frameworks.[48]

In this context, the radical subject is less interested in the specific manifestations of biopower and more in the relational dynamics and "weights" of various struggles that transcend a simplistic victim-perpetrator dyad. They leverage the legitimacy of other movements with a priori centrality on the world stage to elucidate aspects of their political predicament that might otherwise be unaccounted for. The collective outrage at the death of George Floyd serves as an entry point into an explicitly political dialogue from which they have often been excluded. Black Lives Matter has served as a powerful mise-en-scène for reflections on solidarity, coalition building, and legal, moral, and political responsibility for injustice within contemporary politics. As the "social justice yellow brick road" of social movements,[49] this offers Black Lives Matter a moral clarity that orients the audience toward other radical liberatory struggles. In situating their struggle alongside that of others, radical subjects remedy injustices of erasure of revolutionary teleology through enriching the registers through which racial injustice might be advanced.

Conclusion

Raed Fares, the mastermind of the Kafranbel banners, once said of their solidarity-making sentiments, "We wanted to be special."[50] Perhaps paradoxically, being "special" was achieved not through the denial of others, or in a rhetoric of incommensurability, but through the self-conscious implication of oneself alongside others. Solidarity does not reside solely in what is common between here/there, nor does it erase the distinctive, sovereign nature of each struggle. Global solidarity is an unsettling process that must navigate the tensions that arise when those abandoned at the periphery address one another in a collective sense of struggle.

Yet, even when struggles cannot fully coalesce, an affective approach invites us to seek connections and differences productive in the pursuit of solidarity. From this emerges a project of worldmaking—born of the decolonial and antiracist sensibilities of radical subjects in revolutionary practice—without regard for borders, straight lines, or ordered movement. In the multifaceted, multilocal, and affective manifestations of solidarity, we create a space in which struggles come together, even if only ephemerally. This spatial economy

48. Bardawil, "Critical Theory."
49. Binning, "How Black Lives Matter," iv.
50. Griswold, "Free Radio Syria."

of affect maximizes possibilities of connection between those who inhabit the world from places of difference, be it racialized, gendered, or nationalized.

Budour Hassan, in the epigraph of this chapter, captures the spirit of this intersubjective affect when she reminds us, "I am Palestinian until decolonisation; Syrian until the triumph of the revolution; Saharawi until liberation; Kashmiri until independence," and on and on the list may go. At its heart, this is what Judith Butler calls "precariousness," the condition of living socially, reciprocally, and vulnerably with others. Through exceeding the solitary focus on the perpetrator, and the spectacle of bare life, radical subjects craft a supple affective politics that allows them to matter alongside others. This is especially effective when some forms of radical politics are privileged over others. The elastic peripheral is not just a turn in the grammar of political claims-making from the default lexicon of "the Global South" but a purposeful affective alignment (with those who match one's liberatory ethos of dismantling systems of oppression) that expands the spatialities from which solidarity might occur. It does not emphasize a theory of homogenized oppression or equivalence so much as make struggles relational, taking us out of ratified pathways into unexpected forms of engagement and responsibility with those seeking decolonization.

In the next chapter, I examine the radical subject's hope as an affective practice that makes and remakes itself into the warp and weft of radical politics. As we navigate this terrain, we come to ascertain the potential of hope to forge a relationality that leads us to desire, and invest in, a collective inhabitation with others amid the tractive force of revolution over the *longue durée*.

CHAPTER 5

On Hope

Bloom-Spaces and the Circulation of Solidarity

Has it ever occurred to an artist
To sketch a blue, tear-filled sky
Wearing a veil of barbed wire
Anyone destined to stand in a courtyard of Tadmur Prison
And steal a fleeting glance up above
Will see this oppressive portrait
And realize then, what genius nurtures our reality and our dreams!

—Faraj Bayraqdar, *Khiyanat al Lugha Wa l Samt*
[The Betrayals of Language and Silence]

In the documentary *Our Memory Belongs to Us,* three activists—Yadan, Odai, and Rani—now refugees in the "City of Lights" in France, stand on an empty stage watching footage from years past.[1] They stand awkwardly, worlds apart from the footage captured in another time, a time in which they had basked in togetherness and belonging, to the land and to a common cause. The footage captures *sahra thawriyeh,* a late-night congregation of revolutionaries in Daraa broadcast live on *Al Jazeera.*

In the scene, the activists, masked for anonymity with black, white, and green balaclavas of the revolution, sit shoulder to shoulder on the floor of an undisclosed location. Behind them, wall-sized flags of the Syrian Revolution dominate the space. Arabic coffee is served in a coffee pot on a small table in the center, draped with the revolution's flag. Their hands are raised resolutely in the V-shaped sign of victory (see figure 10).

A man's voice bellows an earnest call for revolution, "a revolution for all Syrians, not just for one sect. Syria is not a place for states to work out their sectarian differences." After locating themselves in the footage, the men reminisce sentimentally about that night, but their conversation takes a heated turn when an argument ensues between them:

---

1. Farah, *Our Memory.*

FIGURE 10. Revolutionary late-night gathering. From *Our Memory Belongs to Us.*

DIRECTOR: How do you think this footage was perceived by those watching *Al Jazeera*? How did people see it?

YADAN: *Bashe'a*! Ugly, ugly. An ugly picture.

ODAI: It was not ugly at all! Not at all! It was not ugly at all.

RANI: No, no!

YADAN: Well, we understand something, and the people understand something else.

ODAI: First, the flag behind us was the flag of the revolution. That's the first thing! I am identifying my identity through my flag!

YADAN: But only you know what that means!

ODAI: No, people know it too! The flag of the terrorists was different than our flag.

YADAN: Who are the people who know what our flag means?

ODAI: You are saying because we had our faces hidden, it was an ugly sight? No, it is a beautiful sight! I was afraid for my family, you were scared for your family . . . we were all scared for our families. This video is from the end of 2011, there was not even a terrorist or extremist group in Syria at that time! It was a revolution, and everyone knew it was a revolution!

RANI: [nodding in agreement] 100 percent, 100 percent.

YADAN: An American citizen doesn't know these details! They don't even know where Syria is on a map, people! You have to tell them Syria is next to Israel for them to even know us!

The conversation intimates how grand narratives that discredit one's truths are internalized, whilst those in liberatory struggle rummage to manage and organize their narratives so others might stand in solidarity with their struggle. It also underscores the central question driving this book: *How might one resolve the dissonance between revolution as lived and experienced by radical subjects and how it is received by the outside world? How might the betweenness which comes so easily between those in revolutionary struggle circulate beyond their worlds?* As explored throughout, affect plays a cardinal role in the contagious process of creating this betweenness and alleviating some of the realities that oppress and invisibilize struggles.

One premise that has not been explicitly stated but which underlies this argument is belief as a communal practice of radicality. Belief is the leap required to transcend forces that pull in directions contrary to the pursuit of solidarity, to actualize the capacity to be affected. In this chapter, I explore how we might realize the potentialities of the radical subject's hopeful opening. By refining this aspect in the terminus of this book, I argue that *belief* is the response necessitated by the radical subject's organization of and capacity for hope, one that makes us permeable to their affect. Through marking hope at the heart of the radical subject's affect, we access a feeling of possibility of what could or might be, one that matches their motifs of hope and resistance in confronting injustice. To put it differently, when we *believe* the radical subject, we become open to their affective intensities and articulations of hope.

After this, I track the circulation and distribution of the affect of the radical subject—the ways in which they move and move others. To this end, I develop an explicit vocabulary of hopeful affect to concretize some of the discursive operations and affective attachments of radical subjects as part of the process of arriving at solidarity. Here I am concerned with the interaffectivity that occurs between radical subjects and others. In particular, I think of "hope talk" as an affectively imbued process that produces collectivities both within and beyond the parameters of liberatory struggle. Although hope may be easily identified in radical subjects, this chapter expands on the taking-place of hope as well as its mode of operation in plaiting together the larger-scale collective flows of hope and desire to bring solidarity into being.

Belief and Hopeful Affect

In this section, I bring to the fore *belief* as an emotional and intellectual disposition toward those in liberatory struggle and their affective registers of hope.

Without belief, there is no hope for solidarity. Solidarity is an inherently hopeful act. Here, I theorize belief from the Islamic philosophy of *iman*, though
belief for our purposes is more of an ethical statement than a necessarily theological one. In the Greek tradition of rhetorical thought, belief is construed
as doxa, that is, common opinion or point of view. *Iman*, on the other hand,
though translated literally into "belief," signifies an ethereal belief in which
one manifests submission and humility, which links to the heart. Though *iman*
alludes to a mental state of conviction and acceptance of something unseen,
it is based on proof, reason, or knowledge, which is to say, it acquires an epistemological ethos. According to Imam al-Ghazali, one of the most prominent
Islamic philosophers of the eleventh century, the intellect or knowledge of
"real things" is knowledge whose "site is the heart."[2]

Belief and the intellect are never fully separable—belief is not the enemy
of reason. In other words, belief is rooted in an intellect able to build upon
systems of knowledge, such that belief is adduced as a result of judgment
and the deliberate study of several possibilities. This is a cognitive effort that
stands in contrast to traditional ways of knowing within a Western, Cartesian
perspective, which keeps "the heart a long way from the brain."[3] Here, belief
is in the vein of *sentipensar*, a term used by Latin America activists to suggest
the union of reason (*pensar*) and feeling (*sentir*).[4]

By connecting belief to episteme of the radical subject, an alternative to
the atheistic "refusal to believe," one reaches down into that buried place
inside oneself to access the loathing of alterity that lives there. The refusal to
believe constitutes a hegemonic act unwilling to bridge the abyss between ourselves and the radical subject. This refusal is premised on the implicit assumption of the superiority of one's own worldview and access to hidden affairs in
the world. The radical subject's subjectivity is relegated to doxa, obscure and
unverifiable. As Syrian writer and journalist Samar Yazbek words it, a disbe-
lieving mindset tells us it is impossible for such subjects to "organize something so perfect, so beautiful, so brilliantly orchestrated."[5] In some ways, the
radical subject is an abstraction, an ideal that cannot be realized in any actual
person, *except that sometimes it is.*

By introducing belief into schemas of meaning-making, we supplant skepticism with a willingness to believe those so often met with social, civil, and
biological death and radical exclusion from structures of knowledge. When
skepticism becomes an end in and of itself, there is no substantive telos at the

---

2. Al-Ghazali, *Mukhtasar Iḥyā ' 'Ulūm al-Dīn*, 241.
3. Head and Harada, "Keeping the Heart."
4. Escobar, *Pluriversal Politics.*
5. Yazbek, *Woman in the Crossfire*, x.

end of its practice. We are kept within the control of a rationality that will not release us from automated judgments toward the other. Belief as a practice of solidarity yields one to the affective force of the radical subject, and at its epitome, makes one oblivious of their own self.[6] Though he does not use the word *belief*, Brian Massumi, the political theorist and philosopher, describes how affect, if approached strategically, can pass one into a threshold into the unknown: "Thinking through affect is not just reflecting on it. It is thought taking the plunge, consenting to ride the waves of affect on a crest of words, drenched to the conceptual bone in the fineness of its spray. Affect is only understood as enacted."[7] Believing the radical subject is not a passive experience but a process of immersion—a leap of faith that surrenders one to affect's flow, beyond the familiar into the realm of possibility.

Belief therefore articulates a new set of demands of critical theory, positioning radical subjects as originators of a powerful hopeful affect to which one might be sensitive. Belief grants determinacy to the radical subject, while also affirming their deeply relational radical politics. Relational because their affect exists for continuation—it is trans-situational as a connecting thread of experience.

Importantly, belief is not the suspension of criticism, or anti-intellectualism, but rather a redirection of our wakeful alertness to open up our relational capacities. It is evaluative and cognizant of the existential actualities of human life that should be taken account of by criticism. Considering actualities is challenging precisely because of commanding temptations, which exert pressure and shape the contemporary situation in ways that become the norm. From this perspective, belief does not call for the end of critical thinking or for the dictum "solidarity before criticism," but rectifies practices of critical thinking that validate the status quo. It is not antithetical to our critical capabilities; indeed, by being alive to our critical consciousness, we realize the delusion of all-knowingness. We become epistemologically and ontologically humble. We become privy, in unexpected ways, to another's "inner vision."[8] When doubt gets in the way of hope, it is the best possible antidote to the metaphysics of separation from those in liberatory struggle.

Belief goes hand in glove with the radical subject's motifs of hope and corporeal acts of resistance in confronting injustice. The radical subject is a "hoping subject"[9] whose future-orientation and sacrificial investment is meaningful

---

6. In Sufism, *iman* causes the heart to be consumed with truth, such that it "ansani thekra nafsi" (made me oblivious of myself). See al-Ghazali, *Mukhtasar Iḥyāʾ ʿUlūm al-Dīn.*

7. Massumi, *Politics of Affect*, vii.

8. Al-Ghazali, *Mukhtasar Iḥyāʾ ʿUlūm al-Dīn*, 396.

9. Hage, *Against Paranoid Nationalism.*

to their affect. Jasbir Puar words this best when she says, "Affect is precisely the body's hopeful opening, a speculative opening not wedded to the dialectic of hope and hopelessness, but rather a porous identification of what could or might be."[10] To believe is to become permeable—to offer ourselves to the "availability, the circulation, and the exchange of hope"[11] toward those acting for another world possible in the now. Thus, belief not only requires an orientation toward the radical subject (as explained in chapter 1) but a pausing of skepticism, which attunes us to their affective energies and allows us to be affected. And so, beyond just an orientation toward the radical subject and an intentional "angle of arrival," belief meets the radical subject's felt intensities so an affective "bloom-space" might materialize. The angle of arrival, when coupled with belief, fosters an intersubjective reciprocity with those in struggle.

I pause here on the story of Bassel Shehadeh, a Syrian Christian filmmaker and activist.[12] Born in 1984, Bassel was around twenty-seven years old when the revolution started, but his curly long hair, freckles, and cheeky smile made him seem much younger. Bassel's story exemplifies how the radical subject's affective registers of hope weave a hermeneutically rich rhetoric of emancipatory action that also have the power to generate affective allegiances. Reading Bassel's story takes us to the heart of the relation between hope, its percolation as hope talk, and its capacity to move beyond the radical subject and affect others. Bassel, committed to nonviolent activism and civil disobedience, had been previously arrested and detained in July 2011 in a demonstration of artists and intellectuals in the Meydan neighborhood of Damascus. A month after his release, he decided to travel to the United States to start school in the fall semester of 2011 as a Fulbright scholar pursuing a master's degree in filmmaking at the Syracuse University in New York. The movie he used for his application was called *Saturday Morning Gift*—based on his interactions with a Lebanese child on his memories of the 2006 Israeli-Lebanese war.[13] He completed the semester, but during winter break left his studies in New York to return to Syria to join the revolution.

Once back in Syria, he dedicated himself to documenting the uprising, capturing various civil initiatives and the regime's siege of Homs, the Capital of the Revolution. He organized filmmaking workshops, training activist-photographers and -videographers on how to use the camera to capture the

10. Puar, *Right to Maim*, 19.
11. Hage, *Against Paranoid Nationalism*, 9.
12. Bassel Shehadeh would often call himself a "Christian Muslim." Syrian Voices UK, "Syrian Hero."
13. Wind, "Inside and Outside."

shelling of civilians and in the art of montage editing to craft compelling visual narratives. On his resolve to return, he questioned the possible:

> Imagine, how many times will we have a revolution in our lives? How can I leave a dream that is coming true? And what will I tell my children when they ask me about my work in it? Will I answer them "When the revolution started, I left my country and went to take care of my future." How could there be a future without a free homeland?[14]

His visionary determinism, in characteristic radical subject fashion, at times bordered on nihilism and irrational recklessness. Hope is not a soft, elusive concept or a passivity-inducing wish but extends corporeally to how radical subjects behave, feel, and think toward the likelihood of another world possible in the now. It was not Bassel's first time gambling with his life. In 2010, he drove his grandfather's old Russian motorcycle, which he called Lenin, all the way from Damascus to New Delhi, inspired by Che Guevara's *Motorcycle Diaries*.[15] He pioneered the Currency of Freedom project, where activists printed counterfeit 1,500 SYP bills and distributed them in the streets, one side of which were perfect fakes, but on the other side were leaflets calling Syrians to convene and protest in the streets of Aleppo and Damascus.[16] He reported to the international press, at one point appearing anonymously on *Democracy Now!* under only his first name. With the sounds of guns and the whizzing of bullets in the background, one can make out the tense and tenuous nature of hope that tethers between corporeal vulnerability and the compulsion to bear witness:

> BASSEL SHEHADEH: I just got back from Homs yesterday, after spending one week there. The heavy bombing and shelling of the city continued for several days, 'til the night of the Arab League delegation's arrival. I witnessed tanks withdraw from Homs the morning before the observers arrived. . . . Now, I am calling you from Al-Midan area in Damascus. Activists have called for a protest in this area, and they expected the monitor—the delegations, the monitors, to come and see the protest. But no one arrived here. And the security forces are cracking down [on] the protestors. I can hear them running in the streets now. . . . I can hear . . . the security forces outside of the room I am in now. So I'm, like, keeping

---

14. 100 Faces of the Syrian Revolution, "Ghiath Matar"; and McEvers, "Slain Syrian."
15. Kanaan, "Bassel Shehade"; and Shehadeh, "Bassel and Lenin."
16. Donauskyte et al., "Syria Through a Lens"; and MBC, "Surprise of the Currency."

my voice a little bit low. They are outside . . . so I need to keep my voice a little bit low. Sorry for that.

AMY GOODMAN: We can hear you just fine Bassel, but we want you to be very careful. You can tell us you can't talk. That is fine. . . . I do want to ask you about who is killing who . . .

BASSEL SHEHADEH: I witnessed—and actually, I was shot by snipers when I was trying to cross to these areas. People are forced to fight back to block out the security forces and make their way out to provide food and supplies. . . . They are putting the people in the position like they have to defend themselves. This is what I saw in Homs. . . . The snipers are for the army, actually.[17]

As explicated earlier in this book, the radical subject's testimony is critical when independent media and nongovernmental observers do not arrive. In such times, the radical subject organizes hope into movement. As oppressors work to circumvent witnessing, the testimony of radical subjects forges an agency born of hope as a category of struggle as the future unfolds in the now. His hope endured amid disheartening setbacks and palpable danger to his life. Gambling with his life, he was blinded by a future goodness that obliviated the present and impelled himself and others to revolutionary action. One of the activists he trained recalls, "One day the shelling was so heavy, I told Basel: It is too dangerous, better not to go out today. His answer was: This training is more important than anything else."[18]

On the 28th of May 2012, at twenty-eight years old, Bassel was killed in his car under shelling in the Bab Sibaa neighborhood in Homs. That day, even as rebels took refuge inside people's homes, he decided to conduct interviews on-site, determined to counter the complete media blackout that took place in the area in the aftermath of the Houla massacre. At his funeral, his peppered body, covered in a white shroud, was carried along with those of the four comrades who died with him. Small flashlights luminated Shehadeh's face in the dark of the night while mourners sang, "Oh heaven, open your gates, your students have come to visit you. . . . The revolution and the revolutionaries will be alive!" During his memorial service, the regime cut off access to the church where friends and family gathered, and later sieged his family's home. Father

17. *Democracy Now!*, "Syrian Activist Speaks Out."

18. Anonymous, "Basel Shehadeh." Several of those trained by Bassel Shehadeh became well-known camerapeople, such as Ahmad al-Assam (known as Ahmed Abu Ibrahim), who filmed key news reports on Syria. For more on Bassel Shehadeh, see Anonymous, "Basel Shehadeh"; MsSamero10, "Celebration of a New Constellation"; Syrian2011x, "Standing Homs"; and Syria Campaign, "Bassel Shehadeh."

Paolo Dall'Oglio, a Jesuit Italian priest who ran the desert monastery at Deir Mar Mousa (the Monastery of Saint Moses) for over three decades, presided over the funeral. When the regime prevented the memorial service from taking place inside the church, the mourners boldly collected outside, standing on the church walls and bidding Bassel adieu with songs of the revolution. As news of the dancing and liturgical music became heard, those who had not been able to join earlier pulled themselves out of bed and fled to the church into the early hours of the night.

Hope Talk

Bringing Bassel's story full circle, Syrians who had never protested were stirred to join the revolution after witnessing Shehadeh's funeral—they were incarnated into radical subjects. His death made waves across the country. The short film *I Will Cross Tomorrow*, although credited to Shehadeh himself, was in fact pieced together by others with footage Shehadeh had taken of himself crossing the street breathlessly as he ducked snipers standing on the rooftops. Bassel had filmed the footage to illustrate what life was like for everyday civilians in Homs.[19] Another film of his, *Streets of Freedom*,[20] which he dreamed would be his best work, was never completed. In what the Abounaddara Collective term "emergency cinema," activists patched the footage into a twenty-four-minute version of the film.[21] In the wake of Bassel's death, Father Paolo Dall'Oglio, the Italian priest who delivered Bassel's funeral oration, became more vocal in speaking out about regime violence. Aside from meeting and praying with Free Syrian Army commanders,[22] he released an open letter demanding a transition to democracy in Syria and condemning the killing and imprisonment of dissidents. After he was driven out of Syria by the regime, he felt bitter to be exiled from the land he now considered his own, telling the world, "I consider myself homeless until I go back."[23] He

---

19. Shehadeh, *I Will Cross Tomorrow*.

20. Elsewhere, the film is referred to as *Singing to Freedom*. See Wind, "Inside and Outside," 58.

21. Shehadeh, *Streets of Freedom*.

22. Father Paolo Dall'Oglio was exiled by the regime in 2012, after which he left to live in Italy. But it was not long before he returned to Syria to participate in prorevolutionary activities. In July 2013, it is believed, he was killed by Daesh militants after he traveled to Raqqa to carry out good-faith negotiations to urge them to release prisoners. See Yassin-Kassab and al-Shami, *Burning Country*.

23. Friedman, "Out of Syria."

would return illegally across the border to rebel-held Syria to continue Bassel's legacy of a free Syria.

Digging into the past to retrieve Bassel's story, I could not help but come undone at the flourishing of hope into the perilous praxis of revolution. Bassel's affective intensity, even after death, was capable of overthrowing an entire order of discourse resistant to radicality. His radical affect made for a permeable way of mobilizing others—a conduit to push against systems that seem immovable. His affect was contagious—both informing and emboldening others on how to be in solidarity. The ability of the radical subject to transcend the current reality to understand what it is and to move others within seemingly all-encompassing systems of power bounds us likewise to transcend our realities, in the hope that we might believe too.

From the above, one recognizes the symbiotic nature of radical subjectivity and, more specifically, the circulation and exchange of hope among radical subjects past death, across borders, and across populations. Through thinking about hope relationally, one can decipher rituals of "hope talk," which are affectively productive to the radical subject's shifting between temporalities and geographies, between bodies and borders. As an intersubjective affect, hope talk engenders the production and exchange of hope, even when the path toward revolutionary success appears to be an uphill battle. The radical subject's ontological politics therefore draws on radical relationality with others, in contrast to modernist politics, which presume an ontology of separation.

How the revolutionary past is resourced for hope is pertinent not only to the lifetime of liberatory struggle but for insight into the forces which anchor devotion when hope is lost. It allows us to comprehend some of the ways in which radical subjects create conditions of possibility for reconstituting hope. Within the ecology of social movements, it is part of the complex interplay of processes and purposes that interpellate others, lend longevity to revolution, and draw it into futurity.

Hope talk allows for the continued belief in hope. Through hope talk, radical subjects transcend realities and defy the confinement of disappearance, debilitation, and death. It orients radical subjects, even operates in their formation, whilst making loss bearable. Take for instance the affective performativity of individual protestors dancing *dabkeh* in unison—a folkloric circle dance entitled "dancing of the feet"—amid the raining of bombs in the public sphere: their bodies are one human mass or body politic. The singular, simultaneous, yet collective entity is obdurate—asserting itself while disaffirming the modus operandi of death. As protestors dance with interlaced arms and lyrical chants, with each rhythmic stomp on the ground, they reclaim spaces, taking on a resistive quality of vociferous reclamation of the land. Protestors reckon with death as a form of thanatopolitics: "They protest. They are killed. They mourn the dead while they are protesting. They are killed. They protest. And the camera keeps rolling, so they may say the revolution goes on."[24] With revolutionary rupture, hope is insurrected in productive opposition to biopolitics and its reductive ontologies of political death, so revolution might "go on." In their dreams, as Subcomandante Marcos puts it, they "have seen another world, an honest world, a world decidedly more fair than the one in which we are now live."[25] Hope talk leaps from body to body, moving beyond the death of the radical subject and contending with the politics of death to reach what Achille Mbembe cites as the highest ethical horizon of "giving death to death."[26]

Ghiath Matar, a tailor from the Damascus suburb of Daraya, known for gifting regime forces red roses and water amid their violence against his townsfolk, underscores this form of hope as a radical sacrificial act. Before he was killed in detention and his mutilated corpse returned to his pregnant wife, he wrote a final message in his will: "Remember me when you celebrate the fall of the regime. And remember that I gave my soul and blood for that moment."[27] In honoring his memory, the living carry forward his dreams. Reading radical subjectivities for hope suggests there is no impeccable separation of ontologies between radical subjects. Their affectivity permeates and enters into others as a series of overlapping affective fields. Their affect is sticky—sustaining and preserving connections, especially when we are in intimate contact, but even when we are not. As an intersubjective practice, hope talk speaks to the way struggle comports people one to another—and how in-betweenness and interrelationality transpires when hope is in a condition of existential suspension. Wafa Mustafa observes the symbiotic nature of radical subjectivity and the creation of hope from the ashes of others. For her, hope is a discipline she must practice each day:[28]

> Sometimes I feel there is no hope. . . . But then, I believe, the largest hopes can never be defeated, but they can be reshaped. The motive for me to go on is not hope. I don't find that hope exists now. I wake up in the morning, and I create hope with my hands and teeth, but it is not there. What I have is an incalculable amount of sorrow, pain, and anger. But so that they don't

24. Farah, "Our Memory."
25. Marcos, *Our Word Is Our Weapon*, 18.
26. Mbembe, *On the Postcolony*.
27. 100 Faces of the Syrian Revolution, "Ghiath Matar."
28. For more on hope as a discipline, read Mariane Kaba's *We Do This 'til We Free Us: Abolitionist Organizing and Transforming Justice.*

dominate me, I create hope each day when it is not there . . . and it is "*selseleh bashariyyeh*," a human chain that gives hope to others and then comes back to me. . . . It saves me from the belief in no hope.[29]

Hope talk as an affective form can be germinal and unacknowledged, in the tradition of what the French sociologist Pierre Bourdieu would call *collusio*, an agreement that is not contractual or overt as much as based on mutual understanding between those who share habitus.[30] As a political strategy of everyday survival and adaptability, it is at once subversive and seditious, making visible new strains of political activity forged in the crucible of death, debilitation, and adversity.

One senses this kind of hope talk in the Abounaddara Collective,[31] the anonymous group of self-taught filmmakers who produced some of the most mesmerizing portraits of the revolution. The movies were often close-ups, brief and offered jarringly without any narration or frames of reference. The collective calls for "the right to a dignified image," refusing to publish graphic images of tortured Syrian bodies, with the intention of averting the Western desire to witness victimhood and the suffering of others. Inspired by a lyric in "Song of the Partisans" from World War II, "Friend, if you fall from the shadows on the wall, another steps into your place," they take the uncompleted work of radical subjects after forced disappearance, debility, or death and furtively present it as if it had been completed by the radical subjects themselves. Along with over three hundred short videos published each Friday, they made the film *I Will Cross Tomorrow* after Bassel Shehadeh's death and introduced it as his to prove to the regime that Bassel lives on in his work. They dedicated the film to the sniper who murdered Bassel, renaming it "Brother Sniper." When releasing the movie to the public, they directly addressed the sniper in the imagined tongue of Bassel, writing: "I will cross tomorrow. You can kill me, but your children will see my images. With love, Bassel Shehadeh."[32]

This kind of hope talk is also exemplified in other acts that subvert the regime's brutal attempts to silence dissent. After the regime broke the fingers of the political cartoonist Ali Ferzat, the Abounaddara Collective drew a portrait of Ali Ferzat in his hospital bed. His left eye is seriously injured, and his hands are bandaged except for an intransigent middle finger (see figure 11).[33] The signature of Ali Ferzat in the portrait was faked to make it appear

29. Mustafa, "Activist Wafa Mustafa" (emphasis added).
30. Bourdieu, *Pascalian Meditations*.
31. *Abounaddara* translates into "the man with the glasses," or, the person who can, with lenses, see clearly. For more about the collective, see Ryzik, "Syrian Film Collective."
32. Bayoumi, "Civil War in Syria."
33. Kenner, "Assad's Cartoonish Crackdown."

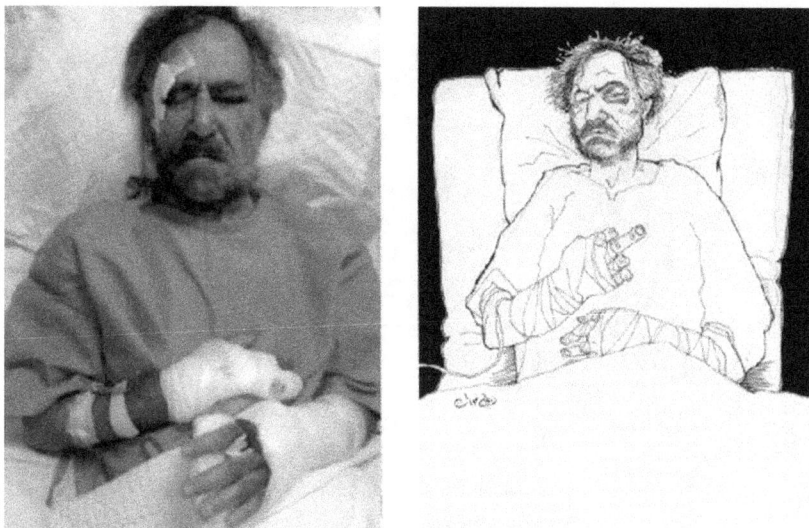

FIGURE 11. A photograph of Ali Ferzat and a portrait of Ali
Ferzat. Used with permission from Ali Ferzat.

that it was Ali Ferzat himself who had drawn it. A member of the collective expounds on the logic of attributing the drawing to Ali Ferzat, who was clearly unable to draw a caricature of himself at that time:

> People were shocked because just two days prior every Syrian had seen Ali Farzat totally broken and in the hospital. Suddenly, here's a self-portrait signed Ali Farzat? How could it be? This is resistance. . . . In this gesture is how our society is resisting. *There will always be someone else who will do the fighting.*[34]

In its own way, the collective addresses a Spinozist "yet-ness" of the radical subject's affectual doings and undoings,[35] that is, their ability to persist in affecting and being affected despite being rendered seemingly powerless.

In other instances, hope talk is a tangible discursive practice that drives affect in other ways, such as the *wasiyya* (will), *amaneh* (a valuable in

---

34. Bayoumi, "Civil War in Syria."

35. This is from Baruch Spinoza's oft-cited quotation "No one has yet determined what the body can do." Spinoza, *Ethics,* 87. A Spinozist "yet-ness" is an acknowledgment of the persistence of possibility, potential, and continuity within the unfolding nature of reality. It draws from Spinoza's philosophy, particularly his notions of immanence, conatus (the striving to persist in one's being), and the interconnectedness of all existence. It encapsulates a sense of endurance and transformative potential, even amid adversity or incompletion.

FIGURE 12. Ghalia al-Rahhal surrounded by the women
of Mazaya. From *Syria's Rebellious Women.*

safekeeping), *ahed* (oath or trust), or *iltizam dam* (blood contract).[36] This
hope talk is also anticipatory—predicting the need to rectify the conduct of
others in the future. Ghalia al-Rahhal and her son Khaled al-Issa engaged in
this form of hope talk with one another. Khaled was a young photojournalist from Kafranbel who documented the violations of the regime, traveling to
areas like the Shaar neighborhood in rebel-held eastern Aleppo, where coverage of the revolution was scant. The target of several assassination attempts,
he was killed at twenty-five years old by an explosive targeting him and his
best friend, the journalist Hadi al-Abdallah, in their home. A few years earlier,
his mother, Ghalia, had converted her hair salon into an underground shelter
so that woman could hide from persistent bombs. Before long, the basement
turned into a place where women would gather to talk about their lives after
the revolution, huddled together and sheltering in place from bombing by the
Assad regime and Russian forces. By June 2014, it became a women's organization called the Mazaya Center for Women's Empowerment, under the Union
of Revolutionary Bureaus (URB), an organization founded by the civil society
leader Raed Fares (see figure 12). Under Ghalia's leadership, Mazaya became a
place for the practice of anarchist feminist politics, including vocational training of women to learn reading, knitting, and journalism; paramedic and first
aid training; economics; photography; law; and political activism. Over the

---

36. In *Our Memory Belongs to Us,* the activists from Daraa memorialize *iltizam dam* (the
blood contract with the dead or disappeared).

years, Mazaya expanded to include seven centers, including medical clinics and childcare centers, and once they acquired a printer, a news center publishing a magazine on women's empowerment. Because of their revolutionary work and, in particular, their empowerment of women, Mazaya was the target of several arson attacks, and Ghalia herself narrowly escaped an assassination attempt by armed groups when her car was rigged by a bomb.[37]

After her son's death, in several interviews, Ghalia explained how her steadfastness was brought about by her son's *wasiyya*—his will before death. In an eerie premonition of his own fate, he recorded a video telling the camera: "All I can tell my mother is—remain steadfast. If you feel something shift within—if despair begins to creep in—resist it. Remain steadfast. At the same time, if something happens to me, don't be sad."[38] Elsewhere, Ghalia stoically refers to potency of the *ahed,* the pact that took place between herself and her son:

> He used to always tell me, if any of us dies, the other must continue. Our path won't stop. If I die, you continue and if you die, I will continue your path. Not many people will understand this agreement. It was an *ahed,* a pact with those who were martyred, with those incarcerated, with our friends who were exiled, and with those who forcibly disappeared, whose whereabouts no one knows and whom we have lost. This gave me motivation to continue my path, even if we are displaced from our lands and endure hardships. The oath we made to each other before he was martyred keeps me going.[39]

Khaled's prophecy exemplifies the mobilizing nature of his distinct orientation toward the scarcity of hope, instilling in his mother a resilience to transcend her grief after his death. He crafts an affective attachment that is patterned—and organized—by his refusal of the status quo and the distribution of hope across temporalities. As the civil society leader Raed Fares once put it, "Revolution is an idea, and an idea cannot be killed."[40]

---

37. In 2019 Mazaya's offices were bombed and destroyed during an attack on Kafranbel by the Assad regime and Russian forces. All residents were forced to flee. Ghalia relocated to the town of Selqeen in northern Idlib and started over from scratch. Rebuilding was incredibly challenging, as the team of over two hundred people was scattered across different areas, but they managed to reestablish the center with just seven team members.

38. Syria Plus, "Ghalia al-Rahhal."

39. Halab Today TV, "Stories from the Revolution."

40. Vidwans, "Ideas Cannot Be Killed."

Conclusion

I leave you with the peroration of the journalist Hadi al-Abdallah—Khaled al-Issa's closest friend and activist companion—on the affective alliances between radical subjects in liberatory struggle. His story highlights the boundary-dissolving affective hope of radical subjects—how they can be affectively present even when physically absent or displaced. When an interviewer prods Hadi on whether he regrets revolution, he conveys with candor the infuriating quandary he is confronted with—torn between oaths made to comrades and the need to stay safe for his family, in this case, his daughter, Bissan. He ponders a world in which staying alive for his daughter is a breach of trust. He contemplates the reignition of revolution each time from the ashes:

> Every action we took, we did because we had no other choice. We were forced into it. That is not to say that anyone threatened us, but we had to be true to ourselves, to not betray the blood of the martyrs killed with us in protest or the screams of those detained when we were protesting together. I am still living in Syria, and if there is one *sheber* [five fingers' width] outside of regime control, I will stay there and I will live in this *sheber* to be loyal to the people who I once made a promise to. I will put one foot there and stand with one foot, because both my feet would not fit in that *sheber*. I am not selling rhetoric. These are the realities and these are our truths.[41]

In the passing of radical subjects, we track their affective attachments and dust their words for teleological tracks, all that is left of them. The dead, the dying, and the disappeared unflinchingly rise up and speak. Structures of hope persist. Loss and suffering are made meaningful a posteriori. If nothing else, Hadi's words speak not only to the affective power of the radical subject but their ability to draw others to the cause. Like the portrait Bayraqdar sketches in *The Betrayals of Language and Silence,* where even a tear-filled sky imprisoned by barbed wire reflects the endurance of revolutionary dreams, the radical subject's hope serves as a critical resource for liberation. It sutures the *décalages*—the temporal and affective gaps—not only among radical subjects themselves but, more importantly, for those who receive and are moved by their affective transmissions in acts of solidarity.

Radical movements themselves often emerge from pivotal moments of solidarity. Before the Syrian Revolution ignited, there was a sense of anticipation among Syrians, with some half-joking in frustration, "Does anybody

---

41. Al-Abdallah, "For the Syrian Revolution."

smell something burning? I'm just saying," alluding to the Tunisian street vendor Mohamed Bouazizi's act of self-immolation, which sparked the Tunisian revolution.[42] The revolution would not take on its full force until the repression of Daraa by the regime. It is then that Syrians went out in a collective resolve not to abandon Daraa to its fate. The revolutionary anthem by Wasfi Massarani echoed this sentiment, "Darana Tunadi"—"Our Daraa Is Calling." And the dominos continued to *rise*. Even as the regime dedicated all its might to repressing one neighborhood, all the other neighborhoods rose in revolt. Syrians were inexorably drawn into radicality, compelled by an acute resolve not to leave Daraa alone in its struggle. Solidarity begets solidarity. Each act of solidarity sparks another, in an unyielding chain reaction. As Hadi poignantly described it, they were "stuck" in the overwhelming affective embrace of radicality. Though their organizing began as a simple expression of solidarity, it soon unfolded into a formidable force of its own.

Hadi's short soliloquy goes on to tell a story of how intersubjective experiences are brought into collective signification: "In the end, we raised our hands and said, 'We are simple revolutionaries facing the strongest armies in the world.'"[43] As "simple revolutionaries" take on "the world," they talk to the world. Though it may be natural to exchange solidarity among those who share the revolutionary milieu, the question is whether one might rise to the occasion and traverse a path to the hopes and truths of the radical subject when they knock at our door. Hope, as an affective practice, has the potential to create the kind of relationality that leads us to desire, and invest in, the liberatory struggle of others. The affective contagions of hope, which bring the "not yet" to the "next" to the "now," are not only deciphered and delineated in and between radical subjects, they can be nurtured within us. This is where belief becomes consequential for solidarity, as the slim interval through which we access the hope of radical subjects, produce it within ourselves, and relieve some, if not all, of the constraints upon solidarity.

---

42. Yazbek, *Woman in the Crossfire*, 235.
43. Al-Abdallah, "For the Syrian Revolution."

CONCLUSION

The sound of our songs were louder than their bombs.
—Waad al-Kateab, "For Sama"

The thrust of this book has been to think through possibilities for solidarity creation within the fragile political economy of emotion, intensified atmospherics of suspicion, and proliferation of fake news and sophisticated disorientation campaigns about those in resistance. In these pages, solidarity has been theorized as an affective phenomenon arising out of the radical subject and their affective force field. A solidarity that is cross-cultural, decolonizing, and transnational in nature and that transcends geographical and cultural boundaries.

With this in mind, this book puts forth a new subject for critical theory, one who might contest the conditions for "negative solidarity," defined as the absence or rejection of solidarity with those resisting oppression and advocating for liberatory visions of the world. To put it differently, solidarity is an emotional, ethical, and political capacity that blossoms through our attentive regard for specific individuals—the "radical subjects" at the heart of revolutionary journey. These subjects nourish what we do not know, wielding an affective force that transcends circumscribed spaces and extracts us out of our insular realities to contemplate the lives of others from afar. They are nonhierarchical, coming together through shared passions, revolutionary aspirations, and an agency that exceeds them. They are actants, and in our attending to them, we are rhizomatically able to cut through competing and contradictory framings of informational distortion fields. Each chapter proffers an aspect of the affective life and affectivity of the radical subject provocative for solidarity. The radical subject induces, compels, and otherwise affects us to become "partners in word and deed to change power."[1] In the preceding pages, we have considered the most productive dimensions of their affect—testimony, knowledge, postmemory, peripherality, and hope—as integral for the emergence, disclosure, and practice of solidarity, with those we are likely never to encounter in our lifetime.

•

It is clear from the outset that I side unequivocally with the Syrian Revolution, taking it as a litmus test of our ability to stand in solidarity with those struggling against imperialism, authoritarianism, and colonialism, under current paradigms. My scholarly interest in social movements only strengthened my persuasion that the Syrian Revolution is the most radical social movement of the last century, one that resulted in a complete collapse of the state and its attendant intelligence services, secret police, prisons, and military.

Before the regime fell, revolutionary fervor had waned among Syrians. In light of the depressing reality at the time, observers were claiming the revolution's outcomes were that of a nightmare. Pervasive fear, collective trauma, economic collapse, sectarian divisions, and persistent injustice all seemed insurmountable. The anniversary of the revolution came and went each year, as fewer and fewer of my friends and acquaintances chose to celebrate it. For them, revolution was a phenomenon to be exorcized rather than commemorated. In view of the impasse of international law and the normalization of the Assad regime by several Arab and European countries that were rebuilding diplomatic ties with the regime, cynicism and demoralization took over. The innumerable times our hopes had been raised and dashed allowed for bitter disillusionment and privately shared ambiguity about what brought us here.[2] Shortly before he was killed resisting the advance of the regime into the countryside of Hama in 2019, Abdul Baset al-Sarout was at the front lines carrying arms against the regime but was nostalgically recollecting the *rawnaq*

---

1. Al-Haj Saleh, "Letters to Samira."

2. In the urgency to make sense of the revolution's trajectory was a magnification of failures and a construction of hopelessness, which threatened to eradicate the revolutionary dream, at one point reaching a disenchantment mirroring the West's erasure of radical subjects, though at times these sentiments were only shared in less guarded conversations with comrades. Conversations gravitate toward *jald al zaat*, self-critique or whipping of oneself for mistakes made, in a tendency to direct blame as much at oneself as against the oppressor.

of the earlier days of the revolution, a word which most closely translates into "splendor, brilliance, and purity."[3]

And yet, on the 8th of December 2024, the revolution's arc came full circle, ending as it had begun, with the immense joy and intensity that defined its inception. The astonishing fall of the Assad regime following ten historic days of revolutionary battle on the ground marked the culmination of a long and arduous struggle. It was a victory forged by Syrians for Syrians, without the international solidarity they had so fervently sought. One might say that the final sobering lesson is this: while solidarity is desirable—achingly so—it is not always essential for liberatory outcomes. In the end, it was radical subjects, the men and women of the liberatory moment, who took freedom with their own hands. The cost of this freedom is unfathomable, but radical subjects have not lost hope in solidarity, continuing to make bids for support as they rebuild their country and confront the formidable challenges that lie ahead.

Having said this, this book has not meant to idolize the radical subject as above reproach, nor suggest they embody pure innocence or are immune to moral compromise. Neither does it assume that they are homogenous and aligned on all issues. Nor have I meant to circumvent internal critiques of revolution, all of which have their place and have been discussed at length elsewhere. The radical subject does not preclude an acknowledgment of paradoxes within struggle. Embracing the ideological idealism of radical subjects does not obscure the fact that are those who abuse revolution for personal gain. Not all who took part in the revolution always and already qualify as radical subjects. There are many unscrupulous actors who take advantage of revolution or who do not live up to its standards.[4]

Nevertheless, "accentuating the greyness must not lead straight toward a path of moral ambiguity; it must not lead to a blindness toward the victim."[5] The very moralizing nature of critique often prevents affective connection and contact with other moving dimensions of their experience. As Syrian filmmaker Mohammad Ali Atassi tactfully puts it, there might be an obligation to critique, but not to "put a knife in (the) back."[6] And so, I have wanted to think through the possibilities of what it might mean to acknowledge those who brave the storm, to speak with and alongside them. To bear witness to seismic

---

3. Al-Sarout, "Al-Sarout Talks."
4. This includes for example those who take up arms to conduct kidnappings or dishonest smuggling of goods under the banner of revolution. For instance, the official and political representation of the Syrian opposition (self-titled the *nukhab*, "elite shadow" or "exile government") are separate from the "internal" radical subject, with some of the former having been compromised by political interests and agendas of foreign donors.
5. Bouris, *Complex Political Victims*, 115.
6. Bello, "Mohammad Ali Atassi."

moments of the "storm brewing"—as the Zapatistas describe it—an unflinching awareness of the catastrophe we all feel, and an unhidden awakening to the storm's abusive matrixes of power.

Lest readers detect too straightforward a determinism in the picture of solidarity I have put forth in this book, I admit, it is an unsettling task—it behooves scholars, journalists, activists, chroniclers, and international solidarity groups to transcend themselves and their epistemic fortress to attend to the vestiges of meaning collected in the wake of Others. It is no doubt even more daunting in the context of those with whom we have limited shared practices, dialogue, and social meanings and traditions, as well as in light of the information technologies and authoritarian systems that sow confusion, polarization, and paralysis among people. Their experiences are at times incommensurable with our own. I have sought to bridge this divide in my writing, given my positionality both as an unapologetic insider with an incisive commitment to my revolution but also a melancholic outsider yearning for a participation that eluded me.

This is the very challenge of solidarity—the process through which one becomes open to the affective bonds and vulnerabilities radical subjects weave in their emancipatory struggle. It encapsulates the "aporia of solidarity"—as feminist scholars Judith Butler and Athena Athanasiou put it: "How are we to struggle for a desire to exist and to be free, when this desire is not exactly "ours," in fact can never be exclusively "ours"?[7] Locating when and how to be in solidarity in situations of revolutionary rupture is never entirely predictable or perfectible. In the era of fake news and conspiracy theories, it is a tall order to sift through all the lies, half-truths, and alternative facts that mark our post-truth era. There are no ultimate guarantees or promises that capacities to affect solidarity will be yielded or that the radical subject will precipitate something more than slight, or move us to overcome indifference to present conditions. It is an uneasy process, one requiring a combination of intuition and judgment as we enter into the extraordinary terrains of the lived realities of others.

Submitting one's sensorium to the radical subject therefore demands conceptual effort and hard labor in discerning the flux of forces which make us impervious to certain struggles and subjectivities. There is constant vigilance required in reflexivity about our epistemic privilege. As the great Persian-Islamic philosopher al-Ghazali put it, to become a believer (and put oneself on the road to solidarity), one must "open [their] inner vision" with "concentrat[ion]" and "direct[ion]."[8] Another important thing to anticipate:

---

7. Butler and Athanasiou, *Dispossession*, 184.
8. Al-Ghazali, *Mukhtasar Iḥyā ' 'Ulūm al-Dīn*.

the worlds of others will sit uncomfortably within our own ethos. Conscious striving is arduous entirely because of space, culture, or ideology—put simply, we have unequal access to the radical subject. This creates a challenge in locating the radical subject in unfamiliar territory, compelling us to stay on the lookout for those whom we instinctively think of as different. Not all of us belong to historical moments of liberatory struggle and we may not always find something antecedently shared by "us" on which solidarity might be built. Their voices speak in languages we don't ordinarily hear. Yet, by orienting ourselves toward their exiled excess, we open the possibility for interpretive intervention, allowing affect not only to proceed through our body and senses but to map out an entirely different atmosphere from which we might forge solidarity.

Finally, this book centers Syria as a case study from which we can derive practices of solidarity. The writing is tied to the constellations of thought and life visions of Syrian radical subjects as a lived context of struggle. In this moment of rupture in the dominant order, we have been privy to specific ways of sense-making and doing arising from the Syrian liberatory struggle. I wanted to break the scholarly tendency to operate from an Archimedean perspective—of "dislocated, disembodied, and disengaged abstraction"[9]—writing I find too often devoid of the political urgency of real subjects in struggle. However, the details coloring every page risk relegating the ideas to the jurisdiction of ethnographic locality, as a theory "contaminated" by historical and political specificities, and as a result of and in relation only to certain events. But the theoretical reflections formulated from the particulars of struggle and exclusion are no less transposable to a variety of spatiotemporal contexts that do not operate from explicitly intersectional contexts. Such theories are not to be ensconced to liminal or exceptional spaces, though they operate most visibly in highly policed (and exceptional) spaces such as that of the authoritarian state, prison systems, ghettos, and refugee camps.

As Robin D. G. Kelley says, "Once we strip radical social movements down to their bare essence and understand the collective desires of people in motion, freedom and love lay at the very heart of the matter."[10] Struggles against capitalism, fascism, militarism, patriarchy, systemic racism, colonialism, and anti-Blackness are unified by the demand for human dignity. Syria is not an aberration on the world stage. The erasure of local contingencies, from Hong Kong, to Sudan, to Yemen, to Mexico, to China, to Egypt, to Ukraine, to Standing Rock, and beyond, speaks to the conditions of life that move

---

9. Mignolo and Walsh, *On Decoloniality*.
10. Kelley, *Freedom Dreams*, 12.

similarly for peoples around the world struggling for liberation and living within abolitionist and decolonial imaginaries. Forms of radical insurgency can be seen in rock-throwing, strikes, civil disobedience, community organizing, artistic and cultural resistance, and worker cooperatives, all which grapple with and disrupt systemic injustice in a variety of ways. The universal nature of the quest to end one's precarity renders imperative the theoretical recourse to paradigms that nurture solidarity with the other.

In closing, the ideas in this book find a home in all struggles for emancipation anchored in the vernacular, in the nonnormative, and in embodied resistance to omnipresent historical oppressors. As the revolutionary actress Fadwa Suleiman puts it: "Syria is not a country, a geography. It's an idea."[11] An idea that invites us to walk freely with others in their struggle, to perhaps see our fates as intertwined, even as it does not assure the reconciliation of grievances or the foreclosure of sorrow. For the time being, let us honor those brave souls—the radical subjects of the past, present, and future—who risk their lives to lift veils of exception and create otherwise worlds. Their struggles cannot be circumscribed either to the particular or the universal, for they are far greater than both.

---

11. Roberts, "Fadwa Suleiman."

CODA

On Exile

Reclaiming the Space that is ours. Forgetting
the Fragility of being alone
In this rose-colored existence, I am enchanted
at the world's wondrousness
Yet, the flesh is tender to the touch. Memory lingers long
The Syrian is a refugee. She has left the *watan,*
the Land of Jasmine and Pistachio
The Land of Honking Taxis and Salted Butter Corn on the Street
Cracked Shells, Broken Windows, and Sarin Gas, drove her out
She sits on the curb, staring at the stars. She Longs. For. Home.
Staring at the stars, I am wondrous again
Memories of wrought-iron balusters on an
Aleppan veranda with a minty breeze
Where nana drinks hot chai with sugar cubes
Basking in her warmth, in the Togetherness, in
the Belonging Of that Immortal Place
Scrolls, write down this prayer
Take me back to the Land of the Citadel, to Halab, to that Moat
And let me sit by the curb with those that yearn too.
—Noor Ghazal Aswad

Even the deepest commitment to justice at home sometimes requires movement beyond its boundaries in order that one might flourish. In the epilogue
of this book, I will briefly pose another question that has begun to trouble
me: *What happens to the affect of the radical subject when they "leave" their
affective environments to become "refugees" in exile?* Aside from the awesome
death toll, over half of Syria's prewar population was pushed into exile, with 11
million either internally displaced or beyond the country's border in the most
substantial forced displacement of individuals since World War II.[1] Thousands upon thousands lost their lives while attempting to cross the Mediter-
ranean Sea. In this "Great Syrian Exodus," refugees are viewed in profoundly

---

1. Ignatieff, "United States and the Syrian Refugee Crisis."

distortive terms—as noble sufferers, apolitical victims, statistics, or political pawns. But rarely as radical subjects.

This "strategic essentialism" bespeaks an agony rooted in reality, though incurring serious costs for a solidarity based on a genuine recognition of the revolution and those who drove it. Within the spectacle of suffering and violence, indeed within the very antipolitical nature of contemporary human rights discourse, the refugee and the radical subject are incompatible, if not antithetical, to one another. This false dichotomy is an impossible one—closing avenues of inquiry and separating us from larger ideological questions tied to the "refugee" figure. This clipped acknowledgment of the "refugee" obliterates the more starkly revolutionary strata of their history, the force of their affecting body (*affectus*) and the impact it leaves on the one affected (*affectio*).[2]

While, naturally, not all refugees are necessarily radical subjects as defined in this book, in many a case, they are "refugees trained in revolution."[3] To mark refugees as radical subjects entails the willingness to see with their "inner eyes,"[4] without containing or retreating from their stories. While a "humanitarian" approach attends to the immediate crisis at or beyond the border, it ignores how refugees are entangled with the liberation struggle in their homeland.[5] It has limited potentiality in enacting solidarity: "[The] nonpolitical stance . . . permit[s] access to populations in need of aid, convincing countries to sign on to refugee conventions—but it also gives humanitarianism a sometimes cruelly narrow focus, able to keep people alive but entirely incapable of changing the conditions that have put them at such great risk."[6] The revocation of the refugee status of over four hundred Syrian refugees in Denmark (after Damascus was declared no longer sufficiently dangerous to provide grounds for international protection) prompts us to more seriously contemplate the interconnections and imbrications that defy strict border delineations. Involuntary repatriation violates international law, and for years, there were multiple reports of arrest, detention, torture, and extrajudicial killing of returnees under the Assad regime.[7] Even after Syria's liberation,

2. See Spinoza, *Ethics*.

3. Yassin-Kassab and al-Shami, *Burning Country*, 225. For more on the risks of apolitical representations of refugees, see Ghazal Aswad, "Biased Neutrality"; Ghazal Aswad, "Fragmented Paradigms" and Ghazal Aswad, "On World Refugee Day."

4. Wynter, "No Humans Involved."

5. "Homeland" might be a problematic term, but I use it following the footsteps of Bassel Shehadeh and Abdul Baset al-Sarout.

6. Feldman, "Difficult Distinctions," 139.

7. Amid the forced repatriation of Syrian refugees, activists promoted the hashtag #SyriaNotSafe to highlight the dangers returnees face, such as detention, disappearance, and torture, notwithstanding the toxic environmental aftermath of the war and the destruction of Syrian homes. See Ghazal Aswad, "Unsafe Homecoming"; and Zakaria, "Syria Is Not Safe," for more on this topic.

the premature and forced return of refugees—absent meaningful support and heedless of the country's ongoing hardships—reflects a shortsightedness divorced from any broader vision of justice or return with dignity.

Moreover, the distinction between the "radical subject" and the "refugee" opens space to explore the convergences and contradictions between these two "figures." Those who rose up in the struggle for freedom do not necessarily find safety—or the freedom they fought for—in exile. Notwithstanding the conditions of attrition or wearing out over time, refugees who engaged in liberatory struggle, the radical subjects of this book, hold an affective subjectivity that extends to various environments or milieus, a state of being less centered on certain "scapes." The "affective economies" of the radical subjects speaks to the ways in which their affective dispositions are valued, circulated, and recalibrated in exile.

Wafa Mustafa, a refugee and fierce activist in Germany advocating for the release of her father, Ali Mustafa, who was forcibly disappeared by the regime in 2013, accentuates the profound affective bonds between radical subjects in exile and the liberatory struggles and loved ones they were forced to leave behind. One time, Wafa was asked to speak at an event with the Red Cross. In preparation for the event, she asked what topics they wanted her to discuss. In response, they requested that she focus only on the "emotional aspect of your separation from your father" and deny the "political side of things, because it is a humanitarian event." Wafa refused such a splitting, stating in no uncertain terms that to deny the liberatory struggle at the heart of their displacement would be "committing a crime against my father. And I do not have the ability to do that."[8] Her words resonate with an unequivocal resolve: crossing borders does not compromise the revolutionary commitments of radical subjects. She echoes the words of Suhail al-Hammoud, a Free Syrian Army rebel, who on the ninth anniversary of the revolution, extended his congratulations to all radical subjects, both inside and inside outside Syria: "Every year that passes, may the revolutionaries in Syria be well. Every year that passes, may the revolutionaries outside of Syria be well."[9]

Simultaneously, exile marks the opportunity to demarcate new territories of hope and fresh predicaments to resistance. For one, refugees resettled in democratic countries are more freely able to publicly share testimonies

---

8. Mustafa, "Activist Wafa Mustafa."

9. Syria TV, "For the First Time." Suhail al-Hammoud, a Free Syrian Army rebel famous for his skill in operating the BGM-71 TOW antitank missiles that neutralized military targets (giving him the nickname Abu Tow), has been the subject of eight assassination attempts, most recently on the 18th of March 2020.

about the barbaric and traumatic past they witnessed during the revolution. We gained unprecedented insight into the regime's inner operations as survivors in exile spoke out about their experiences. The first ever comprehensive account of the "Syrian Gulag," that is, the Assad regime's vast system of arrest, imprisonment, and torture, has been published recently based on the testimonies of those who lived it.[10] One notable example is the landmark court case of Anwar Raslan, a former colonel in Bashar al-Assad's forces, who was arrested in Germany in 2019 after having successfully sought asylum there. Anwar al-Bunni, a Syrian human rights lawyer and refugee, recognized Anwar Raslan when he walked into a Turkish grocery store, finding himself face-to-face with the man who had interrogated and jailed him a decade earlier. Anwar Raslan was found guilty of crimes against humanity after being tried in the Higher Regional Court of Koblenz under the legal principle of universal jurisdiction, which allows the prosecution of crimes in one country even if they happened in another country.[11] Al-Bunni is now part of a network of survivors and legal activists organizing to testify about abuses and their imaginings of freedom.

Alongside witness testimonies, the "Caesar files," a harrowing archive of 53,275 photographs smuggled out of Syria by a regime whistleblower, laid bare the emaciated bodies of thousands tortured and killed in detention. These images are crucial evidence in efforts to prosecute the regime for war crimes. Syrian American activists leveraged the photographic evidence to advocate for the Caesar Act, which imposed sanctions on Bashar al-Assad and the Syrian government for crimes against their own people. Families for Freedom is another trailblazing organization, spearheaded by Amina Khoulani, dedicated to demanding the release and freedom of every Syrian forcibly disappeared or detained by the Assad regime and other armed factions.

Revolutionary politics are always and already protean and cannot be molded into nonnegotiable interpretive frameworks. Exile may compound the inherently unstable state of being in revolution and the amorphous character of the radical subject. A new generation of affinities, loyalties, and subjectivities may emerge, alongside new sites of struggle. Liberatory aspirations take unknown avenues amid the anxieties of prolonged exile and consternation about the degree to which one thinks the thoughts and speaks the words of

10. Baker and Üngör, *Syrian Gulag*.

11. Alaa Mousa, a military doctor in the regime's 251st branch, has been charged with crimes against humanity at the Higher Regional Court in Frankfurt, Germany. Following Syria's liberation, a handful of military and regime officials have been arrested domestically, but there has yet to be any comprehensive movement toward transitional justice—whether through national or international mechanisms.

FIGURE 13. Yassin al-Haj Saleh embracing Ziad Homsi. From *Our Terrible Country*.

those in the "homeland."[12] Practices of radical politics might be invented that did not exist. Yassin al-Haj Saleh, just after his exile to Turkey, muses on the disquiet of displacement, and the potential for growth within the struggle:

> I don't know exactly what I will do in exile. I have long felt claustrophobic over this term. It is more like a mockery coming from those who remained in the country. Today, its meaning might change to include our overwhelming experience, the experience of uprooting, escape, and dispersal. And the hope of return.[13]

The affective weight of estrangement goes beyond just physical displacement to encompass the ambiguity about "what to do" in exile. It might form an affective disruption or counter-affect that generates alternative forms of belonging and politics.

The shifting affective state of the radical subject is captured in the documentary *Our Terrible Country*, a movie that chronicles a tale of inadvertent exile. The last scene vividly portrays the migratory dilemma—the conflict between the desire to stay versus the desire to escape—through a conversation

12. The refugee Félix Pyat, a revolutionary French political activist and representative of the National and Legislative Assemblies of 1848–49, envisioned exiles as intrinsically connected to France, writing: "We think its thoughts, we speak its words" like a "distant but faithful echo." Neudorf, "Reconciling with Rupture."

13. Atassi and Homsi, *Our Terrible Country*.

between twenty-four-year-old Free Syrian Army fighter Ziad Homsi and the fifty-two-year-old writer Yassin al-Haj Saleh (see figure 13). Ziad has left his mother, brother, and detained father in Syria, while Yassin left his wife, Samira Khalil, and his brother Firas al-Haj Saleh. After extricating themselves from mortal danger in their odyssey from Douma to Raqqa to Istanbul, the two men, generations apart, find themselves in a restaurant in Turkey, fighting tears in a poignant moment as they wrestle with the pangs and shame of leaving Syria and leaving their loved ones.

While on the road, they learned that both Ziad's father and Yassin's brother were arrested by the regime. Yassin—whom Ziad calls "doctor"—would soon discover that his wife, Samira; along with Razan Zaitouneh; Razan's husband, Wael Hamadeh; and Nazem Hammadi, were kidnapped by extremists. Ziad's heart-wrenching soliloquy defends his mother's decision to leave Syria, even while he wrestles with the shame of abandoning his imprisoned father and brother.[14] He unpacks the affective labor of choosing to flee. It deserves quotation at length:

> I felt ashamed of myself and worried Yassin would see me and my family differently [for leaving Syria]. I will tell you honestly: I wanted my family to be safe. To get them out of death's way [long pause, wells up in tears]. Damn it, hold on, let me finish. Listen, my father was imprisoned for thirteen years and my mother waited for him patiently. I don't want to cry. She endured it. I was arrested twice. She endured it. My brother Eyad was arrested four times during the revolution. She endured it. And now he has been arrested again. I told her, "That's enough. I am going to get you out." But she said she wouldn't leave without me. I told her, "Okay, I promise—I'll leave with you." When I got back to Raqqa, she said, "Enough, let's carry out our plan and leave together." When she said this, I was shocked because my mother adores my father! How could she want to leave when he was still in prison? Do you know why she said that? Just so she could get me out. So she said, "Get us out!"

The existential decision of whether to cross borders prompts new forms of subjectivity, evident in the affective transactions between "giving enough," "going back," and "getting out," and thoughts of those left behind. The transition to exile is fraught and ever-shifting in terms of the negotiations that take place—when should old men leave and young men stay? Ziad continues: "I want to go back . . . but there is something called a will to live . . . People who

---

14. Atassi and Homsi, *Our Terrible Country*.

want to live should get out. Inside, there is death. But doctor, a young man can tolerate being inside, you have given enough, it's enough. Get out."

As can be deciphered from Ziad's address, leaving is an intensely affective process in which the radical subject inhabits multiple and at times contradictory affectivities—shame, self-righteousness, the will to die for a cause, and the simultaneous urge to leave and to one day return. Ziad, a young combatant, looks up to Yassin, whose resistive activities earned him a hefty sixteen-year prison sentence. Ziad finds himself questioning his revolutionary choices: "When I was held by Daesh, I started thinking, is it possible that lot came because of us? . . . It cuts deep to think that they are one of the consequences of the revolution."[15] It is because of this that he decided to relinquish his arms, amid uncertainty about the "idea" he was fighting for: "I was carrying weapons for a political project that I would not agree with completely. I won't take up arms for a political project. The revolution is bigger than that . . . I take up arms for an idea."

Once past the border, they sit in quiet regret, rueful about what has become of their homeland. Their affect stretches across borders, torn between different places and peoples, embodying what might be termed "diasporic lenticularity." Ghassan Hage's ethnographic work on the Lebanese diaspora introduces diasporic lenticularity as the diasporic subject's ability to occupy two spaces, or more, at the same time.[16] In other words, they are able to inhabit both spatial realities at the same time—that of home and that of exile. Fadwa Suleiman, the Alawite actress who shattered gender and sectarian boundaries when she stood side by side with Abdul Baset al-Sarout at revolutionary protests, captures this multiplicity after her exile to Paris. She speaks of her inability to enjoy the beauty of the City of Lights because of it: "In the beginning, I could not communicate with the place. I would see it as Syria. I would think this neighborhood looks like one in Damascus, or this street looks like one in Damascus. I was completely absent from here. In body here, but in the soul, there. My thoughts were there."[17]

Diasporic lenticularity describes the contradictory yearnings of the radical subject, and the fragmentation experienced both spatially and temporally, as a "flickering between one and the other."[18] This flickering is also affective, as the radical subject negotiates the practicalities and material necessities of life as they are now conditioned. Liberatory struggle might take a back seat to the exigencies of everyday survival in the vicissitudes of the diaspora. And the

15. Atassi and Homsi, *Our Terrible Country.*
16. Hage, *Diasporic Condition.*
17. Al Aan TV, "Fadwa Suleiman."
18. Hage, *Diasporic Condition,* 186.

radical subject must reconcile the will to persist in their own being. To carve a life worth living, or what Judith Butler calls a "livable life."[19]

Memory also imparts much in the process of affect accumulation for radical subjects in the diaspora. Different practices of memory come into play, acting as a tool of both resistance and survival. Joman Hasan, a dissident who was detained and electrocuted in prison by the regime, deliberates on how she wields her memory as a form of affective power. For her, remembering unleashes a powerful affect combating the regime's erasure of the past:

> I worry about my psychological state. For me to be well, I need to believe what happened to me was real. The regime told me they did nothing to me, that they were just investigating, *tahqeeq*. Of course, my memory is excellent. For months, I would keep thinking, was that an inspection or was it torture? Until I was able to put things in perspective, I knew it was torture. To this day, when someone denies what happened to Syrians, I think profoundly about it—what if they are not lying? But we need to keep telling them they are liars, for our own protection, not theirs. We will fight them with our memories, with our stories. Our silence gives space for their lies.[20]

While memory has a vital role in accumulation of radical affect, "strategic amnesia" must also be recognized as its own constitutive force—a conscious (dis)engagement from liberatory struggle. This is not the kind of forgetting as when something is just not important enough to remember, so it slips one's mind, but rather the kind of forgetting one exercises to recover from trauma, memories too painful, so they are pushed away. While some are able to make a clean break with the past, for others, their activism is inextricably entrenched in the anguished affect of revolutionary memory in her own life. In this brief passage, Wafa Mustafa articulates her inability to forget and the inescapable pull of revolutionary memory in her life of exile in Germany:

> I am not saying that all people cannot forget; some people can forget. But I have reached an impasse in my inability to forget. Even though I want to forget, I cannot. My life has become so brutal that, I swear on my father's life, I pray, "Oh God, may I have a car accident and wake up, and find that I have forgotten who I am, and forgotten that my father is not here."[21]

---

19. Butler, *Precarious Life*, xv.
20. Quote is from private communication with author and shared with permission.
21. Mustafa, "Activist Wafa Mustafa."

Wafa's words illuminate the toll of carrying forward revolutionary memory in exile—a memory not stored in archives but lived in the body. Within the lifespan of liberatory struggle, radical subjects in the diaspora continue to articulate fantasies of freedom, alongside the dream of return home. Their words reveal hope for another world possible in the now. Their stories speak to their lingering affect and their ability to touch those with whom they share nothing except common humanity. Just as oppressive power does not need the enclosed spaces of disciplinary society to exercise itself, resistance too transcends the enclosures of the nation-state. In the *shattat*—the exilic condition of being dispersed, strewn and detached—the radical subject's very being continues to nudge us toward a shared inhabitation of the world we long for.

For others, their homes in exile are shrines to the land they left behind. Afraa Hashem, the activist and educator who built schools in liberated areas in Syria, now calls London home after years of revolutionary struggle. For her, exile is simply an extension of the revolution. On her mantle, she keeps soil from Syria in a jar, along with bars of Aleppan laurel soap, so she might smell the scent of her homeland whenever she yearns to. They remind her of her right to return:

> Someday we will come back to our city. We are strong enough to complete what we have started, and what our friends who died started. And we will reach our victory someday. We will try Assad as a war criminal one day, and my country is here in my heart.[22]

Her words reflect a truth now unfolding. Some of those once forced to flee are now reclaiming their homes, rebuilding lives amid the ruins, determined to restore what was lost and heal the scars of exile. Others remain haunted about whether—and if—they will return home, and by the memory of what that return has already cost. Regardless, the revolution lives on—not as an end, but as a horizon still unfolding.

---

22. Oxford Human Rights Festival, "For Sama Q&A."

ACKNOWLEDGMENTS

This book would not have been possible without the invaluable support and encouragement of family, friends, colleagues, and mentors. Antonio de Velasco, you were an extraordinary mentor and to you I am deeply grateful. Andre Johnson, Michael Perez, and Gray Matthews: your guidance enriched this project in its formative stages. I have a wonderful intellectual community of friends and trusted colleagues at the University of Alabama, including Josh Pederson, Angela Billings, Anneliese Bolland, Robin Boylorn, Sim Butler, Kaylin Duncan, Sara Hartley, Leah Lefebvre, Mary Meares, Brent Mitchell, Jeonghyun Oh, Caroline Parsons, Cynthia Peacock, Ben Pyle, Jaclyn Shetterly, Sara Hartley, Mizuki Wyant, Abdullah Salehuddin, and Waleed Hazbun. I am especially grateful to my phenomenal colleagues and friends— Jessy Ohl, Darrin Griffin, Adam Brooks, Heather Hayes, Meredith Bagley— for their camaraderie and generosity of spirit. I would like to acknowledge my graduate research assistant, Lavia Walker, for her editorial assistance with the manuscript. I would like to thank Dean Brian Butler and Associate Dean for Research Andrew Billings for providing institutional support that helped bring this book to fruition. Support for this scholarly work was also provided by the University of Alabama Office of Academic Affairs.

I owe much gratitude to the scholars who embraced my work throughout the years and whose companionship I have cherished: Katherine Hendrix, Mandy Young, Wendy Atkins-Sayre, Marina Levina, Georgeta Vidican, Srivi

Ramasubramanian, Mary Stuckey, Michael Lechuga, Phaedra Pezzullo, Stacey Sowards, Lisa Flores, Kent Ono, Karma Chávez, Matthew Houdek, Walid Afifi, Laura Partain, Joshua Trey Barnett, Shereen Yousuf, and Angie Galal. Gratitude to the anonymous reviewers, who later revealed themselves to be Mary Stuckey and Ana Milena Ribero, whose astute feedback was transformative in bringing the book to completion. Mary Stuckey in particular has encouraged me to find my voice and nurtured my writing with much attentiveness and care over the years. I am also indebted to a group of brilliant activists and thinkers whose work has influenced my thinking in formative ways: Yassin al-Haj Saleh, Robin Yassin-Kassab, Leila al-Shami, Arash Azizi, Yasser Munif, Razan Saffour, Uğur Ümit Üngör, Lilie Chouliaraki, Ghassan Hage, Jasbir Puar, and Gregory Seigworth.

The book would not have happened without my editor at The Ohio State University Press (OSUP), Tara Cyphers, whose wisdom sharpened every aspect of this work. The series editor, Karma Chávez, was a champion for this project and for my work. Your friendship has been a gift, and you continue to inspire me with your kindness, which outweighs even your brilliance. Thanks are also due to the rest of the team at OSUP who supported the production of the book. Thank you to Morgan Blue for proofreading and for the index at the end of the book. Thanks to the talented Molly Crabapple for the stunning book cover and for exemplifying solidarity in all her work. I would also like to thank Aziz Asmar, the members of the Occupied Kafranbel Banners, Ali Ferzat, and The Syrian People Know Their Way Collective for permission to reproduce their powerful work. Portions of this book first appeared in *Rhetoric and Public Affairs* and *Quarterly Journal of Speech*. Portions of chapter 4 also appear in the edited book collection, "Used, Abused, and Sidelined: Debating the Declaration" (Penn State University Press).

On a personal note, I am blessed with true friends and family who sustained me and lifted me up throughout this journey: Diana Watkins Dickerson, Laura Sullivan, Rima Yakteen, Zeina Abbas, Deema Alqassar, Sama Habbal, Sawsan Babil, Laila Sabbagh, Deema Hammad, Rafah Kayali, Rawa Ghazal Aswad, Bisher Imam, and Kamal, Sami, and Shannon al-Assar. I am blessed with your presence in my life. To my in-laws, you are not my family by blood, but you are the family I have been blessed with. Thank you for loving me like your own. To baba, my *sanad*—you raised me not with words but through your steadfast example. I am proud to be *bint* Saad. To mama, what you have endured opened my eyes to a world I may never have cared for. I am proud to be *bint* Falak. Nana, your life has not been easy, but the days I spent in your little blue kitchen listening to your stories formed me and have given me the strength to weather life far from you. To Bisher, I would be lost without you—my moral compass. Your principles and intellect shaped me and this book. To Ameera, thank you for being the sweetest presence between us. We are lucky to have you in our midst. To Karam, what would I do without your quick intelligence and sweet presence? Thank you for being a "little brother" I look up to. To Ghena, thank you for being a devoted sister and aunt. Khaleh Nuha, Khalo Fawaz, and Khalo Naji and all my cousins: borders have separated us, but you are here in my heart.

Mohamad, without you, this book would not be. You are the light in my life and my certitude. I could not have asked for a better partner in this journey. To Hassan, Sami, and Serene, being your mother has been the greatest joy of my life. May you one day come to love your ancestral home, that land of jasmine and pistachio, as I do. May you always honor the freedom God granted you, and defend it always fiercely.

Finally, this book has been inspired by revolutionary Syrians, this book's radical subjects. Many of you sacrificed your lives for something bigger than yourself. But you have not died. You live on—in our memory and in every page of this book.

APPENDIX

Letter from Syrian revolutionaries to the Sheikh Jarrah neighborhood

To the steadfast men and women in the Sheikh Jarrah neighborhood and all the neighborhoods of occupied Jerusalem.

For days, we have been following closely and with great anticipation what is happening in Jerusalem, watching your struggle, sharing your voice, and feeling for you. Borders kill us and our diaspora kills us, as they stand in the way of our actual presence with you. That is why we are writing to you, in the hope that it will convey the slightest hint of the feelings of pain, anger, and burning, that rage in our hearts because of your great suffering and pain.

In your revolution we saw our revolution, and in your steadfastness our steadfastness, and in your displacement our displacement. We know, like you, the meaning of the oppression. We faced it at the hands of the Assad regime, as you faced it at the hands of Israel.

We, as an oppressed people, share with you this just battle with all its moral, human, and existential dimensions against Israel and against the normalization regimes.

In your liberation from the occupation, we see our liberation from tyranny, and in your chants, we hear the chants of our martyrs, and in "heaven,

heaven," we remember our voices and our revolution, and in your resistance and steadfastness we hope and are supplied to continue the path.

Greetings to you from the revolution of freedom and dignity,
The undersigned and the undersigned, Sons and Daughters of Syria

BIBLIOGRAPHY

Aba Zeid, Ahmad. "Soleimani: Naked Propaganda." Translated from Arabic. Facebook, January 2, 2020. https://www.facebook.com/abazed89.

al-Abdallah, Hadi. "For the Syrian Revolution's Ten Years (with Hadi al-Abdallah)." YouTube, January 28, 2021. https://www.youtube.com/watch?v=Eq8usxFnJ6c.

al-Abdallah, Hadi. "The Needy and the Trend." Translated from Arabic. Facebook, December 11, 2021. https://www.facebook.com/HadiAlabdallah/videos/384315566717227/.

Abouzeid, Rania. *No Turning Back: Life, Loss and Hope in Wartime Syria.* W. W. Norton, 2018.

Abu Zayd, Osama. "If Support [for Palestine] Is the Standard on Which Our Values Stand . . ." Translated from Arabic. Twitter, January 6, 2020. https://twitter.com/oabozayd/status/1214294411204550656?s=21.

Agamben, Giorgio. *Homo Sacer: Sovereign Power and Bare Life.* Redwood City, CA: Stanford University Press, 1998.

Ahmed, Sara. *The Cultural Politics of Emotion.* Edinburgh: Edinburgh University Press, 2014.

Ahmed, Sara. *Queer Phenomenology: Orientations, Objects, Others.* Durham, NC: Duke University Press, 2006.

Al Aan TV. "Fadwa Suleiman in a Critical Review of the Syrian Revolution." YouTube, March 7, 2015. https://www.youtube.com/watch?v=QY676AnNDss.

Al Jazeera. "The Killing of the Journalist Trad al Zahori." Translated from Arabic. YouTube, February 21, 2014. https://www.youtube.com/watch?v=bbI831KKFeg.

Alarabiya. "The Killing of Abu Furat, the Leader Who Made Syrians Cry in Sorrow." YouTube, December 17, 2012. https://www.youtube.com/watch?v=t-9-QcuiHCo.

Alcoff, Linda. "The Problem of Speaking for Others." *Cultural Critique,* no. 20 (Winter 1991): 5–32.

Aletto, Lucia. "Aziz Asmar. Syrian Painter, Binnish 2020." YouTube, June 17, 2020. https://www.youtube.com/watch?v=itlnY3bhkHo.

Alexander, M. Jacqui. *Pedagogies of Crossing: Meditations on Feminism, Sexual Politics, Memory, and the Sacred*. Durham, NC: Duke University Press, 2006.

Alford, Jules, and Andy Wilson. *Khiyana: Daesh, the Left and the Unmaking of the Syrian Revolution*. Unkant Publishers, 2015.

Al-Jumhuriya. "The Days of Abd al-Basit." June 13, 2019. https://aljumhuriya.net/en/2019/06/13/the-days-of-abd-al-basit/.

Al-Jumhuriya. "Soleimani in Syria: A Legacy of Death and Devastation." 2020. https://aljumhuriya.net/en/2020/01/06/soleimani-in-syria-a-legacy-of-death-and-devastation/.

Allen, Joe. "How to Revive the Antiwar Movement." *Jacobin*, January 10, 2020. https://jacobinmag.com/2020/01/iran-antiwar-movement-united-states-iraq-afghanistan.

Alloush, Ibrahim. "If Only Syria Had Killed Him!" Translated from Arabic. *Enab Baladi*, May 1, 2020. https://www.enabbaladi.net/archives/353541.

AlRifai, Oula. "In Memoriam: Raed Fares and the Banners of Kafranbel." *Journal of Middle Eastern Politics and Policy*, 2018. https://studentreview.hks.harvard.edu/in-memoriam-raed-fares-and-the-banners-of-kafranbel/.

Amnesty International. "Human Slaughterhouse: Mass Hangings and Extermination at Saydnaya Prison." 2017. https://www.amnesty.org/en/wp-content/uploads/2021/05/MDE2454152017ENGLISH.pdf.

Amnesty International. "Syrian Blogger Arrested as Crackdown Continues." December 6, 2011. https://www.amnesty.org/en/latest/news/2011/12/syrian-blogger-arrested-crackdown-continues/.

Anonymous. "Basel Shehadeh: Where Words Fall Short in Front of Such a Soul." *The Syrianist* (blog), May 29, 2012. https://thesyrianist.blogspot.com/2012/05/basel-shehadeh-rip-1984-2012-where.html.

Anzaldúa, Gloria. *Borderlands / La Frontera: The New Mestiza*. San Francisco: Aunt Lute Books, 1987.

al-Aqeedi, Rasha. "The World Paid Attention to the Wrong Iraqi Protests." *The Atlantic*, January 7, 2020. https://www.theatlantic.com/ideas/archive/2020/01/iraqs-real-protesters-are-caught-in-the-middle/604537/.

Arendt, Hannah. *Eichmann in Jerusalem: A Report on the Banality of Evil*. New York: Viking Press, 1963.

Arendt, Hannah. *The Human Condition*. University of Chicago Press, 1958.

Arendt, Hannah. *On Revolution*. London: Penguin Books, 2006.

Armanazi, Ghayth. *The Story of Syria*. London: Gilgamesh, 2017.

Atassi, Mohammad Ali, dir. *Ibn al-Amm* [The Cousin]. YouTube, 2001. https://www.youtube.com/watch?v=ZN_Hix9RB-I.

Atassi, Mohammad Ali, dir. *Ibn al-Amm Online* [The Cousin Online]. YouTube, 2012. https://www.youtube.com/watch?v=BFOdOdCVKiE.

Atassi, Mohammad Ali, and Ziad Homsi. *Our Terrible Country*. Syria: Bidayyat for Audiovisual Arts, 2014.

Atlantic Council. "Germany Has Sentenced a Syrian Colonel to Life for Crimes Against Humanity. Will Others Face the Same Fate?" January 14, 2022. https://www.atlanticcouncil.org/blogs/new-atlanticist/germany-has-sentenced-a-syrian-colonel-to-life-for-crimes-against-humanity-will-others-face-the-same-fate/.

Atlantic Council. "Russia's Disinformation Campaign Has Changed How We See Syria." September 4, 2018. https://www.atlanticcouncil.org/blogs/syriasource/russia-s-disinformation-campaign-has-changed-how-we-see-syria/.

Ayoub, Elia J. "On Erasures and 'Discourse.'" *I Write Stuff* (blog), May 21, 2021. https://iwritestuff.blog/2021/05/21/on-erasures-and-discourse/.

Aziz, Omar. "A Discussion Paper on Local Councils in Syria." *Anarchist Library,* 2013. https://theanarchistlibrary.org/library/omar-aziz-a-discussion-paper-on-local-councils-in-syria.

Azizi, Arash. *The Shadow Commander: Soleimani, the U.S., and Iran's Global Ambitions.* London: One World Publication, 2020.

Bader Eddin, Eylaf. *Translating the Language of the Syrian Revolution.* Berlin: Walter de Gruyter, 2023.

Badiou, Alain. "On a Finally Objectless Subject." In *Who Comes After the Subject?,* edited by E. Cadava, P. Connor, and J.-L. Nancy, 24–32. New York: Routledge, 1991.

Baker, Jaber, and Uğur Ümit Üngör. *Syrian Gulag: Inside Assad's Prison System.* London: Bloomsbury, 2023.

Bakkour, Samer. "Emergence, Development, and Impact of Population Displacement in Damascus During Syria's Civil War." *Middle East Critique,* May 2024: 1–22. https://doi.org/10.1080/19436149.2024.2347147.

Bardawil, Fadi A. "Césaire with Adorno: Critical Theory and the Colonial Problem." *South Atlantic Quarterly* 117, no. 4 (2018): 773–89.

Bardawil, Fadi A. "Critical Theory in a Minor Key to Take Stock of the Syrian Revolution." In *A Time for Critique,* edited by Didier Fassin and Bernard E. Harcourt, 174–92. New York: Columbia University Press, 2019.

Bardawil, Fadi A. *Revolution and Disenchantment: Arab Marxism and the Binds of Emancipation.* Durham, NC: Duke University Press, 2020.

Barthes, Roland. *Rhetoric of the Image.* Fontana, 1977.

Batatu, Hanna. "Syria's Muslim Brethren." *Middle East Research and Information Project,* November/December 1982. https://merip.org/1982/11/syrias-muslim-brethren/.

Batatu, Hanna. *Syria's Peasantry, the Descendants of Its Lesser Rural Notables, and Their Politics.* Princeton, NJ: Princeton University Press, 1999.

Bayat, Asef. *Revolution Without Revolutionaries: Making Sense of the Arab Spring.* Redwood City, CA: Stanford University Press, 2017.

Bayoumi, Moustafa. "The Civil War in Syria Is Invisible—but This Anonymous Film Collective Is Changing That." *The Nation,* June 29, 2015. https://www.thenation.com/article/archive/the-civil-war-in-syria-is-invisible-but-this-anonymous-film-collective-is-changing-that/.

Bayraqdar, Faraj. *Khiyanat al Lugha Wa l Samt* [The Betrayals of Language and Silence]. Beirut: Dar al-Jadid, 2006.

BBC. "Mayday." *BBC News,* 2021. https://www.bbc.co.uk/programmes/p04sj2pt/episodes/downloads.

BBC. "Syria Should Be Referred to ICC, UN's Navi Pillay says." *BBC News,* December 13, 2011. https://www.bbc.com/news/world-middle-east-16151424.

Bellingcat. "Chemical Weapons and Absurdity: The Disinformation Campaign Against the White Helmets." December 18, 2018. https://www.bellingcat.com/news/mena/2018/12/18/chemical-weapons-and-absurdity-the-disinformation-campaign-against-the-white-helmets/.

Bello, Grace. "Mohammad Ali Atassi: Syria in Its Own Image." *Guernica,* February 16, 2015. https://www.guernicamag.com/syria-in-its-own-image/.

Bergland, Renée L. *The National Uncanny: Indian Ghosts and American Subjects.* Hanover, NH: University Press of New England, 2000.

Berlant, Lauren. *Cruel Optimism.* Durham, NC: Duke University Press, 2011.

Berlant, Lauren. *The Queen of American Goes to Washington City.* Durham, NC: Duke University Press, 1997.

Bhabha, Homhi. *The Location of Culture.* New York: Routledge, 1994.

Bido, Yakeen Yaser. "Sayra Sayra . . ." Translated from Arabic. Facebook, January 3, 2020. https://www.facebook.com/100003941110556/posts/1550336168441072/?d=n.

Binning, Arelle A. "How Black Lives Matter Has Influenced and Interacted with Global Social Movements." Master's thesis, City University of New York, 2019. https://academicworks.cuny.edu/cgi/viewcontent.cgi?article=4182&context=gc_etds.

Bishara, Marwan. *The Invisible Arab: The Promise and Peril of the Arab Revolutions.* New York: Nation Books, 2012.

Borri, Francesca. *Syrian Dust: Reporting from the Heart of the Battle for Aleppo.* New York: Seven Stories Press, 2015.

Bourdieu, Pierre. *Language and Symbolic Power.* Translated by Gino Raymond and Matthew Adamson. Cambridge, MA: Harvard University Press, 1991.

Bourdieu, Pierre. *Pascalian Meditations.* Redwood City, CA: Stanford University Press, 2000.

Bouris, Erica. *Complex Political Victims.* Bloomfield, CT: Kumarian Press, 2007.

Boutros, Julia. "Oh Stories." YouTube, December 3, 2013. https://www.youtube.com/watch?v=xcJqArTAFjE.

Bratta, Phil, and Malea Powell. "Entering the Cultural Rhetorics Conversations." *Enculturation,* April 20, 2016. https://enculturation.net/entering-the-cultural-rhetorics-conversations.

Butler, Judith. *Frames of War: When Is Life Grievable?* London: Verso, 2009.

Butler, Judith. *Notes Toward a Performative Theory of Assembly.* Cambridge, MA: Harvard University Press, 2015.

Butler, Judith. *Precarious Life: The Power of Morning and Violence.* London: Verso, 2004.

Butler, Judith. *Senses of the Subject.* New York: Fordham University Press, 2015.

Butler, Judith, and Athena Athanasiou. *Dispossession: The Performative in the Political.* Cambridge, MA: Polity Press, 2013.

Campbell, Karlyn Kohrs. "Agency: Promiscuous and Protean." *Communication and Critical/Cultural Studies* 2, no. 1 (2005): 1–19.

CBS News. "Former Prosecutor: More Evidence of War Crimes Against Syrian President Assad than There Was Against Nazis." February 18, 2021. https://www.cbsnews.com/news/bashar-al-assad-syria-60-minutes-2021-02-18/.

Chávez, Karma. "Beyond Inclusion: Rethinking Rhetoric's Historical Narrative." *Quarterly Journal of Speech* 101, no. 1 (2015): 162–72.

Chenoweth, Erica, and Maria J. Stephan. *Why Civil Resistance Works: The Strategic Logic of Nonviolent Conflict.* New York: Columbia University Press, 2011.

Chomsky, Noam, and Edward Herman. "Distortions at Fourth Hand." *The Nation,* June 6, 1977. https://chomsky.info/19770625/.

Chouliaraki, Lillie. *The Ironic Spectator: Solidarity in the Age of Post-Humanitarianism.* Cambridge, MA: Polity Press, 2013.

Chouliaraki, Lillie, and Omar al-Ghazzi. "Beyond Verification: Flesh Witnessing and the Significance of Embodiment in Conflict News." *Journalism* 23, no. 3 (2022): 649–67.

CNN. "Bernie Sanders: Trump Administration Hasn't a Clue About What It's Doing." January 6, 2020. https://www.youtube.com/watch?v=GxyXrezEfLo.

Combahee River Collective. "The Combahee River Collective Statement." 1977. https://www.blackpast.org/african-american-history/combahee-river-collective-statement-1977/.

Conduit, Dara. *The Muslim Brotherhood in Syria.* Cambridge: Cambridge University Press, 2019.

Cooke, Miriam. *Dancing in Damascus: Creativity, Resilience, and the Syrian Revolution.* New York: Routledge, 2017.

Daher, Joseph. *Syria After the Uprisings: The Political Economy of State Resilience.* Chicago: Haymarket Books, 2019.

Davis, Angela. "Freedom Is a Constant Struggle: Angela Davis on Ferguson, Palestine and the Foundations of a Movement." *Democracy Now!,* March 28, 2016. https://www.democracynow.org/2016/3/28/freedom_is_a_constant_struggle_angela.

Davison, Derek. "Donald Trump and the Foreign Policy Establishment Want War with Iran." *Jacobin,* January 3, 2020. https://www.jacobinmag.com/2020/01/iran-united-states-drone-strike-qassem-soleimani-death.

Davison, Derek. "The Rogue State Is on the Rampage Again." *Jacobin,* January 13, 2020. https://www.jacobinmag.com/2020/01/donald-trump-united-states-imperialism-iraq-iran.

Democracy Now! "Syrian Activist Speaks Out from Hiding as Arab League Mission Fails to Slow Deadly Crackdown." YouTube, December 29, 2011. https://www.youtube.com/watch?v=DokZOu4_pjI&t=337s.

Dom Tak. "Janna, Janna, Janna [heaven, heaven, heaven]." Sowt Podcast, August 16, 2022. https://www.sowt.com/episodes/dom-tak-dum-tak---jnw-jnw-jnw.

Donauskyte, Kristina, Grace Holme, Kristina Landry, and Lewis Smith. "Syria Through a Lens: The Life and Works of Filmmaker Bassel Shehadeh." YouTube, July 3, 2012. https://www.youtube.com/watch?v=Nem33Ow8wb4.

Dyer, Richard. *White: Essays on Race and Culture.* New York: Routledge, 1977.

Ear, Sophal. "The Khmer Rouge Canon 1975–1979: The Standard Total Academic View on Cambodia." Undergraduate thesis, University of California–Berkeley, 1995.

Edwards, Jason A., and David Weiss. *The Rhetoric of American Exceptionalism: Critical Essays.* Jefferson, NC: McFarland, 2014.

Erhaim, Zaina. *Syria's Rebellious Women.* YouTube, January 7, 2017. https://www.youtube.com/watch?v=bh1HtLr-WEo.

Escobar, Arturo. *Pluriversal Politics: The Real and the Possible.* Durham, NC: Duke University Press, 2020.

Euronews. "Victory: This Is How Syrian Refugees in Idlib See the Killing of Qasem Soleimani." Translated from Arabic. *Euronews Arabic.* YouTube, January 10, 2020. https://www.youtube.com/watch?v=lF_6zJ2rxOM.

Euronews. "Watch: Syrians in Idlib Distribute Sweets to People in Celebration of Soleimani's Killing." Translated from Arabic. *Euronews Arabic.* YouTube, January 3, 2020. https://www.youtube.com/watch?v=i1-s-oXJNMA.

Fanon, Frantz. *The Wretched of the Earth.* New York: Grove Press, 1963.

Farah, Rami. *Our Memory Belongs to Us.* Final Cut for Real, 2021.

Farrell, Thomas B. "The Weight of Rhetoric: Studies in Cultural Delirium." *Philosophy and Rhetoric* 41, no. 4 (2008): 467–87.

Featherstone, Liza. "Neocons Don't Regret the Iraq Disaster—And Now They Want War with Iran." *Jacobin,* January 18, 2020. https://www.jacobinmag.com/2020/01/iraq-war-iran-media-bret-stephens-goldberg-bolton-friedman.

Feldman, Ilana. "Difficult Distinctions: Refugee Law, Humanitarian Practice, and Political Identification in Gaza." *Cultural Anthropology* 22, no. 1 (2007): 129–69.

Fernández, Belen. "The Mainstream Media Is a Cheerleader for War with Iran." *Jacobin,* January 4, 2020. https://www.jacobinmag.com/2020/01/war-iran-qassem-soleimani-drone-strike-death-mainstream-media.

Ferzat, Ali. "Trump and Soleimani." Facebook, January 12, 2021. https://www.facebook.com/photo?fbid=5192492234124644&set=a.175684052472179.

Fisk, Robert. "Syria's 'Moderates' Have Disappeared . . . and There Are No Good Guys." *The Independent,* October 4, 2015. https://www.independent.co.uk/voices/syria-s-moderates-have-disappeared-and-there-are-no-good-guys-a6679406.html.

Fiumara, Gemma C. *The Other Side of Language: A Philosophy of Listening.* New York: Routledge, 1990.

Flowes, Sali. "They All Ate Sweets on the Killing of Soleimani, but Yakeen and I did not . . . ! And so, We Have Decided to Drink Matte Instead and to Pour on the Sugar." Translated from Arabic. Facebook, January 3, 2020. https://www.facebook.com/100012868031263/posts/830360174069576/?d=n.

Foucault, Michel. *Discipline and Punish: The Birth of the Prison.* New York: Pantheon Books, 1977.

Foucault, Michel. *History of Sexuality Volume 1: An Introduction.* New York: Vintage Books, 1980.

Friedman, Amy. "Out of Syria: An Expelled Italian Priest Calls for Peace and Reconciliation." *Time,* August 8, 2012. https://world.time.com/2012/08/08/out-of-syria-an-expelled-italian-priest-calls-for-peace-and-reconciliation/.

Frontline Defenders. "Interview: Razan Ghazzawi." YouTube, February 18, 2013. https://www.youtube.com/watch?v=ZBJVYUSLqWM.

Gardner, David. "Syria Is Witnessing a Violent Demographic Re-Engineering." *Financial Times,* October 2, 2019. https://www.ft.com/content/e40cb754-e456-11e9-b112-9624ec9edc59.

Ghazal Aswad, Noor. "Biased Neutrality: The Symbolic Construction of the Syrian Refugee in the *New York Times.*" *Critical Studies in Media Communication* 36, no. 4 (2019): 357–75. https://doi.org/10.1080/15295036.2019.1628996.

Ghazal Aswad, Noor. "Cultivating Radical Care and Otherwise Possibilities at the End of the World." *Quarterly Journal of Speech* 110, no. 2 (2024): 313–19. https://doi.org/10.1080/00335630.2024.2323672.

Ghazal Aswad, Noor. "Fragmented Paradigms of Transculturality: Negotiating Equivocal Agency in Refugee Representations in Refugee Resettlement Organizations." In *Negotiating Identity and Transnationalism in Middle Eastern and North African Communication and Critical Cultural Studies,* edited by Haneen Ghabra, Fatima Zahrae Chrifi Alaoui, Shadee Abdi, and Bernadette Marie Calafell, 31–47. New York: Peter Lang, 2020.

Ghazal Aswad, Noor. "On World Refugee Day, Let's Remember Syria's Revolutionary Refugees." *New Arab,* June 18, 2020. https://english.alaraby.co.uk/opinion/world-refugee-day-lets-remember-our-revolutionary-refugees.

Ghazal Aswad, Noor. "Unsafe Homecoming: Unraveling Environmental Injustice and Land Dispossession in the Syrian Refugee Crisis." *Environmental Communication* 18, nos. 1–2 (2024): 35–42. https://doi.org/10.1080/17524032.2023.2296831.

Ghazal Aswad, Noor, and Matthew Houdek. "Radical Rhetorics at/and the World's End: Epistemologies, Ontologies, and Otherwise Possibilities." *Quarterly Journal of Speech* 110, no. 2 (2024): 263–69. https://doi.org/10.1080/00335630.2024.2330577.

Ghazal Aswad, Noor, and Michael Lechuga. "Led by the Land: Recovering Land Agency and Interconnectedness in Social Movement Scholarship." *Rhetoric and Public Affairs* 27, no. 2 (2024): 25–44. https://doi.org/10.14321/rhetpublaffa.27.2.0025.

Ghazal Aswad, Noor, and Laura Partain. "Gift or Gilded Cage? Performing Gratitude and the Respectability Politics of Refuge." *Communication and Critical Cultural Studies* 22, no. 2 (2025): 180–98. https://doi.org/10.1080/14791420.2025.2505630.

al-Ghazali, Imam. *Mukhtasar Iḥyā ʾ ʿUlūm al-Dīn* [Abridged Revival of the Religious Sciences]. Lympia: Spohr, 2020.

al-Ghazzi, Omar. "'Forced to Report': Affective Proximity and the Perils of Local Reporting on Syria." *Journalism* 24, no. 2 (2021): 280–94.

Gregg, Melissa, and Gregory J. Seigworth. *The Affect Theory Reader.* London: Duke University Press, 2010.

Griswold, Eliza. "Radio Free Syria." *New York Times,* December 7, 2014. https://www.nytimes.com/2014/12/07/magazine/radio-free-syria.html.

Hage, Ghassan. *Against Paranoid Nationalism.* London: Pluto Press, 2003.

Hage, Ghassan. *The Diasporic Condition: Ethnographic Explorations of the Lebanese in the World.* Chicago: University of Chicago Press, 2021.

al-Haj Saleh, Yassin. "The Dark Path of Minority Politics: Why Privileging Minorities Will Only Perpetuate the Syrian Catastrophe." Century Foundation, 2019. https://tcf.org/content/report/dark-path-minority-politics/?agreed=1.

al-Haj Saleh, Yassin. *The Impossible Revolution: Making Sense of the Syrian Tragedy.* Chicago: Haymarket Books, 2017.

al-Haj Saleh, Yassin. "Letters to Samira (12)." *Al-Jumhuriya,* January 2, 2019. https://aljumhuriya.net/en/2019/02/01/letters-to-samira-12/.

al-Haj Saleh, Yassin. "Syria, Iran, ISIS and the Future of Social Justice." *Radio Zamaneh,* 2015. https://en.radiozamaneh.com/24107/.

al-Haj Saleh, Yassin. "Syria and Western Powers: A Global Problem." *Al Quds,* September 19, 2015.

al-Haj Saleh, Yassin. "The Syrian Cause and Anti-Imperialism." *Al-Jumhuriya,* May 5, 2017. https://aljumhuriya.net/en/2017/02/24/the-syrian-cause-and-anti-imperialism/.

Halab Today TV. "Stories From the Revolution—Episode 20 (Ghalia al-Rahhal—A Revolutionary Who Devoted Her Activism to Empowering Women in Idlib)." Translated from Arabic. YouTube, May 6, 2021. https://www.youtube.com/watch?v=eZdqhsdfOSM.

Halasa, Malu, Zaher Omareen, and Nawara Mahfoud. *Syria Speaks: Art and Culture from the Frontline.* London: Saqi Books, 2014.

Hamad, Sam. "You Want the Truth? A Correspondence with Noam Chomsky on Syria." *Here Comes the Tumbleweed* (blog), April 30, 2017. https://herecomesthetumbleweed.wordpress.com/2017/04/30/you-want-the-truth-a-correspondence-with-noam-chomsky/.

Hamid, Shadi. "American Self-Criticism Borders on Narcissism." *The Atlantic,* January 9, 2020. https://www.theatlantic.com/ideas/archive/2020/01/the-us-isnt-as-important-as-the-left-thinks/604642/.

Hanano, Alam. "From Hama to Daraya." In *Syria,* edited by Ziauddin Sardar and Robin Yassin-Kassab, 85–94. C. Hurst & Co., 2014.

Hasan, Mehdi. "'We Fought Alone, We Dreamed Alone': Former Syrian Prisoner on the Historic Fall of Bashar Al Assad." *Zeteo,* December 8, 2024. https://zeteo.com/p/we-fought-alone-we-dreamed-alone.

Hashem, Afraa. "The Regime's Crimes Did Not Stop at Imprisonment, Bombing and Forced Displacement, but They Have Not Refrained from Any Action Which Makes Us Strangers in Our Own Land and by Stealing Our Lands and Belongings." Translated from Arabic. Facebook, 2020. https://www.facebook.com/afraa.hashem.944/.

Hashemi, Nader, and Danny Postel. *The Syria Dilemma.* Cambridge, MA: Boston Review, 2013.

Hassan, Budour. "Global Voices." *Budour Hassan* (blog), 2013. https://budourhassan.wordpress. com/about/.

Hassan, Budour. "Radical Lives: Omar Aziz." *Novara Media,* February 23, 2015. https://novaramedia.com/2015/02/23/radical-lives-omar-aziz/.

Hassan, Hassan. "The Army of Islam Is Winning in Syria and That's Not Necessarily a Bad Thing." *Foreign Policy,* October 1, 2013. https://foreignpolicy.com/2013/10/01/the-army-of-islam-is-winning-in-syria/.

Head, Lesley, and Theresa Harada. "Keeping the Heart a Long Way from the Brain: The Emotional Labour of Climate Scientists." *Emotion, Space and Society* 24, no. 1 (2017): 34–41.

Hensman, Rohini. *Indefensible: Democracy, Counter-Revolution, and the Rhetoric of Anti-Imperialism.* Chicago: Haymarket Books, 2018.

Hincks, Joseph. "In Solidarity and as a Symbol of Global Injustices, a Syrian Artist Painted a Mural to George Floyd on a Bombed Idlib Building." *Time,* June 6, 2020. https://time. com/5849444/george-floyd-mural-idlib-syria/.

Hirsch, Marianne. *The Generation of Postmemory.* New York: Columbia University Press, 2008.

Hoffman, Eva. *After Such Knowledge: Memory, History and the Legacy of the Holocaust.* New York: Public Affairs, 2003.

Houdek, Matthew. "Recontextualizing Responsibility for Justice: The Lynching Trope, Racialized Temporalities, and Cultivating Breathable Futures." *Communication and Critical/Cultural Studies* 18, no. 2 (2021): 139–62.

Houdek, Matthew, and Ersula J Ore. "Cultivating Otherwise Worlds and Breathable Futures." *Rhetoric, Public and Culture* 1, no. 1 (2021): 85–95.

Huber, Makenzie, and Erin Woodiel. "Protesters in Keystone Arrested After Blocking Road to Mount Rushmore for Hours." *USA Today,* July 4, 2020. https://www.usatoday.com/story/ news/politics/2020/07/03/keystone-south-dakota-protesters-anti-trump-demonstration-mount-rushmore-rally-fireworks/5374418002/.

Human Rights Watch. "Torture Archipelago: Arbitrary Arrests, Torture, and Enforced Disappearances in Syria's Underground Prisons Since March 2011." July 3, 2012. https://www.hrw. org/report/2012/07/03/torture-archipelago/arbitrary-arrests-torture-and-enforced-disappearances-syrias.

Hume, David. *A Treatise of Human Nature.* Oxford: Oxford University Press, 1978.

Huneidi, Sarah. "Iran's Wars Kill Innocents Just Like America's Do." *BuzzFeed News,* January 16, 2020. https://www.buzzfeednews.com/article/sarahhunaidi/oppose-all-wars-iran-not-just-american-ones.

Idlbi, Qutaiba. "The Man Who Came Looking for His Family After the Chemical Massacre." Translated from Arabic. Twitter, February 29, 2020. https://twitter.com/Qidlbi/status/ 1233788313368219649?s=20.

Ignatieff, Michael. "The United States and the Syrian Refugee Crisis: A Plan of Action." Shorenstein Center on Media, Politics, and Public Policy, January 2016. https://shorensteincenter. org/wp-content/uploads/2016/01/Syria-Crisis-Plan-of-Action.pdf.

International Center for Transitional Justice. "Gone Without a Trace: Syria's Detained, Abducted, and Forcibly Disappeared." May 2020. https://www.ictj.org/sites/default/files/ ICTJ_PolicyPaper_Syria_Gone_Without_a_Trace_web.pdf.

Ismail, Salwa. *The Rule of Violence: Subjectivity, Memory and Government in Syria.* Cambridge: Cambridge University Press, 2018.

Jamal, Ahmed. "Soleimani's Movements Along Syrian Map Documented with Illustrations." *Enab Baladi,* September 1, 2020. https://english.enabbaladi.net/archives/2020/01/ soleimanis-movements-along-syrian-map-documented-with-illustrations/?so=related.

Jaspers, Karl. *The Question of German Guilt.* New York: Capricorn Books, 1961.

Kaba, Mariame. *We Do This 'til We Free Us: Abolitionist Organizing and Transforming Justice.* Chicago: Haymarket Books, 2021.

Kadi, Sam. *Little Gandhi.* Samer K Productions, 2016.

Kaepernick, Colin. "There Is Nothing New About American Terrorist Attacks Against Black and Brown People for the Expansion of American Imperialism." Twitter, January 4, 2020. https://twitter.com/Kaepernick7/status/1213552939786096640?ref_src=twsrc%5Etfw%7Ctwcamp%5Etweetembed%7Ctwterm%5E1213552939786096640&ref_url=https%3A%2F%2Ffanbuzz.com%2Fnfl%2Fcolin-kaepernick-iran-reaction%2F.

Kanaan, Wissam. "Bassel Shehade: Syria's Motorcycle Diarist." *Al Akhbar,* May 30, 2012. https://web.archive.org/web/20131224120449/http://english.al-akhbar.com/content/bassel-shehade-syria's-motorcycle-diarist.

Karam, Zeina. "Iran's Role in Syria Key Item at Trump-Putin Summit." *AP News,* July 13, 2018.

al-Kateab, Waad, and Edward Watts, dirs. *Frontline.* Episode 17, "For Sama." Channel 4 News / ITN Productions, 2019. https://www.pbs.org/wgbh/frontline/film/for-sama/.

Katerji, Oz. "The West's Leftist 'Intellectuals' Who Traffic in Genocide Denial, from Srebrenica to Syria." *Haaretz,* November 24, 2017. https://www.haaretz.com/opinion/the-west-s-leftist-male-intellectuals-who-traffic-in-genocide-denial-1.5626759.

Katouh, Zoulfa. *As Long as the Lemon Trees Grow.* New York: Little, Brown, 2022.

Kelley, Robin. *Freedom Dreams.* Boston: Beacon Press, 2002.

Kenner, David. "Assad's Cartoonish Crackdown." *Foreign Policy,* 2011. https://foreignpolicy.com/2011/08/25/assads-cartoonish-crackdown/.

al-Khalidiya District Coordination in Homs. "Heaven, Heaven, My Homeland Is Heaven." YouTube, August 20, 2013. https://www.youtube.com/watch?v=tocBLyhcXlc.

Kilani, Chams al Din. "Introduction to Syrian Political Life: From Entity's Formation to Revolution." Translated from Arabic. Arab Center for Research and Policy Studies, 2017.

King, Martin Luther, Jr. *The Trumpet of Conscience.* Edited by Coretta Scott King. Boston: Beacon Press, 1968.

King, Tiffany L., Jenell Navarro, and Andrea Smith. *Otherwise Worlds: Against Settler Colonialism and Antiblackness.* Durham, NC: Duke University Press, 2020.

Lazare, Sarah, and Michael Arria. "Trump Is Pushing War on Iran—but Democrats Laid the Groundwork." *Jacobin,* January 4, 2020. https://www.jacobinmag.com/2020/01/donald-trump-war-iran-democrats-qassem-soleimani-drone-strike.

Lefevre, Raphael. *Ashes of Hama: The Muslim Brotherhood in Syria.* Oxford: Oxford University Press, 2013.

Lenin, Vladimir I. *Imperialism: The Highest Stage of Capitalism.* Mansfield Centre: Martino, 1939.

Levander, Caroline, and Walter Mignolo. "The Global South and World Dis/Order." *Journal of Anthropological Research* 67, no. 2 (2011): 165–88.

Levina, Marina. "Whiteness and the Joys of Cruelty." *Communication and Critical/Cultural Studies* 15, no. 1 (2018): 73–78.

Levinas, Emmanuel. *Beyond the Verse: Talmudic Readings and Lectures.* Bloomington: Indiana University Press, 1994.

Levinas, Emmanuel. *Existence and Existents.* Pittsburgh, PA: Duquesne University Press, 2001.

Linfield, Susie. *The Lion's Den: Zionism and the Left from Hannah Arendt to Noam Chomsky.* New Haven, CT: Yale University Press, 2019.

Liu, Roseann, and Savannah Shange. "Toward Thick Solidarity: Theorizing Empathy in Social Justice Movements." *Radical History Review,* no. 131 (2018): 189–98.

Mansel, Philip. *Aleppo: The Rise and Fall of Syria's Great Merchant City*. London: I. B. Tauris, 2016.

Marcetic, Branko. "The Imperial Presidency Helped Bring Us to the Brink of War in Iran." *Jacobin*, January 3, 2020. https://www.jacobinmag.com/2020/01/iran-qassem-soleimani-killing-drone-donald-trump-war.

Marcos. *Our Word Is Our Weapon: Subcomandante Insurgente Marcos*. New York: Seven Stories Press, 2001.

Margalit, Avishai. *The Ethics of Memory*. Cambridge, MA: Harvard University Press, 2002.

Massey, Eli. "The Most Important Thing Missing from Coverage of Syria: The Perspectives of Syrians Themselves." *In These Times*, May 3, 2016. https://inthesetimes.com/article/19099/syria-burning-country-noam-chomsky-robert-fisk-patrick-cockburn.

Massumi, Brian. *Parables for the Virtual: Movement, Affect, Sensation*. Durham, NC: Duke University Press, 2002.

Massumi, Brian. *Politics of Affect*. Cambridge, MA: Polity Press, 2015.

Massumi, Brian. *Semblance and Event: Activist Philosophy and Occurent Arts*. Cambridge, MA: MIT Press, 2011.

MBC. "Surprise of the Currency of Freedom Project (MBC Report)." YouTube, 2012. https://www.youtube.com/watch?v=pDkj2bUv3ss.

Mbembe, Achille. *Critique of Black Reason*. Durham, NC: Duke University Press, 2017.

Mbembe, Achille. *On the Postcolony*. Oakland: University of California Press, 2001.

McCrisken, Trevor B. *American Exceptionalism and the Legacy of Vietnam: US Foreign Policy Since 1974*. London: Palgrave Macmillan, 2003.

McEvers, Kelly. "Slain Syrian Filmmaker Traded Study for 'Revolution.'" *NPR*, May 29, 2012. https://www.npr.org/2012/05/29/153937342/student-helped-the-world-see-inside-a-ravaged-syria.

McKittrick, Katherine. *On Being Human as Praxis*. Durham, NC: Duke University Press, 2015.

MEMRI. "Studies by Arab Researchers of Distribution of Foreign Bases Across Syria." January 18, 2018. https://www.memri.org/reports/studies-arab-researchers-distribution-foreign-bases-across-syria.

Mignolo, Walter, and Catherine E. Walsh. *On Decoloniality: Concepts, Analytics, Praxis*. Durham, NC: Duke University Press, 2018.

Million, Dian. *Therapeutic Nations: Healing in an Age of Indigenous Human Rights*. Tempe: University of Arizona Press, 2013.

Moore, Michael. "Hello Fellow Americans. Do You Know this Man? Did You Know He Was Your Enemy? What? Never Heard of Him? By the End of Today You Will be Trained to Hate Him. You will be Glad Trump Had Him Assassinated. You Will Do As You Are Told." Twitter, January 3, 2020. https://twitter.com/mmflint/status/1213084631530196992?lang=en.

Moore, Michael. "I Know it's Bothersome that I'm Speaking Some Awful Truths & Asking These Questions, so I'll Just Continue: Can Someone Name the Building in the US that the 'Bad Guy' General Soleimani Ordered Blown Up?" Twitter, January 8, 2020. https://twitter.com/MMFlint/status/1214900138453409792.

Moore, Michael. "Just Wondering—Is There an American General for Whom Millions of us Would Turn Out for His Funeral? Mad Dog? Kelly? Colin Powel? William Westmoreland? Can Anyone Even Name the Chair of the Joint Chiefs?" Twitter, January 8, 2020. https://twitter.com/MMFlint/status/1214881961564606464.

Morland, Paul. *Demographic Engineering: Population Strategies in Ethnic Conflict*. New York: Routledge, 2015.

Mouffe, Chantal. *Agonistics: Thinking the World Politically.* London: Verso, 2013.

MsSamero10. "Celebration of a New Constellation of Homs Martyrs." Translated from Arabic. YouTube, May 28, 2012. https://www.youtube.com/watch?v=C72qh2AXV7w.

Munif, Yasser. *The Syrian Revolution: Between the Politics of Life and the Geopolitics of Death.* London: Pluto Press, 2020.

Mustafa, Wafa. "The Activist Wafa Mustafa." Episode 52, *Tak Tak* (podcast). Translated from Arabic. YouTube, January 13, 2022. https://www.youtube.com/watch?v=S70nB_XzpXQ.

Mustafa, Wafa. "The Syrian Revolution 10 Years On: What Does the Future Hold?" Syrian Revolt, May 31, 2021. https://www.youtube.com/watch?v=c1Y7h4N_Uhq.

Naprushkina, Marina. "Surviving Monstrosities: An Interview with Yassin al-Haj Saleh." *Al-Jumhuriya,* June 25, 2020. https://www.aljumhuriya.net/en/content/surviving-monstrosities-interview-yassin-al-haj-saleh.

Neudorf, Atlanta Rae. "Reconciling with Rupture: The Impact of Exile on Revolutionary Thought." *Journal of the History of Ideas Blog,* December 15, 2021. https://www.jhiblog.org/2021/12/15/reconciling-with-rupture-the-impact-of-exile-on-revolutionary-thought/.

Obama, Barack. "Statement by the President on Syria." Obama White House Archives, August 31, 2013. https://obamawhitehouse.archives.gov/the-press-office/2013/08/31/statement-president-syria.

Occupied Kafranbel Banners. "We stand in solidarity. . . ." Facebook, May 26, 2020. https://www.facebook.com/kafrnbl/photos/3092542220839197.

Ohl, Jessy. "In Pursuit of Light War in Libya: Kairotic Justifications of War That Just Happened." *Rhetoric and Public Affairs* 20, no. 2 (2017): 195–222.

100 Faces of the Syrian Revolution. "Ghiath Matar." *100 Faces of the Syrian Revolution* (blog), April 13, 2020. https://100facesofthesyrianrevolution.wordpress.com/2020/04/13/ghiath-matar.

Orient TV. "Orient TV News Cameras Collects the Opinions of the Syrian Street Around the Killing of Soleimani." Translated from Arabic. YouTube, January 4, 2020. https://www.youtube.com/watch?v=Am8nDIMl2ac.

Oweis, Khaled Y. "Mother of Young Syrian Blogger Appeals for Her Release." *Reuters,* September 1, 2010. https://www.reuters.com/article/us-syria-internet-blogger-idUSTRE68073J20100901.

Oxford Human Rights Festival. "For Sama Q&A with Afraa Hashem." YouTube, December 15, 2020. https://www.youtube.com/watch?v=FaI-C1CWNc4.

PAX and the Syria Institute. *No Return to Homs: A Case Study on Demographic Engineering in Syria.* 2017. https://scm.bz/wp-content/uploads/2017/10/pax-tsi-no-return-to-homs.pdf.

PBS. "The President Blinked: Why Obama Changed Course on the 'Red Line' in Syria." *PBS,* May 25, 2015. https://www.pbs.org/wgbh/frontline/article/the-president-blinked-why-obama-changed-course-on-the-red-line-in-syria/.

Pearlman, Wendy. "Mobilizing from Scratch: Large-Scale Collective Action Without Preexisting Organization in the Syrian Uprising." *Comparative Political Studies* 54, no. 10 (2020): 1786–817.

Pearlman, Wendy. *We Crossed a Bridge and It Trembled: Voices from Syria.* New York: HarperCollins, 2017.

Pletts, Adam. *The Revolution Is Being Televised. Al Jazeera,* April 20, 2014. https://www.aljazeera.com/program/witness/2014/4/20/the-revolution-is-being-televised/.

Postone, Moishe. "History and Helplessness: Mass Mobilization and Contemporary Forms of Anticapitalism." *Public Culture* 18, no. 1 (2006): 93–110.

Power, Samantha. *A Problem from Hell: America and the Age of Genocide.* New York: Basic Books, 2013.

Prashad, Vijay. *The Poorer Nations: A Possible History of the Global South*. London: Verso, 2012.

Puar, Jasbir. *The Right to Maim: Debility, Capacity and Disability*. Durham, NC: Duke University Press, 2017.

Radhakrishnan, Rajagopalan. *Theory in an Uneven World*. Hoboken, NJ: Wiley-Blackwell, 2003.

Ratcliffe, Krista. *Rhetorical Listening: Identification, Gender, Whiteness*. Carbondale: Southern Illinois University Press, 2005.

Rizk, Philip, and Leila al-Shami. "Land, Revolutions and Lessons from Syria." *Syria Untold,* May 4, 2021. https://syriauntold.com/2021/05/04/land-revolutions-and-lessons-from-syria/.

Roberts, Sam. "Fadwa Suleiman, Actress and Voice of Syrian Opposition in Exile, Dies at 47." *New York Times*, August 17, 2017. https://www.nytimes.com/2017/08/17/world/middleeast/fadwa-suleiman-actress-and-voice-of-syrian-opposition-dies-at-47.html.

Robinson, Nathan J. "How to Avoid Swallowing War Propaganda." *Current Affairs*, January 5, 2020. https://www.currentaffairs.org/2020/01/how-to-avoid-swallowing-war-propaganda.

al-Romoh, Ahmad. "MB in Syria: From Democracy to Radicalism." MENA Research Center, July 16, 2022. https://www.mena-researchcenter.org/mb-in-syria-from-democracy-to-radicalism/.

Rothberg, Michael. *The Implicated Subject: Beyond Victims and Perpetrators*. Redwood City, CA: Stanford University Press, 2019.

Ryzik, Melena. "Syrian Film Collective Offers View of Life Behind a Conflict." *New York Times*, October 18, 2015. https://www.nytimes.com/2015/10/19/movies/syrian-film-collective-offers-view-of-life-behind-a-conflict.html.

Sadjadpour, Karim. "Iran: Syria's Lone Regional Ally." *Carnegie Endowment for International Peace,* June 9, 2014. https://carnegieendowment.org/2014/06/09/iran-syria-s-lone-regional-ally-pub-55834.

Safwan, Luna. "#Lebanon's Airport Highway with New Qassem Souleimani Pictures on Every Possible Corner—to Some He was a Great Leader, to Others, he was a Mass Murderer, so How Do You Compromise and Make a Country Livable & Bearable, to Both Sides?" Twitter, 2020. https://twitter.com/LunaSafwan/status/1345729454623105024.

Said, Edward W. *Culture and Imperialism*. New York: Random House, 1981.

Said, Edward W. *Reflections on Exile and Other Essays*. Cambridge, MA: Harvard University Press, 2000.

Said, Edward W. *The World, the Text, and the Critic*. Cambridge, MA: Harvard University Press, 1983.

Salahi, Amr. "Will We Ever Really Know How Many People Have Died in Syria Since 2011?" *New Arab*, January 28, 2020. https://english.alaraby.co.uk/english/indepth/2020/1/28/how-many-people-have-died-in-syria-since-2011.

Santos, Boaventura de Sousa. *Epistemologies of the South: Justice Against Epistemicide*. New York: Routledge, 2014.

al-Sarout, Abdul. "Al-Sarout Talks About His Painful Memories, Sacrifice and Hope in the Revolution." Translated from Arabic. YouTube, June 8, 2019. https://www.youtube.com/watch?v=gzpxMoWOfMo.

al-Sarout, Abdul. "Syria Feature: Hope and Tragedy of an Uprising—An Interview with Abdul Baset Sarout." *EA Worldview,* June 10, 2019. https://eaworldview.com/2019/06/syria-feature-hope-tragedy-uprising-interview-abdul-baset-sarout/.

Scaff, May. "I Won't Lose Hope . . . I Won't Lose Hope . . . It's the Great Syria, not Assad's Syria." Facebook, July 21, 2018. https://www.facebook.com/may.scaff.7.

Seale, Patrick. *Asad of Syria: The Struggle for the Middle East.* Oakland: University of California Press, 1988.

Sergie, Lina. *Recollecting History: Songs, Flags and a Syrian Square.* Cambridge, MA: Massachusetts Institute of Technology, 2003.

Sergie Attar, Lina. "Revolutionary Wit: In Memory of Raed Fares, the Satirist Syria Needed." *New Lines,* November 22, 2020. https://newlinesmag.com/essays/revolutionary-wit/.

Shabo, Rateb. "Exile and the State of the Syrian Left." *Syria Untold,* September 17, 2021. https://syriauntold.com/2021/09/17/rateb-shabo-politics-disappears-amid-violence/.

Shaer, Matther. "One of Syria's Brave Young Photographers Has Been Kidnapped by Islamist Rebels." *New Republic,* November 6, 2013. https://newrepublic.com/article/115494/ziad-homsi-kidnapped-syria-islamist-rebels.

al-Shami, Leila. "Syria and the 'Anti-Imperialism' of Idiots." *Vice,* April 18, 2018. https://www.vice.com/en_uk/article/9kgm3e/syria-and-the-anti-imperialism-of-idiots.

al-Shami, Leila, and Shon Meckfessel. "Why the US Far Right Loves Bashar al-Assad." *New Lines Magazine,* August 1, 2023. https://newlinesmag.com/argument/why-the-us-far-right-loves-bashar-al-assad/.

Shange, Savannah. *Progressive Dystopia: Abolition, Antiblackness, and Schooling in San Francisco.* Durham, NC: Duke University Press, 2019.

Shehadeh, Bassel. "Bassel and Lenin." YouTube, March 19, 2014. https://www.youtube.com/watch?v=52iuuC1Dp3A.

Shehadeh, Bassel. *I Will Cross Tomorrow.* Abounaddara Collective, June 1, 2012. https://vimeo.com/43241736.

Shehadeh, Bassel. *Streets of Freedom.* May 31, 2013. https://www.youtube.com/watch?v=nIqJQEyJSbc.

Shohat, Ella. *Talking Visions: Multicultural Feminism in a Transnational Age.* Cambridge, MA: MIT Press, 1998.

Shupak, Greg. "Stop the War. Stop US Empire." *Jacobin,* January 5, 2020. https://jacobinmag.com/2020/01/donald-trump-war-iran-us-empire.

Shurbaji, Ayman. "The Diary of a Vanguard Combatant in Syria." Translated from Arabic. *Homsrevolution,* December 17, 2011. https://homsrevolution.wordpress.com/2011/12/17/مذكرات-القائد-الشهيد-أيمن-شربجي-رحمه-ا-4. (Site discontinued.)

Shweish, Abdel Aziz. "The Syrian Artist Aziz Asmar Expresses his Solidarity with the Jerusalemites Towards the Attack by the Israeli Forces, by Painting the Dome of the Rock on the Wall of a Destroyed House in the Idlib Governorate, and Confirms That 'The Pain of the Syrian and Palestinian' Peoples is One." *Shwiesh* (blog), May 10, 2021. https://1wwwshwiesh.wordpress.com/2021/05/10/the-syrian-artist-aziz-asmar-expresses-his-solidarity-with-the-jerusalemites-towards-the-attack-by-the-israeli-forces-by-painting-the-dome-of-the-rock-on-the-wall-of-a-destroyed-house-in-the-idlib-go/.

Silk, Sally M. "When the Writer Comes Home: Narrative Failure in Butor's *La modification.*" *Style* 26, no. 2 (1992): 270–86.

Singh, Julietta. *Unthinking Mastery: Dehumanism and Decolonial Entanglements.* London: Duke University Press, 2018.

Smith, Leilani T., Eve Tuck, and K. Wayne Yang. *Indigenous and Decolonizing Studies in Education: Mapping the Long View.* New York: Routledge, 2019.

Smith, Lillian. *Killers of the Dream.* New York: W. W. Norton, 1994.

Solon, Olivia. "How Syria's White Helmets Became Victims of an Online Propaganda Machine." *The Guardian,* December 18, 2017. https://www.theguardian.com/world/2017/dec/18/syria-white-helmets-conspiracy-theories.

South Commission. *The Challenge to the South: The Report of the South Commission.* Oxford: Oxford University Press, 1990.

Spinoza, Benedictus de. *Ethics: On the Correction of Understanding.* London: Everyman's Library, 1959.

Spivak, Gayatri C. "Can the Subaltern Speak?" In *Marxism and the Interpretation of Culture,* edited by Cary Nelson and Lawrence Grossberg, 271–316. Champaign: University of Illinois Press, 1988.

Stauffer, Jill. *Ethical Loneliness: The Injustice of Not Being Heard.* New York: Columbia University Press, 2015.

Syria Campaign. "Bassel Shehadeh." Facebook, May 28, 2021. https://www.facebook.com/TheSyriaCampaign/posts/4096415360450446.

Syrian Network for Human Rights. "The 6th Anniversary of the Breakout of the Popular Uprising Towards Freedom, and the Killing of the First Civilians." March 18, 2017. http://sn4hr.org/blog/2017/03/18/35726/.

The Syrian People Know Their Way. "Palestinian until Freedom." Facebook, August 5, 2012. https://www.facebook.com/Syrian.Intifada/photos/a.148885538508914/396650947065704.

Syrian Voices UK. "Syrian Hero: Bassel Shehadeh." YouTube, February 19, 2019. https://www.youtube.com/watch?v=u6fDV6FCfFo.

Syrian2011X. "Standing Homs: The Hero Bassel Shehadeh." Translated from Arabic. YouTube, 2012. https://www.youtube.com/watch?v=NNvf-Kl7XHg.

Syria Plus. "Ghalia al-Rahhal: An Activist Defies War and Continues Empowering the Syrian Women." Translated from Arabic. YouTube, March 24, 2020. https://www.youtube.com/watch?v=wNwoG3kyCFM.

Syria Plus. "Syrians Distribute Sweets in Celebration of the Killing of Qasem Soleimani." YouTube, January 3, 2020. https://www.youtube.com/watch?v=4X9RFlJh9NE&feature=youtu.be.

Syria Stream. "In Less than Three Minutes, the Most Famous Statements of Waleed al-Muallem." Translated from Arabic. YouTube, November 16, 2020. https://www.youtube.com/watch?v=z6fTDWXTJTU.

Syria TV. "Ahmad Aba Zeid Talks About His Experience in the Siege of Aleppo and the Current Siege on Daraa, with Noor Khanum." Translated from Arabic. YouTube, July 14, 2018. https://www.youtube.com/watch?v=GZ9GcbShE4E.

Syria TV. "For the First Time, Suhail al-Hammoud Abu Tow Speaks in Detail About the Details of His Assassination in Idlib." Translated from Arabic. YouTube, March 19, 2020. https://www.youtube.com/watch?v=cOwRAGZ74IY.

Thomson, Mike. *Syria's Secret Library: Reading and Redemption in a Town Under Siege.* New York: Public Affairs, 2019.

Tuathail, Gearoid O., and John Agnew. "Geopolitics and Discourse: Practical Geopolitical Reasoning in American Foreign Policy." *Political Geography* 11, no. 2 (1992): 190–204.

Tube True. "Rural Aleppo: The Syrian Army, Unit 80, Attacks." Translated from Arabic. YouTube, November 8, 2013. https://www.youtube.com/watch?v=bAIDO3dVRiw&feature=youtu.be.

Uetricht, Micah, and Megan Day. "The US Cannot Retaliate Against Iran's Strikes in Iraq." *Jacobin,* 2020. https://www.jacobinmag.com/2020/01/iran-bombing-us-base-no-war.

Üngör, Uğur Ümit. "Screaming, Silence, and Mass Violence in Israel/Palestine." Preprint, *Journal of Genocide Research,* January 26, 2024. https://doi.org/10.1080/14623528.2024.2309709.

United Nations Human Rights. "Pillay Urges United International Action to Protect Syrians." *United Nations Human Rights: Office of the High Commissioner,* October 14, 2011. https://www.ohchr.org/EN/NewsEvents/Pages/DisplayNews.aspx?NewsID=11493&LangID=E.

Uskowi, Nader. "The Evolving Iranian Strategy in Syria: A Looming Conflict with Israel." *Atlantic Council,* September 27, 2018. https://www.atlanticcouncil.org/in-depth-research-reports/issue-brief/the-evolving-iranian-strategy-in-syria-a-looming-conflict-with-israel/.

Vidwans, Prachi. "Ideas Cannot Be Killed with Weapons: Why the Assassination of Syria's Most Prominent Citizen Journalist Matters." *Time,* November 29, 2018. https://time.com/5466658/remembering-raed-fares-syria/.

Vivian, Bradford. *Commonplace Witnessing: Rhetorical Invention, Historical Remembrance, and Public Culture.* Oxford: Oxford University Press, 2017.

von Einsiedel, Orlando. *The White Helmets.* Netflix, September 16, 2016.

Walker, Margaret U. *Moral Repair: Reconstructing Moral Relations After Wrong-Doing.* Cambridge: Cambridge University Press, 2006.

Wallet, Bart. "Niet Zomaar Een Land." *De Groene Amsterdammer,* November 15, 2023. https://www.groene.nl/artikel/niet-zomaar-een-land.

Walsh, Catherine. *Pedagogías Decoloniales: Prácticas Insurgentes de Resistir, (Re)existir y (Re)vivir.* Quito: Ediciones Abya-Yala, 2013.

Warner, Michael. *Publics and Counterpublics.* New York: Zone Books, 2005.

Wedeen, Lisa. *Ideology, Judgement, and Mourning in Syria: Authoritarian Apprehensions.* Chicago: University of Chicago Press, 2019.

Weheliye, Alexander G. *Habeas Viscus: Racializing Assemblages, Biopolitics, and Black Feminist Theories of the Human.* Durham, NC: Duke University Press, 2014.

Wind, Ella. "Inside and Outside." In *Critical Muslim 11,* edited by Ziauddin Sardar and Robin Yassin-Kassab, 51–62. London: Muslim Institute / Hurst Publishers, 2014.

Wood, Julia T., and Robert Cox. "Rethinking Critical Voice: Materiality and Situated Knowledges." *Western Journal of Communication* 57, no. 2 (1993): 209–20.

Wynter, Sylvia. "No Humans Involved: A Letter to My Colleagues." *Forum NHI: Knowledge for the 21st Century* 1, no. 1 (1994): 42–71.

Yassin-Kassab, Robin. "Literature of the Syrian Uprising." In *Syria Speaks: Art and Culture from the Frontline,* edited by Malu Halasa, Zaher Omareen, and Nawara Mahfoud, 138–44. London: Saqi Books, 2014.

Yassin-Kassab, Robin, and Leila al-Shami. *Burning Country: Syrians in Revolution and War.* London: Pluto Press, 2016.

Yazbek, Samar. *A Woman in the Crossfire: Diaries of the Syrian Revolution.* London: Haus, 2012.

Zahlout, Hanadi. "If Our Eyes Could See the Spirits of Cities." Translated from Arabic. Facebook, January 3, 2020. https://www.facebook.com/hanadi.zahlout [private facebook post shared with permission of author].

Zaitouneh, Razan. "True Vengeance Is in Justice." *Rising for Freedom,* July 8, 2013. https://www.freedomraise.net/en/opinion/true-vengeance-is-in-justice/.

Zakaria, Khudor. "Traditional Opposition Parties in Syria: Positions and Directions." In *The Revolution's Background: Syrian Studies,* 243–68. Arab Center for Research and Policy Studies, 2013.

Zakaria, Zakaria. "Syria Is Not Safe, No Matter What Propagandists and Profiteers Say." Syrian Association for Citizen's Dignity, December 3, 2021. https://syacd.org/syria-is-not-safe-no-matter-what-propagandists-and-profiteers-say/.

al-Zayat, Rama. "It Will Not Leave My Mind the Girl That Was Studying Medicine . . ." Translated from Arabic. Twitter, February 28, 2020. https://twitter.com/Ramalzayat/status/1233492147535589377.

Žižek, Slavoj. "Syria Is a Pseudo-Struggle." *The Guardian,* September 6, 2013. https://www.theguardian.com/commentisfree/2013/sep/06/syria-pseudo-struggle-egypt.

Zollner, Barbara. *The Muslim Brotherhood: Hasan Al-Hudaybi and Ideology.* New York: Routledge, 2009.

INDEX

Aba Zeid, Ahmad, 29, 94

Abbas, Hamed, 80

al-Abdallah, Hadi, 55, 138, 140–41

Abounaddara Collective, 133, 136

Abu Zayd, Osama, 32

affect, 7–11, 55–57, 91–99; belief and, 17, 127–30, 134, 141, 145; etho-affect, 16, 57, 75; global geographies and, 17, 101–6, 110–12, 120–24, 134, 148–56; hope talk and, 17, 127, 130, 133–41; joy and celebration, 6, 12, 18–19, 25–27, 81, 99, 135, 143–44; loss, 4, 27–28, 39, 75, 92, 99, 111, 114n26, 132–35, 139–40; in tenets of radical subjectivity, 14–15; towardness and, 16, 21–22, 42–43. *See also* embodiment; memory; resistance; solidarity

affect theory, 10

Agamben, Giorgio, 122n45

agency, 3, 11–12, 45n3, 46, 69, 101, 142; denial of, 15, 23–24, 37, 39–41, 51, 59–61; hope and, 132; significance to radical subjectivity, 51–52

Ahmed, Sara, 11, 16, 21

Alawites, 62, 63n73, 76, 80, 83, 121, 154

Alcoff, Linda, 52

al-Dumari (*The Lamplighter*), 26

Aleppo, Syria, 1, 5, 25, 28, 32, 54, 85, 131, 138; Aleppo Artillery School, 80; Aleppo Media Centre, 53; falling to Assad regime, 31, 115; as Halab al-Muhtalla (Aleppo the Occupied), 115; Muslim Brotherhood in, 78–80, 88

Alexander, M. Jacqui, 48

al-Ali, Naji, 110

Al-Jumhuriya, 24

"All Lives Matter" rhetoric, 68

Al-Qaeda, 29, 61

AlShogre, Omar, 6

Althusser, Louis, 90

anti-imperialism, 15, 18, 36, 113–14, 117; Soleimani and, 32–33, 39–40

Anzaldúa, Gloria, 66

Arab League, 5n13, 131

Arab Spring of 2011, 2–3, 72, 74, 97

Arabic language, 25, 97, 99, 109, 115; author's notes on translation, 13n32, 29n30, 48n9, 71n1, 100n3, 107

Arendt, Hannah, 9, 24n17, 90

Aristotle, 75n10

INTERSECTIONAL RHETORICS
KARMA R. CHÁVEZ, SERIES EDITOR

This series takes as its starting point the position that intersectionality offers important insights to the field of rhetoric—including that to enhance what we understand as rhetorical practice, we must diversify the types of rhetors, arguments, frameworks, and forms under analysis. Intersection works on two levels for the series: (1) reflecting the series' privileging of intersectional perspectives and analytical frames while also (2) emphasizing rhetoric's intersection with related fields, disciplines, and research areas.

9 780814 259603